The American Philological Association
Series of Classical Texts

TIBULLUS: *A Commentary*

MICHAEL C. J. PUTNAM

TIBULLUS
A Commentary

Published by the University of Oklahoma Press, Norman, in co-operation
with the American Philological Association

By Michael C. J. Putnam

The Poetry of the Aeneid (Cambridge, Mass., 1965)
Virgil's Pastoral Art (Princeton, 1970)
Tibullus: A Commentary (Norman, 1973)

PA
6789
.P8

Library of Congress Cataloging in Publication Data

Putnam, Michael C   J
    Tibullus: a commentary.

    "Commentary is limited to the sixteen poems which com-
prise the first two books of the Corpus Tibullianum"; with the
Latin text of books 1−2.
    Bibliography: p.
    1.   Tibullus, Albius.
PA6789.P8   478'.6'421   72-9255
ISBN: 0−8061−1560−2

Tibullus: A Commentary is Volume 3 in The American Philological Association Series.

5   6   7   8   9   10   11   12   13   14   15   16   17

FOR *Charles* and *Polly Chatfield*

PREFACE

This commentary is limited to the sixteen poems which comprise the first two books of the *corpus Tibullianum*, that is, to poems authentically by Tibullus. In this age of completeness, the absence of the third and fourth books may seem a drawback, but, other rare exceptions apart, the Sulpicia cycle alone cannot redeem the non-Tibullus segments of the *corpus* from general dullness or grandiloquence. The notes focus on the needs of the student approaching Latin elegy for the first time, yet they may still prove useful for the more experienced graduate student or for scholars in other languages. I have tried to balance matters of fact with occasional sallies of interpretation. These latter, while open to the accusation of subjectivity, aim to reveal aspects of the poet's style and ideas which the modern critic's arsenal of weapons can capture. Those seeking greater documentation, especially in the matter of parallels from ancient and modern literature, should turn to the splendid edition of Tibullus by Kirby Flower Smith which I have found a constantly enlivening guide.

The notion to undertake a commentary was first suggested to Professor J. P. Elder and me in 1963. Unfortunately the pressures of administration prevented Dean Elder from lending more than moral support, but even for this I am extremely grateful. The major portion of the work was finished during a sabbatical leave from Brown University for the academic year 1969–70. For a six months' period at that time I was privileged, through the kind invitation of Professor Frank E. Brown, to be Scholar in Residence at the American Academy in Rome. I must thank the staff of the Academy library and especially Mrs. Inez Longobardi for her efficient and kindly hospitality.

I have received help from many colleagues and students, in particular Mrs. Christina Sorum and Miss Nancy Wiggers. With her usual competence, my secretary, Mrs. Frances Eisenhauer, has brought polish to a complex manuscript. Once again Professor and Mrs. Cedric Whitman have not failed in offering sympathetic advice and encouragement. On one matter I turned to Professor Lily Ross Taylor who responded with her accustomed knowledge and warmth. I have benefited from the careful scrutiny of Professor Helen North, editor of the College Textbook Series for the American Philological Association. Professors Charles Babcock and Katherine Geffcken have given time far beyond the ordinary claims of *amicitia*. What is worthwhile in the pages that follow owes much to their wisdom and counsel. The blemishes and lapses which remain are the author's responsibility alone.

MICHAEL C. J. PUTNAM

Providence, Rhode Island

CONTENTS

TIBULLUS: *A Commentary*

Documentation for the life of Albius Tibullus is meager.[1]
If we may trust Ovid's list of elegists—Gallus, Tibullus,
Propertius, and himself—as chronological, then Tibullus'
birthdate would logically rest somewhere between 60 and
55 B.C.[2] An epigram, attached to the manuscripts and
ascribed to Domitius Marsus, points to contemporary death
dates for Vergil and Tibullus. This would place his demise
not long after September, 19 B.C.[3] The *vita*, a brief "life"
also in the manuscript tradition, itself probably a much
later abridgment of the Suetonian "life," appeals to the epigram as evidence for an early death. Postulating date of
birth around 55 B.C., we would conjecture for Tibullus a life
span of some thirty-six years.

The *vita* entitles him *eques Romanus*, a rank he shared
with the other three elegists.[4] This implies not only social
stature but a certain economic worth as well. References
in the poems themselves suggest ancestral acres diminished,
like those of Propertius or Vergil, by the depredations of
civil war.[5] But the Vergilian literary tradition for loss of
land and the poet's own admission at the end of the first
elegy that he was not penniless imply that we should not
take his protestations of poverty (and attacks on wealth)

1 We know of no *praenomen*. The *nomen*, in itself of an obscure *gens*,
is documented only by Horace (assuming here and elsewhere that *Carm.*
1.33 and *Epist.* 1.4 refer to our Albius) and his commentators, by the
grammarian Diomedes, by the manuscripts, and the *vita*. Tibullus in-
variably refers to himself by his *cognomen* alone (1.3.55; 1.9.83).

2 Gallus was born c. 69 B.C. (and died in 26 B.C.), Propertius probably between 54 and 47 B.C.

3 For a review of the data and critique of several other recent dis-
cussions, see M. J. McGann "The Date of Tibullus' Death," *Latomus*
29 (1970), 774–80.

4 See L. R. Taylor, "Republican and Augustan Writers Enrolled in
the Equestrian Centuries," *TAPA* 99 (1968), 469–86, esp. 479–80.

5 E.g. 1.1.5, 19–20, 37; 1.10.15–20.

4 TIBULLUS: *A Commentary*

too literally or seriously. Poverty was a stock elegiac attitude, necessary to establish contrast with a wealthy rival
and to stress the poet's difficulty in providing rich presents
to satisfy a greedy mistress.[6]

Horace places Tibullus *in regione Pedana* (*Epist.* 1.4.2),
and it is reasonable to associate him with lands in the Alban
hills east of Rome, near the deserted village of Pedum.[7]

Both poems[8] and *vita*[9] connect Tibullus closely with the
orator, soldier, and statesman M. Valerius Messalla Corvinus (64 B.C.–A.D. 8).[10] Poem 1.7 celebrates ? triumph
which Messalla held in September, 27 B.C. (This is the only
exact date we can garner from any poem in the first book,
but it is plausible to assume that it was published not long
thereafter.) Tibullus (1.7.9ff.) and the *vita* state directly
that he accompanied Messalla on the Aquitanian part of the
latter's campaigns following the battle of Actium, in which
Messalla took part. The opening of 1.3 finds the poet on
the island of Corcyra (modern Corfu), roughly seventy
miles to the northwest of Actium, ill and unable to continue
with his patron. Otherwise, since the chronology of Messalla's actions between September 2, 31 B.C. (the date of
Actium) and September 25, 27 B.C. (the date of his triumph) is still in doubt, speculation on the poet's doings is
hazardous (especially when extracted indirectly from the
poems themselves).[11]

6 Horace, in *Epist.* 1.4, speaks of Tibullus' *divitias* (7) and his *mundus
victus non deficiente crumena* (11). The implication is confirmed by
Statius (*Silv.* 1.2.255) who calls him *dives foco lucente,* perhaps a reference to 1.1.6.

7 Evidence favors the location of Pedum near modern Gallicano, between Palestrina (ancient Praeneste) and Tivoli (ancient Tibur, beyond
which lay Horace's own farm). See further R. M. Ogilvie on Livy 2.39.4;
L. R. Taylor, *The Voting Districts of the Roman Republic* (Rome, 1960),
37, 44f. A detailed map of the area may be found in *Roma e dintorni*
("Guida d'Italia del Touring Club Italiano," Milan, 1962) after p. 608.

8 1.1, 3, 5, 7; 2.1, 5.

9 ". . . ante alios Corvinum Messalam [*sic*] oratorem dilexit, cuius
etiam contubernalis Aquitanico bello militaribus donis donatus est."

10 He was consul in 31 B.C. to replace Antony. For a detailed exami-
nation of his life with full bibliography see R. Hanslik, *RE* 8a (1955),
131–57 (147f., for the campaigns; 152f., for the triumph).

11 *Canam* (1.7.13) does not preclude Tibullus' involvement in any

Poem 2.5 honors Messallinus, Messalla's oldest son, on the occasion of his induction as a member of the *quindecimviri sacris faciundis* whose primary charge was to care for and read the Sibylline books. An inscription dating from 17 B.C. places his name at the bottom of a listing of these fifteen either because of his age or because his election was recent.[12] In any case the event should probably be placed near the end of Tibullus' life.

Because of their common enjoyment of Messalla's patronage, Tibullus must have been intimately connected with Lygdamus, Sulpicia, and the author of the *Panegyricus Messallae*, whose works follow Tibullus' sixteen poems in the manuscripts and form, with two *priapeia*, *vita*, and epigram, the so-called *corpus Tibullianum*.[13] Ovid, who never knew Tibullus personally (*Tr.* 4.10.51–52), also acknowledges his indebtedness to Messalla's inspiration in a poem addressed to Messallinus (*Ex Pont.* 1.7.27–30).

Five poems of the first book mention a certain Delia.[14] Apuleius (*Apol.* 10), discussing the pseudonyms under which Roman poets disguised their mistresses' names, says that when Tibullus mentions Delia *in versu* he had Plania *in animo*. The *gens Plania* is otherwise unknown.[15] Beyond this it is dangerous here also to take traditional elegiac conventions (that she had a *coniunx*, for instance) to build up a biography. Of the boy Marathus, who figures in two poems and whose presence is implied in a third, of Tibullus' friend

eastern campaigns, but the contrast with the boast of the preceding lines intimates that he did not take part. The *vita* singles out the Aquitanian campaign as the source of Tibullus' military honors.

12 On Messallinus and his election as *quindecimvir*, see D. von Lunzer, *RE* 8a (1955), 159–62 (159f. for the inscription).

13 See further R. Hanslik, "Der Dichterkreis des Messalla," *AAWW* 89 (1952), 22–38. According to the younger Pliny (*Epist.* 5.3.5) Messalla wrote erotic verse.

14 1.1, 2, 3, 5, 6.

15 Propertius (whose first book of elegies was probably published in 28 B.C.) chose as pseudonym Cynthia, another island epithet of the goddess Diana. The name Delia suggests specifically clarity, more generally mythic perspective, creativity, poetry, and the feminine principle of the moon. For further speculation on the choice see E. N. O'Neil "Cynthia and the Moon," *CP* 53 (1958), 1–8, esp. 7f.

Cornutus, and the girl Nemesis, the poet's *amour* in book
two, the poems speak for themselves.[16]

Tibullus' connection with Messalla raises less factual
considerations. First is the matter of style. Messalla was a
speaker and writer of note. The elder Seneca says of him
that he was "exactissimi ingenii quidem in omni studiorum
parte, sed Latini utique sermonis observator diligentissi-
mus" (*Contr.* 2.4.8). Cicero (*Ad Brut.* 1.15.1) writes to
Brutus that Messalla will explain to him in the choicest
manner (*elegantissime*) what has been happening in Rome.
Finally Tacitus, comparing him to his great contemporary,
judges that "Cicerone mitior Corvinus et dulcior et in
verbis magis elaboratus" (*Dial.* 18). This last attribute can
be taken pejoratively ("exquisite," "over polished"),[17] but
it is more discreet to see a unified portrait in the references
—his style was smooth, with words always well chosen.[18]

Tibullus' own stylistic proclivities present reasons for his
friendship with Messalla. It is primarily to style that Quintilian is alluding in his critical comparison of Tibullus with
Propertius (*Inst.* 10.1.93): "Elegia quoque Graecos provocamus, cuius mihi tersus atque elegans maxime videtur
auctor Tibullus. Sunt qui Propertium malint. Ovidius utro-
que lascivior sicut durior Gallus." Style as well as intimacy
with Messalla also help explain Ovid's deep, sustained
affection for Tibullus. Ovid designates Propertius *blandus*
and *tener*.[19] The adjective with which he singles out Tibullus
is *cultus*, polished as a writer, cultivated as a person. His

[16] Marathus: 1.4, 8 and, by implication, 9; Cornutus: 2.2, 3; Nemesis:
2.3, 4, 5, 6. There may be a connection between Pholoe, Marathus' girl
mentioned at 1.8.69, and a girl of the same name who appears prominently in Horace *Carm.* 1.33.

[17] Hanslik, above n. 10, 155.

[18] For an example of Messalla's simple, "plain" style see Suetonius
Aug. 58.1–2 (References to his speeches are collected in H. Malcovati,
ORF, 2d ed. [Turin, 1955], 529–34). An instance of his interest in words is
documented by the elder Seneca (*Suas.* 1.7—on *desultor*).

Quintilian (10.1.113) is negative only about his lack of persuasive and
forceful projection: "At Messalla nitidus et candidus et quodam modo
praeferens in dicendo nobilitatem suam, viribus minor." *Nitidus* and
candidus may connote aspects of *elegantia*. (Cf. also Quintilian 1.7.35.)
Among "plain" stylists, Caesar alone apparently did not lack *vis*.

[19] *Blandus*: *Tr.* 2.465, 5.1.17; *tener*: *Ars Amat.* 3.333.

wit Ovid calls smooth.[20] Finally—and here we are beyond all questions of style—Tibullus' death forms the subject of one of Ovid's most moving poems (*Am.* 3.9).[21]

The two poems which Horace addresses to Tibullus reveal keen understanding of his subject as a human being.[22] Both pieces (*Carm.* 1.33; *Epist.* 1.4) depict a person who takes himself too seriously and tends to escape from confrontation with life, characteristics even an initial reading of Tibullus' verses confirms. The ode shows Tibullus unable to take love easy and to concede that the only permanence in an elegist's erotic adventures is change. The epistle is a closer portrait. It represents Tibullus as wealthy and handsome, graceful in bearing and mode of living.[23] But, says Horace, his powers do not depend merely on superficial traits. He has mind as well as body, wisdom along with sensitivity, and contemplates thoughtfully "what is worthy of a wise and good man." Nevertheless Horace must urge him, in the midst of hope and care, of his moments of fear and anger, to ponder death. This is the lyricist's underhand way, touched with saving humor, of urging life on his elegist friend. Aloof meditation in a silent sylvan retreat is not enough.

Horace reveals another fact of note. He wonders whether Tibullus is writing something to vie with the *opuscula* of Cassius of Parma.[24] What these are is dubious. Cassius fought in the army of Brutus and the more famous Cassius Longinus at Philippi, with Sextus Pompeius in Sicily and Antony at Actium. The last surviving assassin of Julius Caesar (Velleius Paterculus 2.87.3), he fled to Athens

20 *Ingenium mite*: *Tr.* 5.1.18; *cultus*: *Am.* 1.15.28; 3.9.66.

21 Velleius Paterculus (2.36.3) honorifically links Tibullus and Ovid (*perfectissimi in forma*) with no mention of Propertius.

22 Horace, in spite of their common inclusion among the intimates of Maecenas, never mentions Propertius by name, but it is likely that he alludes to him indirectly and negatively (*Epist.* 2.2.97ff.). Propertius' third book provided ready reasons for his irony.

23 He possesses *forma* (6), *artem fruendi* (7), *gratia* (10). The first is confirmed by the *vita* which describes him as *insignis forma cultuque corporis observabilis*.

24 "Scribere quod Cassi Parmensis opuscula vincat . . . ?" (*Epist.* 1.4.3). For details on Cassius' life see F. Skutsch, *RE* 3.2 (1899), 1743–44.

where he was executed at the order of Octavian. We know that he wrote a play about the tyrannicide Brutus, whose murder of Tarquin traditionally ushered in the republic, and that he lampooned Octavian.[25] The portrait would seem that of a republican and conservative. It has elements in common with the life of Messalla Corvinus which we know more clearly. He too fought along with Brutus and Cassius but, after a brief liaison with Antony, sided with Octavian to whom he offered tempered allegiance thereafter. He proposed the title *Pater Patriae* for Augustus (2 B.C.) but he has another side. Already around the year 25 B.C. he had resigned the post of *praefectus urbis* after only a few days, claiming, according to St. Jerome, that the power he possessed was *incivilis*.[26]

We may therefore plausibly though speculatively suggest political as well as stylistic sympathy between Messalla and Tibullus. In his only poem whose subject is partially Roman and historical (2.5), Tibullus alludes only indirectly to the crucial battle of Actium. Now that Saturn has been exiled and Jupiter holds sway, Apollo can return to his purely intellectual role as god of song, claims Tibullus. But the poem has its ironies. There was once an ideal, rural Rome, a Rome of Panpipes and amorous shepherds, before Romulus built walls and killed Remus. Once, prior to Rome's assumption of universal rule, cattle cropped her grassy seven hills, a moment in civilization halted only by Aeneas battling with Turnus and Ilia deserting Vesta for Mars. Tibullus feels no need to eulogize the Rome of Augustus and even his treatment of Messalla has its ambiguities.

Certainly time and again throughout the poems Tibullus makes his own deep affection for the countryside felt. In praising peace, especially in 1.10, he shares fully the sentiments of his colleagues Vergil and Horace.[27] In less skillful hands such themes might become only propaganda. With

25 Varro *De Ling. Lat.* 6.7, 7.72; Suetonius *Aug.* 4.

26 Tacitus *Ann.* 6.11.3. Tacitus (*Ann.* 4.34) is also witness that Messalla continued to speak of his republican sympathies without in the least incurring Augustus' wrath. His was a detached involvement.

27 Cf. F. Solmsen, "Tibullus as an Augustan Poet," *Hermes* 90 (1962), 295–325.

Tibullus one senses something more universal than Augustan—an unwilling warrior with an intense dislike of war, the devotee of an urban (and urbane) poetic genre who found intense satisfaction in the literal concerns of rural living and ancient ritual, and, in common with his great contemporary poets, saw landscape as a metaphor for essential aesthetic and ethical continuities.

In general Tibullus is concerned with topics he shares with Propertius, a poet who is also writing subjective love elegy at the same time. Propertius, by admitting his devotion to Mimnermus and Callimachus, places himself squarely in a tradition that runs from seventh-century Greece to the most influential poet of the Hellenistic era. Tibullus expresses no such loyalties directly, but his debt is equally clear. The difficulty is that the origin of Latin subjective erotic elegy remains still a subject of debate. Quintilian states that "elegia quoque Graecos provocamus," implying rivalry more than originality. Yet the rhetorician is thinking not of content but of style and meter (we have examples of elegiac meter preserved from c. 650 B.C.). Ovid, on the other hand (*Tr.* 4.10.53–54), and Quintilian himself by insinuation place the origin of the poetic tradition with Cornelius Gallus whose works, save for one line, have perished but whose material and tone can be gauged well by Vergil's description of him in *Eclogue* 10. His words there (and Vergil may well have quoted from Gallus' own writing) clearly look forward to the later elegists.[28]

We have no fragments of Hellenistic personal love-elegy. Since Hellenistic authors preferred to speak of personal and erotic matters in epigram and since the first subjective erotic poetry in Latin—the few poems of Valerius Aedituus, Porcius Licinus, and Lutatius Catulus, dating from c. 100 B.C.

[28] There is probably a grain of truth in Servius' exaggerated comment on *Ecl.* 10.46: "hi autem omnes versus Galli sunt, de ipsius translati carminibus."

The question of origin is carefully discussed by A. A. Day, *The Origins of Latin Love-Elegy* (Oxford, 1938) and G. Luck, *The Latin Love Elegy*, 2d ed. (London, 1969), esp. ch. 2 and 3. We must not forget that the *Eclogues* were published around 35 B.C. This leaves only seven or eight years until Propertius and Tibullus published their first books, at which time Gallus himself was still alive.

—is epigrammatic, the traditional modern interpretation still seems wiser—first to see elements evolving toward the subjective elegy in Catullus' longer epigrams and in at least one of his lengthier elegiac poems (68), then to assume from later references a profoundly creative (but undocumented) influence emanating from Cornelius Gallus.

Which leaves Tibullus, in Ovid's chronology, Rome's premier elegist. We may easily trace traditional elements in his poetry: 1.2, for instance, is a *paraklausithyron* or song of an excluded lover before his mistress' door. The idea goes back at least to Aristophanes, but Tibullus rings his own variations on tradition.[29] Poem 1.4 contains elements common to all *priapeia*, but Tibullus combines them with a brilliant *ars amandi* while the whole can be seen as a humorous parody of serious didactic poetry. We find in 1.7 elements of birthday poem, heroic ode, panegyric, and hymn caught in easy solution. Even the stock themes common to all the Roman elegists—the rich rival, the negligent *lena*, the dilatory mistress, for example—are given special turns.

The way the poems are ordered also reveals Tibullus' special reliance on variation in the ordering of elegies. Intensely personal elegies are juxtaposed with poems which expand on broader topics, oriented toward philosophy or history.[30] Tibullus sick on Corcyra, dreaming of Elysium and return to Delia, precedes Priapus' disquisition on the virtues of pederasty. Tibullus complaining of fortune's foibles and Delia's disaffection adjoins the praises of Messalla. And there are meticulous verbal echoes and arrangements which not only help structure individual elegies but in many instances clearly link one poem with another.

Some special personal elements deserve brief mention.[31]

29 See F. O. Copley, *Exclusus Amator: A Study in Latin Love Poetry* (Am. Phil. Assoc. monograph 17, 1956), *passim*.

30 Book 1 was certainly arranged by the poet. Book 2 may or may not have received the poet's *ultima manus*. It is unwise to theorize on the chronology of composition (as most recently W. Wimmel in *Der frühe Tibull*). Evidence that the poems are to be read in the traditional order is paramount.

31 For broader appreciations of the poet's art see especially J. P. Elder, "Tibullus: Tersus atque Elegans," in *Critical Essays on Roman Literature*, ed. by J. P. Sullivan (Cambridge, Mass., 1962), 65–105; G. Luck, *The*

There is a very idealistic side to Tibullus' poetry—a yearning for peace and reliance on hope, the creation of a dream world of perfected love in a perfected setting (whether past or future), which serves as touchstone against which present reality is measured. Common to both factual and ideal (and often effecting a transition from gloom to happiness or vice versa) is a typically Roman fascination with magic and religion which not only permeates the poems' subject matter but surfaces also in Tibullus' constant reliance on figures of speech such as assonance, alliteration, and anaphora. These, along with his constant reliance on invocation and on themes of advent and discovery, lend a ritualistic tone which in hymnic passages verges on litany. And poetic ceremony has its counterpart in the firm traditions of country living which itself contrasts with love's urbanities and petty trials.

Basic tensions in Tibullus' poetry range from the most universal—love and hatred, life and death, motion and rest, nearness and remoteness, acceptance and rejection—to more personal predilections when noise challenges silence, binding release, supplication daring. Even more than we might expect from an elegist, Tibullus is fascinated with the idea of touch (tactile words such as hands, feet, hair abound in his verse). Nevertheless, in spite of dependence on the world of sensation, his nature seems reserved, not to say retiring. He resorts to prayer, submits to force, accepting the *status quo* with endurance, anxiety, and occasionally complaint. Frequently he will interweave a series of characters in a single poem as necessary relieving factors, whereas the bolder Propertius regularly faces his subject squarely. And while Propertius will deepen our awareness of his present concerns by reference to mythology, Tibullus analogizes by withdrawal into make-believe or yearning.

Stylistically the ease with which Tibullus moves from theme to theme is remarkable.[32] This smoothness unfailing-

---

Latin Love Elegy, ch. 4 and 5. Shorter articles on individual poems are listed in the bibliography.

[32] Tibullus' style is elaborately discussed by R. Bürger, "Beiträge zur Elegantia Tibulls," in *Charites F. Leo* (Berlin, 1911), 371–90; B. Axelson, *Unpoetische Wörter* (Lund, 1945), esp. 114–33.

ly unifies even disparate materials into a graceful whole. The refined elegance and clarity of diction which Quintilian praises so highly control the most careful, complex verbal settings which make broad use of a wide range of figures of sound and sense. Tibullus' is an artful, witty "simplicity." He relies as fully on repetition, ambiguity, irony, and paradox as do any of his great contemporaries.

The meter of Tibullus' poetry, the elegiac couplet or distich, consists of a dactylic hexameter line (the meter of epic) followed by a shorter line misleadingly called the pentameter, which takes the first two and a half feet of the hexameter line and then repeats the segment. The scheme is as follows:

$$-\smile\smile \mid -\smile\smile \mid -\smile\smile \mid -\smile\smile \mid -\smile\smile \mid - -$$
$$-\smile\smile \mid -\smile\smile \mid - \parallel -\smile\smile \mid -\smile\smile \mid -$$

The principal caesura (or break between words within a foot) occurs, as usual in epic, after the first syllable of the third foot. There will naturally be also a pronounced pause in the middle of the pentameter. Spondees can replace dactyls except in the second half of the pentameter.[33]

Each distich tends to be self-contained though ideas will often be expanded over a series of distichs. A spreading opening line is resolved in a briefer line whose choppy, jingling quality tends to make the reader pause and take stock, as act becomes aphorism, emotion is soothed through commentary, and life philosophized. Thus in any two lines the tense propulsion of fact is often resolved into abstract comment, the specific becomes generalized and the whole takes on an epigrammatic quality which has its parallels in

[33] For detailed discussion see M. Platnauer, *Latin Elegiac Verse* (Cambridge, 1951); J. W. Halporn, M. Ostwald, and T. G. Rosenmeyer, *The Meters of Greek and Latin Poetry* (London, 1963), esp. 71–72; D. S. Raven, *Latin Metre* (London, 1965), esp. 103–109. Most Latin grammars treat rules governing quantity, rhythm, and versification (e.g. Allen and Greenough, *New Latin Grammar* [Boston, 1931], pp. 401–13).

the English meditative lyric more than the heroic couplet. It is a fitting meter for erotic subjects, as epic and lyric, adventure and exclamation, combine.[34]

The manuscript tradition of Tibullus is uncomplicated and late.[35] We have two chief witnesses to the text. Our earliest and best exemplar, dating from the fourteenth century and once in the possession of the great early Renaissance scholar Coluccio Salutati, is now in the Ambrosian library of Milan (catalogued as Ambrosianus R 26 sup. and regularly called A in the *sigla* of critical editions). Next in importance is Vaticanus Latinus 3270 (V), dating from the fifteenth century. Infrequently lesser manuscripts are of value. Though A is our first preserved manuscript, Tibullus is often quoted in medieval *florilegia* which are also of occasional help in establishing the text. The few places where readings are still insecure (as 1.6.42; 1.9.25) are analyzed in the notes.

I have followed here, closely but not exclusively, the text of Georg Luck (1964).[36] The reader is referred to his *apparatus criticus* for the source of individual readings.

[34] For detailed analyses of specific couplets see M. C. J. Putnam, "Simple Tibullus and the Ruse of Style," *Yale French Studies* 45 (1970), 21–32, esp. 24–26.

[35] Full treatment of the textual tradition and of the history of editions can be found in *Albii Tibulli aliorumque carminum libri tres,* ed. by F. W. Lenz, 2d ed. (Leiden, 1964). See also the review by H. D. Jocelyn, *Gnomon* 38 (1966), 35–40. On the use of medieval *florilegia* in establishing the text see F. L. Newton, "Tibullus in two Grammatical *Florilegia* of the Middle Ages," *TAPA* 93 (1962), 253–86.

[36] *Propertii et Tibulli Carmina* (Zürich, 1964). His *apparatus criticus* for Tibullus is on pp. 481–83. Except for minor questions of punctuation or orthography my own departures from the Luck text are usually explained in the notes.

1. 1.

Divitias alius fulvo sibi congerat auro
　　et teneat culti iugera multa soli,
quem labor assiduus vicino terreat hoste,
　　Martia cui somnos classica pulsa fugent:
5　me mea paupertas vita traducat inerti,
　　dum meus assiduo luceat igne focus.
ipse seram teneras maturo tempore vites
　　rusticus et facili grandia poma manu,
nec Spes destituat, sed frugum semper acervos
10　praebeat et pleno pinguia musta lacu.
nam veneror, seu stipes habet desertus in agris
　　seu vetus in trivio florida serta lapis;
et quodcumque mihi pomum novus educat annus,
　　libatum agricolae ponitur ante deo:
15　flava Ceres, tibi sit nostro de rure corona
　　spicea, quae templi pendeat ante fores,
pomosisque ruber custos ponatur in hortis,
　　terreat ut saeva falce Priapus aves.
vos quoque, felicis quondam, nunc pauperis agri
20　custodes, fertis munera vestra, Lares.
tunc vitula innumeros lustrabat caesa iuvencos,
　　nunc agna exigui est hostia parva soli.
agna cadet vobis quam circum rustica pubes
　　clamet "io messes et bona vina date."
25　iam modo, iam possim contentus vivere parvo
　　nec semper longae deditus esse viae,
sed Canis aestivos ortus vitare sub umbra
　　arboris ad rivos praetereuntis aquae.
nec tamen interdum pudeat tenuisse bidentem
30　aut stimulo tardos increpuisse boves,
non agnamve sinu pigeat fetumve capellae

15

    desertum oblita matre referre domum.
at vos exiguo pecori, furesque lupique,
    parcite: de magno praeda petenda grege.
35 hic ego pastoremque meum lustrare quotannis
    et placidam soleo spargere lacte Palem.
adsitis, divi, neu vos e paupere mensa
    dona nec e puris spernite fictilibus.
fictilia antiquus primum sibi fecit agrestis
40   pocula, de facili composuitque luto.
non ego divitias patrum fructusve requiro,
    quos tulit antiquo condita messis avo:
parva seges satis est, satis est requiescere lecto,
    si licet, et solito membra levare toro.
45 quam iuvat immites ventos audire cubantem
    et dominam tenero continuisse sinu
aut, gelidas hibernus aquas cum fuderit Auster,
    securum somnos igne iuvante sequi.
hoc mihi contingat: sit dives iure, furorem
50   qui maris et tristes ferre potest pluvias.
o quantum est auri pereat potiusque smaragdi,
    quam fleat ob nostras ulla puella vias!
te bellare decet terra, Messalla, marique,
    ut domus hostiles praeferat exuvias:
55 me retinent vinctum formosae vincla puellae,
    et sedeo duras ianitor ante fores.
non ego laudari curo, mea Delia; tecum
    dum modo sim, quaeso segnis inersque vocer.
te spectem, suprema mihi cum venerit hora,
60   te teneam moriens deficiente manu.
flebis et arsuro positum me, Delia, lecto,
    tristibus et lacrimis oscula mixta dabis.
flebis: non tua sunt duro praecordia ferro
    vincta, neque in tenero stat tibi corde silex.
65 illo non iuvenis poterit de funere quisquam
    lumina, non virgo sicca referre domum.
tu Manes ne laede meos, sed parce solutis
    crinibus et teneris, Delia, parce genis.
interea, dum fata sinunt, iungamus amores:
70   iam veniet tenebris Mors adoperta caput,

iam subrepet iners aetas nec amare decebit,
    dicere nec cano blanditias capite.
nunc levis est tractanda Venus, dum frangere postes
    non pudet et rixas inseruisse iuvat.
75 hic ego dux milesque bonus: vos, signa tubaeque
    ite procul, cupidis vulnera ferte viris,
ferte et opes: ego composito securus acervo
    despiciam dites despiciamque famem.

1. 2.

Adde merum vinoque novos compesce dolores,
    occupet ut fessi lumina victa sopor,
neu quisquam multo percussum tempora baccho
    excitet, infelix dum requiescit amor.
5 nam posita est nostrae custodia saeva puellae,
    clauditur et dura ianua firma sera.
ianua difficilis domini, te verberet imber,
    te Iovis imperio fulmina missa petant.
ianua, iam pateas uni mihi, victa querelis,
10   neu furtim verso cardine aperta sones.
et mala siqua tibi dixit dementia nostra,
    ignoscas: capiti sint precor illa meo.
te meminisse decet, quae plurima voce peregi
    supplice, cum posti florida serta darem.
15 tu quoque ne timide custodes, Delia, falle:
    audendum est! fortes adiuvat ipsa Venus.
illa favet, seu quis iuvenis nova limina temptat,
    seu reserat fixo dente puella fores;
illa docet molli furtim decedere lecto,
20   illa pedem nullo ponere posse sono,
illa viro coram nutus conferre loquaces
    blandaque compositis abdere verba notis.
nec docet hoc omnes, sed quos nec inertia tardat
    nec vetat obscura surgere nocte timor.
25 en ego cum tenebris tota vagor anxius urbe,
   . . . .
    nec sinit occurrat quisquam, qui corpora ferro
    vulneret aut rapta praemia veste petat.
quisquis amore tenetur, eat tutusque sacerque

30   qualibet: insidias non timuisse decet.
   non mihi pigra nocent hibernae frigora noctis,
       non mihi, cum multa decidit imber aqua.
   non labor hic laedit, reseret modo Delia postes
       et vocet ad digiti me taciturna sonum.
35 parcite luminibus, seu vir seu femina fias
       obvia: celari vult sua furta Venus.
   neu strepitu terrete pedum, neu quaerite nomen,
       neu prope fulgenti lumina ferte face.
   siquis et imprudens aspexerit, occulat ille
40   perque deos omnes se meminisse neget:
   nam fuerit quicumque loquax, is sanguine natam,
       is Venerem e rapido sentiet esse mari.
   nec tamen huic credet coniunx tuus, ut mihi verax
       pollicita est magico saga ministerio.
45 hanc ego de caelo ducentem sidera vidi,
       fluminis haec rapidi carmine vertit iter,
   haec cantu finditque solum Manesque sepulcris
       elicit et tepido devocat ossa rogo:
   iam tenet infernas magico stridore catervas,
50   iam iubet aspersas lacte referre pedem.
   cum libet, haec tristi depellit nubila caelo,
       cum libet, aestivo convocat orbe nives.
   sola tenere malas Medeae dicitur herbas,
       sola feros Hecatae perdomuisse canes.
55 haec mihi composuit cantus, quis fallere posses:
       ter cane, ter dictis despue carminibus.
   ille nihil poterit de nobis credere cuiquam,
       non sibi, si in molli viderit ipse toro.
   tu tamen abstineas aliis: nam cetera cernet
60   omnia, de me uno sentiet ipse nihil.
   quid? credam? nempe haec eadem se dixit amores
       cantibus aut herbis solvere posse meos,
   et me lustravit taedis, et nocte serena
       concidit ad magicos hostia pulla deos.
65 non ego totus abesset amor, sed mutuus esset,
       orabam, nec te posse carere velim.
   ferreus ille fuit, qui te cum possit habere,
       maluerit praedas stultus et arma sequi.

ille licet Cilicum victas agat ante catervas,
70   ponat et in capto Martia castra solo,
totus et argento contextus, totus et auro
    insideat celeri conspiciendus equo,
ipse boves mea si tecum modo Delia possim
    iungere et in solito pascere monte pecus,
75 et te, dum liceat, teneris retinere lacertis,
    mollis et inculta sit mihi somnus humo.
quid Tyrio recubare toro sine amore secundo
    prodest, cum fletu nox vigilanda venit?
nam neque tunc plumae nec stragula picta soporem
80   nec sonitus placidae ducere possit aquae.
num Veneris magnae violavi numina verbo,
    et mea nunc poenas impia lingua luit?
num feror incestus sedes adiisse deorum
    sertaque de sanctis deripuisse focis?
85 non ego, si merui, dubitem procumbere templis
    et dare sacratis oscula liminibus,
non ego tellurem genibus perrepere supplex
    et miserum sancto tundere poste caput.
at tu, qui laetus rides mala nostra, caveto
90   mox tibi: non uni saeviet usque deus.
vidi ego, qui iuvenum miseros lusisset amores,
    post Veneris vinclis subdere colla senem
et sibi blanditias tremula componere voce
    et manibus canas fingere velle comas,
95 stare nec ante fores puduit caraeve puellae
    ancillam medio detinuisse foro.
hunc puer, hunc iuvenis turba circumterit arta,
    despuit in molles et sibi quisque sinus.
at mihi parce, Venus: semper tibi dedita servit
100   mens mea: quid messes uris acerba tuas?

1. 3.

Ibitis Aegaeas sine me, Messalla, per undas,
    o utinam memores ipse cohorsque mei!
me tenet ignotis aegrum Phaeacia terris,
    abstineas avidas, Mors, modo nigra manus.
5 abstineas, Mors atra, precor: non hic mihi mater

quae legat in maestos ossa perusta sinus,
non soror, Assyrios cineri quae dedat odores
　　et fleat effusis ante sepulcra comis.
Delia non usquam; quae me cum mitteret urbe,
10　dicitur ante omnes consuluisse deos.
　illa sacras pueri sortes ter sustulit, illi
　　rettulit e trinis omina certa puer.
　cuncta dabant reditus: tamen est deterrita numquam,
　　quin fleret nostras respiceretque vias.
15 ipse ego solator, cum iam mandata dedissem,
　　quaerebam tardas anxius usque moras.
　aut ego sum causatus aves aut omina dira,
　　Saturnive sacram me tenuisse diem.
　o quotiens ingressus iter mihi tristia dixi
20　offensum in porta signa dedisse pedem!
　audeat invito ne quis discedere Amore,
　　aut sciat egressum se prohibente deo.
　quid tua nunc Isis mihi, Delia, quid mihi prosunt
　　illa tua totiens aera repulsa manu,
25 quidve, pie dum sacra colis, pureque lavari
　　te—memini—et puro secubuisse toro?
　nunc, dea, nunc succurre mihi—nam posse mederi
　　picta docet templis multa tabella tuis—,
　ut mea votivas persolvens Delia voces
30　ante sacras lino tecta fores sedeat
　bisque die resoluta comas tibi dicere laudes
　　insignis turba debeat in Pharia.
　at mihi contingat patrios celebrare Penates
　　reddereque antiquo menstrua tura Lari.
35 quam bene Saturno vivebant rege, priusquam
　　tellus in longas est patefacta vias!
　nondum caeruleas pinus contempserat undas,
　　effusum ventis praebueratque sinum,
　nec vagus ignotis repetens compendia terris
40　presserat externa navita merce ratem.
　illo non validus subiit iuga tempore taurus,
　　non domito frenos ore momordit equus,
　non domus ulla fores habuit, non fixus in agris,
　　qui regeret certis finibus arva, lapis.

45 ipsae mella dabant quercus, ultroque ferebant
    obvia securis ubera lactis oves.
non acies, non ira fuit, non bella, nec ensem
    immiti saevus duxerat arte faber.
nunc Iove sub domino caedes et vulnera semper,
50   nunc mare, nunc leti mille repente viae.
parce, pater! timidum non me periuria terrent,
    non dicta in sanctos impia verba deos.
quod si fatales iam nunc explevimus annos,
    fac lapis inscriptis stet super ossa notis:
55 "hic iacet immiti consumptus morte Tibullus,
    Messallam terra dum sequiturque mari."
sed me, quod facilis tenero sum semper Amori,
    ipsa Venus campos ducet in Elysios.
hic choreae cantusque vigent, passimque vagantes
60   dulce sonant tenui gutture carmen aves,
fert casiam non culta seges, totosque per agros
    floret odoratis terra benigna rosis;
ac iuvenum series teneris immixta puellis
    ludit, et assidue proelia miscet Amor.
65 illic est, cuicumque rapax Mors venit amanti,
    et gerit insigni myrtea serta coma.
at scelerata iacet sedes in nocte profunda
    abdita, quam circum flumina nigra sonant:
Tisiphoneque impexa feros pro crinibus angues
70   saevit, et huc illuc impia turba fugit:
tum niger in porta serpentum Cerberus ore
    stridet et aeratas excubat ante fores.
illic Iunonem temptare Ixionis ausi
    versantur celeri noxia membra rota,
75 porrectusque novem Tityos per iugera terrae
    assiduas atro viscere pascit aves.
Tantalus est illic, et circum stagna, sed acrem
    iam iam poturi deserit unda sitim,
et Danai proles, Veneris quod numina laesit,
80   in cava Lethaeas dolia portat aquas.
illic sit, quicumque meos violavit amores,
    optavit lentas et mihi militias.
at tu casta precor maneas, sanctique pudoris

assideat custos sedula semper anus.
85 haec tibi fabellas referat positaque lucerna
    deducat plena stamina longa colu,
at circa gravibus pensis affixa puella
    paulatim somno fessa remittat opus.
tunc veniam subito, nec quisquam nuntiet ante,
90   sed videar caelo missus adesse tibi.
tunc mihi, qualis eris, longos turbata capillos,
    obvia nudato, Delia, curre pede.
hoc precor, hunc illum nobis Aurora nitentem
    Luciferum roseis candida portet equis.

1. 4.

"Sic umbrosa tibi contingant tecta, Priape,
    ne capiti soles, ne noceantque nives:
quae tua formosos cepit sollertia? certe
    non tibi barba nitet, non tibi culta coma est,
5 nudus et hibernae producis frigora brumae,
    nudus et aestivi tempora sicca Canis."
sic ego; tum Bacchi respondit rustica proles
    armatus curva sic mihi falce deus:
"o fuge te tenerae puerorum credere turbae,
10   nam causam iusti semper amoris habent.
hic placet, angustis quod equum compescit habenis,
    hic placidam niveo pectore pellit aquam,
hic, quia fortis adest audacia, cepit; at illi
    virgineus teneras stat pudor ante genas.
15 sed ne te capiant, primo si forte negabit,
    taedia: paulatim sub iuga colla dabit.
longa dies homini docuit parere leones,
    longa dies molli saxa peredit aqua;
annus in apricis maturat collibus uvas,
20   annus agit certa lucida signa vice.
nec iurare time: Veneris periuria venti
    irrita per terras et freta summa ferunt.
gratia magna Iovi: vetuit pater ipse valere,
    iurasset cupide quidquid ineptus amor,
25 perque suas impune sinit Dictynna sagittas
    adfirmes crines perque Minerva suos.

    at si tardus eris, errabis: transiet aetas.
        quam cito non segnis stat remeatque dies.
    quam cito purpureos deperdit terra colores,
30   quam cito formosas populus alta comas!
    quam iacet, infirmae venere ubi fata senectae,
        qui prior Eleo est carcere missus equus!
    vidi iam iuvenem premeret cum serior aetas,
        maerentem stultos praeteriisse dies.
35 crudeles divi! serpens novus exuit annos,
        formae non ullam fata dedere moram.
    solis aeterna est Baccho Phoeboque iuventas,
        nam decet intonsus crinis utrumque deum.
    tu, puero quodcumque tuo temptare libebit,
40   cedas: obsequio plurima vincet amor.
    neu comes ire neges, quamvis via longa paretur
        et Canis arenti torreat arva siti,
    quamvis praetexens picta ferrugine caelum
        venturam amiciat imbrifer arcus aquam.
45 vel si caeruleas puppi volet ire per undas,
        ipse levem remo per freta pelle ratem.
    nec te paeniteat duros subiisse labores
        aut opera insuetas atteruisse manus,
    nec, velit insidiis altas si claudere valles,
50   dum placeas, umeri retia ferre negent.
    si volet arma, levi temptabis ludere dextra:
        saepe dabis nudum, vincat ut ille, latus.
    tunc tibi mitis erit: rapias tum cara licebit
        oscula: pugnabit, sed tamen apta dabit.
55 rapta dabit primo, post afferet ipse roganti,
        post etiam collo se implicuisse volet.
    heu male nunc artes miseras haec saecula tractant!
        iam tener adsuevit munera velle puer.
    at tua, qui Venerem docuisti vendere primus,
60   quisquis es, infelix urgeat ossa lapis.
    Pieridas, pueri, doctos et amate poetas,
        aurea nec superent munera Pieridas.
    carmine purpurea est Nisi coma: carmina ni sint,
        ex umero Pelopis non nituisset ebur.
65 quem referent Musae, vivet, dum robora tellus,

dum caelum stellas, dum vehet amnis aquas.
at qui non audit Musas, qui vendit amorem,
    Idaeae currus ille sequatur Opis
et tercentenas erroribus expleat urbes
70   et secet ad Phrygios vilia membra modos.
blanditiis volt esse locum Venus: illa querelis
    supplicibus, miseris fletibus illa favet."
haec mihi, quae canerem Titio, deus edidit ore,
    sed Titium coniunx haec meminisse vetat.
75 pareat ille suae: vos me celebrate magistrum,
    quos male habet multa callidus arte puer.
gloria cuique sua est: me, qui spernentur, amantes
    consultent: cunctis ianua nostra patet.
tempus erit, cum me Veneris praecepta ferentem
80   deducat iuvenum sedula turba senem.
heu heu quam Marathus lento me torquet amore!
    deficiunt artes deficiuntque doli.
parce, puer, quaeso! ne turpis fabula fiam,
    cum mea ridebunt vana magisteria.

1. 5.

Asper eram et bene discidium me ferre loquebar:
    at mihi nunc longe gloria fortis abest.
namque agor ut per plana citus sola verbere turben,
    quem celer adsueta versat ab arte puer.
5 ure ferum et torque, libeat ne dicere quicquam
    magnificum post haec: horrida verba doma!
parce tamen, per te furtivi foedera lecti,
    per venerem quaeso compositumque caput!
ille ego, cum tristi morbo defessa iaceres,
10   te dicor votis eripuisse meis,
ipseque ter circum lustravi sulphure puro,
    carmine cum magico praecinuisset anus;
ipse procuravi, ne possent saeva nocere
    somnia, ter sancta deveneranda mola;
15 ipse ego velatus filo tunicisque solutis
    vota novem Triviae nocte silente dedi.
omnia persolvi: fruitur nunc alter amore,
    et precibus felix utitur ille meis.

at mihi felicem vitam, si salva fuisses,
20   fingebam demens, sed renuente deo:
rura colam, frugumque aderit mea Delia custos,
    area dum messes sole calente teret,
aut mihi servabit plenis in lintribus uvas
    pressaque veloci candida musta pede;
25 consuescet numerare pecus, consuescet amantis
    garrulus in dominae ludere verna sinu.
illa deo sciet agricolae pro vitibus uvam,
    pro segete spicas, pro grege ferre dapem.
illa regat cunctos, illi sint omnia curae:
30   at iuvet in tota me nihil esse domo.
huc veniet Messalla meus, cui dulcia poma
    Delia selectis detrahat arboribus;
et tantum venerata virum hunc sedula curet,
    huic paret atque epulas ipsa ministra gerat.
35 haec mihi fingebam, quae nunc Eurusque Notusque
    iactat odoratos vota per Armenios.
saepe ego temptavi curas depellere vino:
    at dolor in lacrimas verterat omne merum,
saepe aliam tenui: sed iam cum gaudia adirem,
40   admonuit dominae deseruitque Venus.
tunc me discedens devotum femina dixit,
    et pudet et narrat scire nefanda meam.
non facit hoc verbis, facie tenerisque lacertis
    devovet et flavis nostra puella comis.
45 talis ad Haemonium Nereis Pelea quondam
    vecta est frenato caerula pisce Thetis.
haec nocuere mihi: quod adest huic dives amator,
    venit in exitium callida lena meum.
sanguineas edat illa dapes atque ore cruento
50   tristia cum multo pocula felle bibat;
hanc volitent animae circum sua fata querentes
    semper et e tectis strix violenta canat;
ipsa fame stimulante furens herbasque sepulcris
    quaerat et a saevis ossa relicta lupis;
55 currat et inguinibus nudis ululetque per urbes,
    post agat e triviis aspera turba canum.
eveniet: dat signa deus; sunt numina amanti,

saevit et iniusta lege relicta Venus.
at tu quam primum sagae praecepta rapacis
60   desere, nam donis vincitur omnis amor.
pauper erit praesto semper, te pauper adibit
   primus et in tenero fixus erit latere,
pauper in angusto fidus comes agmine turbae
   subicietque manus efficietque viam,
65 pauper ad occultos furtim deducet amicos
   vinclaque de niveo detrahet ipse pede.
heu canimus frustra, nec verbis victa patescit
   ianua, sed plena est percutienda manu.
at tu, qui potior nunc es, mea furta timeto:
70   versatur celeri Fors levis orbe rotae.
non frustra quidam iam nunc in limine perstat
   sedulus, et crebro prospicit ac refugit,
et simulat transire domum, mox deinde recurrit
   solus et ante ipsas excreat usque fores.
75 nescio quid furtivus amor parat. utere quaeso,
   dum licet: in liquida nat tibi linter aqua.

1. 6.

Semper, ut inducar, blandos offers mihi vultus,
   post tamen es misero tristis et asper, Amor.
quid tibi saevitiae mecum est? an gloria magna est
   insidias homini composuisse deum?
5 iam mihi tenduntur casses, iam Delia furtim
   nescio quem tacita callida nocte fovet.
illa quidem tam multa negat, sed credere durum est:
   sic etiam de me pernegat usque viro.
ipse miser docui, quo posset ludere pacto
10   custodes: heu heu nunc premor arte mea!
fingere nunc didicit causas, ut sola cubaret,
   cardine nunc tacito vertere posse fores,
tum sucos herbasque dedi, quis livor abiret,
   quem facit impresso mutua dente venus.
15 at tu, fallacis coniunx incaute puellae,
   me quoque servato, peccet ut illa nihil.
neu iuvenes celebret multo sermone, caveto,
   neve cubet laxo pectus aperta sinu,

neu te decipiat nutu, digitoque liquorem
20 ne trahat et mensae ducat in orbe notas.
exibit quam saepe, time, seu visere dicet
   sacra Bonae maribus non adeunda Deae.
at mihi si credas, illam sequar unus ad aras:
   tunc mihi non oculis sit timuisse meis.
25 saepe, velut gemmas eius signumque probarem,
   per causam memini me tetigisse manum;
saepe mero somnum peperi tibi, at ipse bibebam
   sobria supposita pocula victor aqua.
non ego te laesi prudens: ignosce fatenti,
30 iussit Amor: contra quis ferat arma deos?
ille ego sum, nec me iam dicere vera pudebit,
   instabat tota cui tua nocte canis.
quid tenera tibi coniuge opus? tua si bona nescis
   servare frustra clavis inest foribus!
35 te tenet, absentes alios suspirat amores
   et simulat subito condoluisse caput.
at mihi servandam credas: non saeva recuso
   verbera, detrecto non ego vincla pedum.
tum procul absitis, quisquis colit arte capillos,
40 et fluit effuso cui toga laxa sinu,
quisquis et occurret, ne possit crimen habere,
   stet procul aut alia stet procul ante via.
sic fieri iubet ipse deus, sic magna sacerdos
   est mihi divino vaticinata sono.
45 haec ubi Bellonae motu est agitata, nec acrem
   flammam, non amens verbera torta timet;
ipsa bipenne suos caedit violenta lacertos
   sanguineque effuso spargit inulta deam,
statque latus praefixa veru, stat saucia pectus,
50 et canit eventus, quos dea magna monet:
"parcite, quam custodit Amor, violare puellam,
   ne pigeat magno post didicisse malo.
attigerit, labentur opes, ut vulnere nostro
   sanguis, ut hic ventis diripiturque cinis."
55 et tibi nescio quas dixit, mea Delia, poenas:
   si tamen admittas, sit, precor, illa levis.
non ego te propter parco tibi, sed tua mater

me movet atque iras aurea vincit anus.
haec mihi te adducit tenebris multoque timore
60 coniungit nostras clam taciturna manus,
haec foribusque manet noctu me affixa proculque
cognoscit strepitus me veniente pedum.
vive diu mihi, dulcis anus: proprios ego tecum,
sit modo fas, annos contribuisse velim.
65 te semper natamque tuam te propter amabo:
quidquid agit, sanguis est tamen illa tuus.
sit modo casta, doce, quamvis non vitta ligatos
impediat crines nec stola longa pedes.
et mihi sint durae leges, laudare nec ullam
70 possim ego, quin oculos appetat illa meos,
et siquid peccasse putet, ducarque capillis
immerito pronas proripiarque vias.
non ego te pulsare velim, sed, venerit iste
si furor, optarim non habuisse manus:
75 nec saevo sis casta metu, sed mente fideli;
mutuus absenti te mihi servet amor.
at, quae fida fuit nulli, post victa senecta
ducit inops tremula stamina torta manu
firmaque conductis adnectit licia telis
80 tractaque de niveo vellere ducta putat.
hanc animo gaudente vident iuvenumque catervae
commemorant merito tot mala ferre senem,
hanc Venus ex alto flentem sublimis Olympo
spectat et, infidis quam sit acerba, monet.
85 haec aliis maledicta cadant: nos, Delia, amoris
exemplum cana simus uterque coma.

1. 7.

Hunc cecinere diem Parcae fatalia nentes
stamina, non ulli dissoluenda deo;
hunc fore, Aquitanas posset qui fundere gentes,
quem tremeret forti milite victus Atax.
5 evenere: novos pubes Romana triumphos
vidit et evinctos bracchia capta duces:
at te victrices lauros, Messalla, gerentem
portabat nitidis currus eburnus equis.

non sine me est tibi partus honos: Tarbella Pyrene
10 testis et Oceani litora Santonici,
testis Arar Rhodanusque celer magnusque Garunna,
 Carnutis et flavi caerula lympha Liger.
an te, Cydne, canam, tacitis qui leniter undis
 caeruleus placidis per vada serpis aquis,
15 quantus et aetherio contingens vertice nubes
 frigidus intonsos Taurus alat Cilicas?
quid referam, ut volitet crebras intacta per urbes
 alba Palaestino sancta columba Syro,
utque maris vastum prospectet turribus aequor
20 prima ratem ventis credere docta Tyros,
qualis et, arentes cum findit Sirius agros,
 fertilis aestiva Nilus abundet aqua?
Nile pater, quanam possim te dicere causa
 aut quibus in terris occuluisse caput?
25 te propter nullos tellus tua postulat imbres,
 arida nec pluvio supplicat herba Iovi.
te canit atque suum pubes miratur Osirim
 barbara, Memphiten plangere docta bovem.
primus aratra manu sollerti fecit Osiris
30 et teneram ferro sollicitavit humum,
primus inexpertae commisit semina terrae
 pomaque non notis legit ab arboribus.
hic docuit teneram palis adiungere vitem,
 hic viridem dura caedere falce comam;
35 illi iucundos primum matura sapores
 expressa incultis uva dedit pedibus.
ille liquor docuit voces inflectere cantu,
 movit et ad certos nescia membra modos;
Bacchus et agricolae magno confecta labore
40 pectora tristitiae dissoluenda dedit;
Bacchus et afflictis requiem mortalibus affert,
 crura licet dura compede pulsa sonent.
non tibi sunt tristes curae nec luctus, Osiri,
 sed chorus et cantus et levis aptus amor,
45 sed varii flores et frons redimita corymbis,
 fusa sed ad teneros lutea palla pedes
et Tyriae vestes et dulci tibia cantu

et levis occultis conscia cista sacris.
huc ades et Genium ludis Geniumque choreis
50   concelebra et multo tempora funde mero:
illius et nitido stillent unguenta capillo,
   et capite et collo mollia serta gerat.
sic venias hodierne: tibi dem turis honores,
   liba et Mopsopio dulcia melle feram.
55 at tibi succrescat proles, quae facta parentis
   augeat et circa stet veneranda senem.
nec taceat monumenta viae, quem Tuscula tellus
   candidaque antiquo detinet Alba lare.
namque opibus congesta tuis hic glarea dura
60   sternitur, hic apta iungitur arte silex.
te canet agricola, a magna cum venerit urbe
   serus inoffensum rettuleritque pedem.
at tu, Natalis multos celebrande per annos,
   candidior semper candidiorque veni.

1. 8.

Non ego celari possum, quid nutus amantis
   quidve ferant miti lenia verba sono.
nec mihi sunt sortes nec conscia fibra deorum,
   praecinit eventus nec mihi cantus avis:
5 ipsa Venus magico religatum bracchia nodo
   perdocuit multis non sine verberibus.
desine dissimulare; deus crudelius urit,
   quos videt invitos succubuisse sibi.
quid tibi nunc molles prodest coluisse capillos
10   saepeque mutatas disposuisse comas?
quid fuco splendente genas ornare, quid ungues
   artificis docta subsecuisse manu?
frustra iam vestes, frustra mutantur amictus,
   ansaque compressos colligat arta pedes.
15 illa placet, quamvis inculto venerit ore
   nec nitidum tarda compserit arte caput.
num te carminibus, num te pallentibus herbis
   devovit tacito tempore noctis anus?
cantus vicinis fruges traducit ab agris,
20   cantus et iratae detinet anguis iter,

cantus et e curru Lunam deducere temptat
    et faceret, si non aera repulsa sonent.
quid queror, heu, misero carmen nocuisse, quid herbas?
    forma nihil magicis utitur auxiliis:
25 sed corpus tetigisse nocet, sed longa dedisse
    oscula, sed femini conseruisse femur.
nec tu difficilis puero tamen esse memento:
    persequitur poenis tristia facta Venus.
munera ne poscas: det munera canus amator,
30   ut foveat molli frigida membra sinu.
carior est auro iuvenis, cui levia fulgent
    ora nec amplexus aspera barba terit.
huic tu candentes umero suppone lacertos,
    et regum magnae despiciantur opes.
35 at Venus inveniet puero concumbere furtim,
    dum timet, et teneros conserere usque sinus
et dare anhelanti pugnantibus umida linguis
    oscula et in collo figere dente notas.
non lapis hanc gemmaeque iuvant, quae frigore sola
40   dormiat et nulli sit cupienda viro.
heu sero revocatur amor seroque iuventa,
    cum vetus infecit cana senecta caput!
tum studium formae est, coma tum mutatur, ut annos
    dissimulet viridi cortice tincta nucis,
45 tollere tum cura est albos a stirpe capillos
    et faciem dempta pelle referre novam.
at tu, dum primi floret tibi temporis aetas,
    utere! non tardo labitur illa pede.
neu Marathum torque! puero quae gloria victo est?
50   in veteres esto dura, puella, senes!
parce, precor, tenero! non illi sontica causa est,
    sed nimius luto corpora tingit amor.
vel miser absenti maestas quam saepe querelas
    conicit, et lacrimis omnia plena madent.
55 "quid me spernis?" ait, "poterat custodia vinci:
    ipse dedit cupidis fallere posse deus.
nota Venus furtiva mihi est, ut lenis agatur
    spiritus, ut nec dent oscula rapta sonum,
et possum media quamvis obrepere nocte

60   et strepitu nullo clam reserare fores.
  quid prosunt artes, miserum si spernit amantem
      et fugit ex ipso saeva puella toro?
  vel cum promittit, subito sed perfida fallit,
      est mihi nox multis evigilanda malis.
65 dum mihi venturam fingo, quodcumque movetur,
      illius credo tunc sonuisse pedes."
  desistas lacrimare, puer: non frangitur illa,
      et tua iam fletu lumina fessa tument.
  oderunt, Pholoe, moneo, fastidia divi,
70   nec prodest sanctis tura dedisse focis.
  hic Marathus quondam miseros ludebat amantes
      nescius ultorem post caput esse deum.
  saepe etiam lacrimas fertur risisse dolentis
      et cupidum ficta detinuisse mora:
75 nunc omnes odit fastus, nunc displicet illi
      quaecumque opposita est ianua dura sera.
  at te poena manet, ni desinis esse superba.
      quam cupies votis hunc revocare diem!

1. 9.

  Quid mihi, si fueras miseros laesurus amores,
      foedera per divos, clam violanda, dabas?
  a miser, et siquis primo periuria celat!
      sera tamen tacitis Poena venit pedibus.
5 parcite, caelestes: aequum est impune licere
      numina formosis laedere vestra semel.
  lucra petens habili tauros adiungit aratro
      et durum terrae rusticus urget opus,
  lucra petituras freta per parentia ventis
10   ducunt instabiles sidera certa rates:
  muneribus meus est captus puer, at deus illa
      in cinerem et liquidas munera vertat aquas.
  iam mihi persolvet poenas, pulvisque decorem
      detrahet et ventis horrida facta coma;
15 uretur facies, urentur sole capilli,
      deteret invalidos et via longa pedes.
  admonui quotiens "auro ne pollue formam:
      saepe solent auro multa subesse mala.

divitiis captus siquis violavit amorem,
20   asperaque est illi difficilisque Venus.
ure meum potius flamma caput et pete ferro
    corpus et intorto verbere terga seca.
nec tibi celandi spes sit peccare paranti:
    scit deus, occultos qui vetat esse dolos.
25 ipse deus tacito permisit lene ministro
    ederet ut multo libera verba mero;
ipse deus somno domitos emittere vocem
    iussit et invitos facta tegenda loqui."
haec ego dicebam: nunc me flevisse loquentem,
30   nunc pudet ad teneros procubuisse pedes.
tunc mihi iurabas nullo te divitis auri
    pondere, non gemmis vendere velle fidem,
non tibi si pretium Campania terra daretur,
    non tibi si, Bacchi cura, Falernus ager.
35 illis eriperes verbis mihi sidera caeli
    lucere et puras fluminis esse vias.
quin etiam flebas: at non ego fallere doctus
    tergebam umentes credulus usque genas.
quid faciam, nisi et ipse fores in amore puellae?
40   sit, precor, exemplo, sit levis illa tuo!
o quotiens, verbis ne quisquam conscius esset,
    ipse comes multa lumina nocte tuli!
saepe insperanti venit tibi munere nostro
    et latuit clausas post adoperta fores.
45 tum miser interii stulte confisus amari:
    nam poteram ad laqueos cautior esse tuos.
quin etiam attonita laudes tibi mente canebam,
    at me nunc nostri Pieridumque pudet.
illa velim rapida Vulcanus carmina flamma
50   torreat et liquida deleat amnis aqua.
tu procul hinc absis, cui formam vendere cura est
    et pretium plena grande referre manu.
at te, qui puerum donis corrumpere es ausus,
    rideat assiduis uxor inulta dolis,
55 et cum furtivo iuvenem lassaverit usu,
    tecum interposita languida veste cubet.
semper sint externa tuo vestigia lecto,

et pateat cupidis semper aperta domus;
nec lasciva soror dicatur plura bibisse
60   pocula vel plures emeruisse viros.
(illam saepe ferunt convivia ducere Baccho,
    dum rota Luciferi provocet orta diem;
illa nulla queat melius consumere noctem
    aut operum varias disposuisse vices.)
65 at tua perdidicit, nec tu, stultissime, sentis,
    cum tibi non solita corpus ab arte movet.
tune putas illam pro te disponere crines
    aut tenues denso pectere dente comas?
istane persuadet facies, auroque lacertos
70   vinciat et Tyrio prodeat apta sinu?
non tibi, sed iuveni cuidam vult bella videri,
    devoveat pro quo remque domumque tuam.
nec facit hoc vitio, sed corpora foeda podagra
    et senis amplexus culta puella fugit.
75 cui tamen accubuit noster puer: hunc ego credam
    cum trucibus venerem iungere posse feris.
blanditiasne meas aliis tu vendere es ausus?
    tune aliis demens oscula ferre mea?
tum flebis, cum me vinctum puer alter habebit
80   et geret in regno regna superba tuo.
at tua tum me poena iuvet, Venerique merenti
    fixa notet casus aurea palma meos:
"hanc tibi fallaci resolutus amore Tibullus
    dedicat et grata sis, dea, mente rogat."

1. 10

Quis fuit, horrendos primus qui protulit enses?
    quam ferus et vere ferreus ille fuit!
tum caedes hominum generi, tum proelia nata,
    tum brevior dirae mortis aperta via est.
5 an nihil ille miser meruit, nos ad mala nostra
    vertimus, in saevas quod dedit ille feras?
divitis hoc vitium est auri, nec bella fuerunt,
    faginus adstabat cum scyphus ante dapes.
non arces, non vallus erat, somnumque petebat
10   securus varias dux gregis inter oves.

tunc mihi vita foret vulgi nec tristia nossem
    arma nec audissem corde micante tubam:
nunc ad bella trahor, et iam quis forsitan hostis
    haesura in nostro tela gerit latere.
15 sed patrii servate Lares! aluistis et idem,
    cursarem vestros cum tener ante pedes.
neu pudeat prisco vos esse e stipite factos:
    sic veteris sedes incoluistis avi.
tum melius tenuere fidem, cum paupere cultu
20   stabat in exigua ligneus aede deus.
hic placatus erat, seu quis libaverat uvam,
    seu dederat sanctae spicea serta comae,
atque aliquis voti compos liba ipse ferebat
    postque comes purum filia parva favum.
25 at nobis aerata, Lares, depellite tela,

. . . .

    hostiaque e plena rustica porcus hara.
hanc pura cum veste sequar myrtoque canistra
    vincta geram, myrto vinctus et ipse caput.
sic placeam vobis: alius sit fortis in armis,
30   sternat et adversos Marte favente duces,
ut mihi potanti possit sua dicere facta
    miles et in mensa pingere castra mero.
quis furor est atram bellis accersere mortem?
    imminet et tacito clam venit illa pede.
35 non seges est infra, non vinea culta, sed audax
    Cerberus et Stygiae navita turpis aquae:
illic percussisque genis ustoque capillo
    errat ad obscuros pallida turba lacus.
quin potius laudandus hic est, quem prole parata
40   occupat in parva pigra senecta casa!
ipse suas sectatur oves, at filius agnos,
    et calidam fesso comparat uxor aquam.
sic ego sim, liceatque caput candescere canis,
    temporis et prisci facta referre senem.
45 interea pax arva colat. pax candida primum
    duxit araturos sub iuga curva boves,
pax aluit vites et sucos condidit uvae,

        funderet ut nato testa paterna merum,
    pace bidens vomerque nitent, at tristia duri
50   militis in tenebris occupat arma situs.
    rusticus e lucoque vehit, male sobrius ipse,
        uxorem plaustro progeniemque domum,
    sed Veneris tum bella calent, scissosque capillos
        femina perfractas conqueriturque fores.
55 flet teneras subtusa genas, sed victor et ipse
        flet sibi dementes tam valuisse manus.
    at lascivus Amor rixae mala verba ministrat,
        inter et iratum lentus utrumque sedet.
    a, lapis est ferrumque, suam quicumque puellam
60   verberat! e caelo deripit ille deos.
    sit satis e membris tenuem rescindere vestem,
        sit satis ornatus dissoluisse comae,
    sit lacrimas movisse satis: quater ille beatus,
        quo tenera irato flere puella potest!
65 sed manibus qui saevus erit, scutumque sudemque
        is gerat et miti sit procul a Venere.
    at nobis, Pax alma, veni spicamque teneto,
        perfluat et pomis candidus ante sinus.

2. 1.

    Quisquis adest, faveat: fruges lustramus et agros,
        ritus ut a prisco traditus extat avo.
    Bacche, veni, dulcisque tuis e cornibus uva
        pendeat, et spicis tempora cinge, Ceres!
5 luce sacra requiescat humus, requiescat arator,
        et grave suspenso vomere cesset opus.
    solvite vincla iugis: nunc ad praesepia debent
        plena coronato stare boves capite.
    omnia sint operata deo: non audeat ulla
10   lanificam pensis imposuisse manum.
    vos quoque abesse procul iubeo, discedat ab aris,
        cui tulit hesterna gaudia nocte Venus.
    casta placent superis: pura cum veste venite
        et manibus puris sumite fontis aquam.
15 cernite, fulgentes ut eat sacer agnus ad aras
        vinctaque post olea candida turba comas.

di patrii, purgamus agros, purgamus agrestes:
    vos mala de nostris pellite limitibus,
neu seges eludat messem fallacibus herbis,
20   neu timeat celeres tardior agna lupos.
tunc nitidus plenis confisus rusticus agris
    ingeret ardenti grandia ligna foco,
turbaque vernarum, saturi bona signa coloni,
    ludet et ex virgis exstruet ante casas.
25 eventura precor: viden ut felicibus extis
    significet placidos nuntia fibra deos?
nunc mihi fumosos veteris proferte Falernos
    consulis et Chio solvite vincla cado.
vina diem celebrent: non festa luce madere
30   est rubor, errantes et male ferre pedes.
sed "bene Messallam" sua quisque ad pocula dicat,
    nomen et absentis singula verba sonent.
gentis Aquitanae celeber Messalla triumphis
    et magna intonsis gloria victor avis,
35 huc ades adspiraque mihi, dum carmine nostro
    redditur agricolis gratia caelitibus.
rura cano rurisque deos: his vita magistris
    desuevit querna pellere glande famem;
illi compositis primum docuere tigillis
40   exiguam viridi fronde operire domum,
illi etiam tauros primi docuisse feruntur
    servitium et plaustro supposuisse rotam.
tunc victus abiere feri, tunc consita pomus,
    tunc bibit inriguas fertilis hortus aquas,
45 aurea tunc pressos pedibus dedit uva liquores
    mixtaque securo est sobria lympha mero.
rura ferunt messes, calidi cum sideris aestu
    deponit flavas annua terra comas.
rure levis verno flores apis ingerit alveo,
50   compleat ut dulci sedula melle favos.
agricola assiduo primum satiatus aratro
    cantavit certo rustica verba pede
et satur arenti primum est modulatus avena
    carmen, ut ornatos diceret ante deos,
55 agricola et minio suffusus, Bacche, rubenti

primus inexperta duxit ab arte choros.
huic datus a pleno, memorabile munus, ovili
    dux pecoris: curtas auxerat hircus opes.
rure puer verno primum de flore coronam
60   fecit et antiquis imposuit Laribus.
rure etiam teneris curam exhibitura puellis
    molle gerit tergo lucida vellus ovis.
hinc et femineus labor est, hinc pensa colusque,
    fusus et apposito pollice versat opus:
65 atque aliqua assidue textrix operata Minervae
    cantat, et appulso tela sonat latere.
ipse interque agros interque armenta Cupido
    natus et indomitas dicitur inter equas.
illic indocto primum se exercuit arcu:
70   ei mihi, quam doctas nunc habet ille manus!
nec pecudes, velut ante, petit: fixisse puellas
    gestit et audaces perdomuisse viros.
hic iuveni detraxit opes, hic dicere iussit
    limen ad iratae verba pudenda senem;
75 hoc duce custodes furtim transgressa iacentes
    ad iuvenem tenebris sola puella venit
et pedibus praetemptat iter suspensa timore,
    explorat caecas cui manus ante vias.
a miseri, quos hic graviter deus urget, at ille
80   felix, cui placidus leniter adflat Amor!
sancte, veni dapibus festis, sed pone sagittas
    et procul ardentes hinc, precor, abde faces.
vos celebrem cantate deum pecorique vocate
    voce: palam pecori, clam sibi quisque vocet,
85 aut etiam sibi quisque palam: nam turba iocosa
    obstrepit et Phrygio tibia curva sono.
ludite: iam Nox iungit equos, currumque sequuntur
    matris lascivo sidera fulva choro,
postque venit tacitus furvis circumdatus alis
90   Somnus et incerto Somnia nigra pede.

2. 2.

Dicamus bona verba; venit Natalis ad aras:
    quisquis ades, lingua, vir mulierque, fave!

urantur pia tura focis, urantur odores,
  quos tener e terra divite mittit Arabs.
5 ipse suos Genius adsit visurus honores,
  cui decorent sanctas mollia serta comas.
illius puro destillent tempora nardo,
  atque satur libo sit madeatque mero.
adnuat et, Cornute, tibi quodcumque rogabis.
10   en age, quid cessas? adnuit ille: roga.
auguror, uxoris fidos optabis amores:
  iam reor hoc ipsos edidicisse deos.
nec tibi malueris, totum quaecumque per orbem
  fortis arat valido rusticus arva bove,
15 nec tibi, gemmarum quidquid felicibus Indis
  nascitur, Eoi qua maris unda rubet.
vota cadunt: utinam strepitantibus advolet alis
  flavaque coniugio vincula portet Amor,
vincula, quae maneant semper, dum tarda senectus
20   inducat rugas inficiatque comas.
hic veniat Natalis, avis prolemque ministret,
  ludat ut ante tuos turba novella pedes.

2. 3.

Rura meam, Cornute, tenent villaeque puellam:
  ferreus est, heu heu, quisquis in urbe manet!
ipsa Venus latos iam nunc migravit in agros,
  verbaque aratoris rustica discit Amor.
5 o ego, cum adspicerem dominam, quam fortiter illic
  versarem valido pingue bidente solum!
agricolaeque modo curvum sectarer aratrum,
  dum subigunt steriles arva serenda boves,
nec quererer, quod sol graciles exureret artus,
10   laederet et teneras pussula rupta manus.
pavit et Admeti tauros formosus Apollo,
  nec cithara intonsae profueruntve comae,
nec potuit curas sanare salubribus herbis:
  quidquid erat medicae vicerat artis amor.
15 ipse deus solitus stabulis expellere vaccas

. . . .

et miscere novo docuisse coagula lacte,
    lacteus et mixtis obriguisse liquor.
tum fiscella levi detexta est vimine iunci,
20   raraque per nexus est via facta sero.
o quotiens illo vitulum gestante per agros
    dicitur occurrens erubuisse soror!
o quotiens ausae, caneret dum valle sub alta,
    rumpere mugitu carmina docta boves!
25 saepe duces trepidis petiere oracula rebus,
    venit et a templis irrita turba domum;
saepe horrere sacros doluit Latona capillos,
    quos admirata est ipsa noverca prius.
quisquis inornatumque caput crinesque solutos
30   aspiceret, Phoebi quaereret ille comam.
Delos ubi nunc, Phoebe, tua est, ubi Delphica Pytho?
    nempe Amor in parva te iubet esse casa.
felices olim, Veneri cum fertur aperte
    servire aeternos non puduisse deos.
35 fabula nunc ille est, sed cui sua cura puella est,
    fabula sit mavult quam sine amore deus.
at tu, quisquis is es, cui tristi fronte Cupido
    imperat, ut nostra sint tua castra domo

. . . .

ferrea non Venerem, sed praedam saecula laudant,
40   praeda tamen multis est operata malis.
praeda feras acies cinxit discordibus armis:
    hinc cruor, hinc caedes mors propriorque venit.
praeda vago iussit geminare pericula ponto,
    bellica cum dubiis rostra dedit ratibus.
45 praedator cupit immensos obsidere campos,
    ut multa innumera iugera pascat ove;
cui lapis externus curae est, urbisque tumultu
    portatur validis mille columna iugis,
claudit et indomitum moles mare, lentus ut intra
50   neglegat hibernas piscis adesse minas.
at mihi laeta trahant Samiae convivia testae
    fictaque Cumana lubrica terra rota.
heu heu, divitibus video gaudere puellas:

iam veniant praedae, si Venus optat opes,
55 ut mea luxuria Nemesis fluat utque per urbem
    incedat donis conspicienda meis.
illa gerat vestes tenues, quas femina Coa
    texuit auratas disposuitque vias;
illi sint comites fusci, quos India torret
60   Solis et admotis inficit ignis equis;
illi selectos certent praebere colores
    Africa puniceum purpureumque Tyros.
nota loquor: regnum ipse tenet, quem saepe coegit
    barbara gypsatos ferre catasta pedes.
65 at tibi dura seges, Nemesim qui abducis ab urbe,
    persolvat nulla semina certa fide.
et tu, Bacche tener, iucundae consitor uvae,
    tu quoque devotos, Bacche, relinque lacus.
haud impune licet formosas tristibus agris
70   abdere: non tanti sunt tua musta, pater.
o valeant fruges, ne sint modo rure puellae:
    glans alat, et prisco more bibantur aquae.
glans aluit veteres, et passim semper amarunt:
    quid nocuit sulcos non habuisse satos?
75 tum, quibus adspirabat Amor, praebebat aperte
    mitis in umbrosa gaudia valle Venus.
nullus erat custos, nulla exclusura dolentes
    ianua: si fas est, mos precor ille redi!

. . . .

80   horrida villosa corpora veste tegant.
nunc si clausa mea est, si copia rara videndi,
    heu miserum, laxam quid iuvat esse togam?
ducite: ad imperium dominae sulcabimus agros,
    non ego me vinclis verberibusque nego.

2. 4.

Sic mihi servitium video dominamque paratam:
    iam mihi libertas illa paterna vale,
servitium sed triste datur, teneorque catenis,
    et numquam misero vincla remittit Amor,
5 et seu quid merui seu nil peccavimus, urit.

uror, io! remove, saeva puella, faces!
o ego ne possim tales sentire dolores,
    quam mallem in gelidis montibus esse lapis,
stare vel insanis cautes obnoxia ventis,
10   naufraga quam vasti tunderet unda maris!
nunc et amara dies et noctis amarior umbra est,
    omnia nunc tristi tempora felle madent.
nec prosunt elegi nec carminis auctor Apollo:
    illa cava pretium flagitat usque manu.
15 ite procul, Musae, si non prodestis amanti:
    non ego vos, ut sint bella canenda, colo,
nec refero Solisque vias et qualis, ubi orbem
    complevit, versis Luna recurrit equis.
ad dominam faciles aditus per carmina quaero:
20   ite procul, Musae, si nihil ista valent.
at mihi per caedem et facinus sunt dona paranda,
    ne iaceam clausam flebilis ante domum,
aut rapiam suspensa sacris insignia fanis,
    sed Venus ante alios est violanda mihi:
25 illa malum facinus suadet dominamque rapacem
    dat mihi: sacrilegas sentiat illa manus.
o pereat, quicumque legit viridesque smaragdos
    et niveam Tyrio murice tingit ovem.
hic dat avaritiae causas et Coa puellis
30   vestis et e Rubro lucida concha mari.
haec fecere malas: hinc clavim ianua sensit,
    et coepit custos liminis esse canis.
sed pretium si grande feras, custodia victa est,
    nec prohibent claves, et canis ipse tacet.
35 heu quicumque dedit formam caelestis avarae,
    quale bonum multis attulit ille malis!
hinc fletus rixaeque sonant, haec denique causa
    fecit ut infamis nunc deus erret Amor.
at tibi, quae pretio victos excludis amantes,
40   eripiant partas ventus et ignis opes:
quin tua tunc iuvenes spectent incendia lenti,
    nec quisquam flammae sedulus addat aquam;
seu veniet tibi mors, nec erit qui lugeat ullus,
    nec qui det maestas munus in exequias.

45 at bona quae nec avara fuit, centum licet annos
    vixerit, ardentem flebitur ante rogum,
  atque aliquis senior veteres veneratus amores
    annua constructo serta dabit tumulo
  et "bene" discedens dicet "placideque quiescas,
50   terraque securae sit super ossa levis."
  vera quidem moneo, sed prosunt quid mihi vera?
    illius est nobis lege colendus Amor.
  quin etiam sedes iubeat si vendere avitas,
    ite sub imperium sub titulumque, Lares!
55 quidquid habet Circe, quidquid Medea veneni,
    quidquid et herbarum Thessala terra gerit,
  et quod, ubi indomitis gregibus Venus adflat amores,
    hippomanes cupidae stillat ab inguine equae,
  si modo me placido videat Nemesis mea vultu,
60   mille alias herbas misceat illa, bibam!

2. 5.

  Phoebe, fave! novus ingreditur tua templa sacerdos:
    huc age cum cithara carminibusque veni.
  nunc te vocales impellere pollice chordas,
    nunc precor ad laudes flectere verba meas.
5 ipse triumphali devinctus tempora lauro,
    dum cumulant aras, ad tua sacra veni;
  sed nitidus pulcherque veni: nunc indue vestem
    sepositam, longas nunc bene pecte comas,
  qualem te memorant Saturno rege fugato
10   victori laudes concinuisse Iovi.
  tu procul eventura vides, tibi deditus augur
    scit bene, quid fati provida cantet avis,
  tuque regis sortes, per te praesentit haruspex,
    lubrica signavit cum deus exta notis;
15 te duce Romanos numquam frustrata Sibylla,
    abdita quae senis fata canit pedibus.
  Phoebe, sacras Messalinum sine tangere chartas
    vatis, et ipse, precor, quid canat illa doce.
  haec dedit Aeneae sortes, postquam ille parentem
20   dicitur et raptos sustinuisse Lares:
  (nec fore credebat Romam, cum maestus ab alto

Ilion ardentes respiceretque deos.
Romulus aeternae nondum formaverat urbis
    moenia, consorti non habitanda Remo,
25 sed tunc pascebant herbosa Palatia vaccae,
    et stabant humiles in Iovis arce casae.
lacte madens illic suberat Pan ilicis umbrae
    et facta agresti lignea falce Pales,
pendebatque vagi pastoris in arbore votum,
30   garrula silvestri fistula sacra deo,
fistula, cui semper decrescit arundinis ordo,
    nam calamus cera iungitur usque minor.
at qua Velabri regio patet, ire solebat
    exiguus pulsa per vada linter aqua.
35 illa saepe gregis diti placitura magistro
    ad iuvenem festa est vecta puella die,
cum qua fecundi redierunt munera ruris,
    caseus et niveae candidus agnus ovis)
"impiger Aenea, volitantis frater Amoris,
40   Troica qui profugis sacra vehis ratibus,
iam tibi Laurentes adsignat Iuppiter agros,
    iam vocat errantes hospita terra Lares.
illic sanctus eris, cum te veneranda Numici
    unda deum caelo miserit indigetem.
45 ecce super fessas volitat Victoria puppes,
    tandem ad Troianos diva superba venit.
ecce mihi lucent Rutulis incendia castris:
    iam tibi praedico, barbare Turne, necem.
ante oculos Laurens castrum murusque Lavini est
50   Albaque ab Ascanio condita Longa duce.
te quoque iam video, Marti placitura sacerdos
    Ilia, Vestales deseruisse focos,
concubitusque tuos furtim vittasque iacentes
    et cupidi ad ripas arma relicta dei.
55 carpite nunc, tauri, de septem montibus herbas,
    dum licet! hic magnae iam locus urbis erit.
Roma, tuum nomen terris fatale regendis,
    qua sua de caelo prospicit arva Ceres,
quaque patent ortus, et qua fluitantibus undis
60   Solis anhelantes abluit amnis equos.

Troia quidem tunc se mirabitur et sibi dicet
    vos bene tam longa consuluisse via.
vera cano: sic usque sacras innoxia laurus
    vescar, et aeternum sit mihi virginitas."
65 haec cecinit vates et te sibi, Phoebe, vocavit,
    iactavit fusas et caput ante comas.
quidquid Amalthea, quidquid Marpesia dixit
    Herophile, Phoeto Graia quod admonuit,
quotque Aniena sacras Tiburs per flumina sortes
70   portarit sicco pertuleritque sinu,
(hae fore dixerunt belli mala signa cometen,
    multus ut in terras deplueretque lapis,
atque tubas atque arma ferunt strepitantia caelo
    audita et lucos praecinuisse fugam.
75 ipsum etiam Solem defectum lumine vidit
    iungere pallentes nubilus annus equos
et simulacra deum lacrimas fudisse tepentes
    fataque vocales praemonuisse boves)
haec fuerant olim; sed tu iam mitis, Apollo,
80   prodigia indomitis merge sub aequoribus.
et succensa sacris crepitet bene laurea flammis,
    omine quo felix et sacer annus erit.
laurus ubi bona signa dedit, gaudete coloni:
    distendet spicis horrea plena Ceres,
85 oblitus et musto feriet pede rusticus uvas,
    dolia dum magni deficiantque lacus,
ac madidus Baccho sua festa Palilia pastor
    concinet: a stabulis tunc procul este lupi.
ille levis stipulae sollemnis potus acervos
90   accendet flammas transilietque sacras,
et fetus matrona dabit, natusque parenti
    oscula comprensis auribus eripiet,
nec taedebit avum parvo advigilare nepoti
    balbaque cum puero dicere verba senem.
95 tunc operata deo pubes discumbet in herba,
    arboris antiquae qua levis umbra cadit,
aut e veste sua tendent umbracula sertis
    vincta, coronatus stabit et ipse calix.
at sibi quisque dapes et festas exstruet alte

100   caespitibus mensas caespitibusque torum.
     ingeret hic potus iuvenis maledicta puellae,
          postmodo quae votis irrita facta velit:
     nam ferus ille suae plorabit sobrius idem
          et se iurabit mente fuisse mala.
105 pace tua pereant arcus pereantque sagittae,
          Phoebe, modo in terris erret inermis Amor.
     ars bona, sed postquam sumpsit sibi tela Cupido,
          heu heu, quam multis ars dedit ista malum!
     et mihi praecipue: iaceo cum saucius annum
110   et faveo morbo cum iuvat ipse dolor,
     usque cano Nemesim, sine qua versus mihi nullus
          verba potest iustos aut reperire pedes.
     at tu—nam divum servat tutela poetas—
          praemoneo, vati parce, puella, sacro,
115 ut Messalinum celebrem, cum praemia belli
          ante suos currus oppida victa feret,
     ipse gerens laurus: lauro devinctus agresti
          miles "io" magna voce "triumphe" canet.
     tunc Messalla meus pia det spectacula turbae
120   et plaudat curru praetereunte pater.
     adnue! sic tibi sint intonsi, Phoebe, capilli,
          sic tua perpetuo sit tibi casta soror.

2. 6.

     Castra Macer sequitur; tenero quid fiet Amori?
          sit comes et collo fortiter arma gerat?
     et seu longa virum terrae via seu vaga ducent
          aequora, cum telis ad latus ire volet?
5   ure, puer, quaeso, tua qui ferus otia liquit,
          atque iterum erronem sub tua signa voca.
     quod si militibus parces, erit hic quoque miles,
          ipse levem galea qui sibi portet aquam.
     castra peto, valeatque Venus valeantque puellae:
10   et mihi sunt vires, et mihi facta tuba est.
     magna loquor, sed magnifice mihi magna locuto
          excutiunt clausae fortia verba fores.
     iuravi quotiens rediturum ad limina numquam!
          cum bene iuravi, pes tamen ipse redit.

15 acer Amor, fractas utinam, tua tela, sagittas,
    si licet, extinctas aspiciamque faces!
   tu miserum torques, tu me mihi dira precari
    cogis et insana mente nefanda loqui.
   iam mala finissem leto, sed credula vitam
20   Spes fovet et fore cras semper ait melius.
   Spes alit agricolas, Spes sulcis credit aratis
    semina quae magno faenore reddat ager;
   haec laqueo volucres, haec captat arundine pisces,
    cum tenues hamos abdidit ante cibus;
25 Spes etiam valida solatur compede vinctum:
    crura sonant ferro, sed canit inter opus;
   Spes facilem Nemesim spondet mihi, sed negat illa;
    ei mihi, ne vincas, dura puella, deam!
   parce, per immatura tuae precor ossa sororis:
30   sic bene sub tenera parva quiescat humo.
   illa mihi sancta est, illius dona sepulcro
    et madefacta meis serta feram lacrimis,
   illius ad tumulum fugiam supplexque sedebo
    et mea cum muto fata querar cinere.
35 non feret usque suum te propter flere clientem:
    illius ut verbis, sis mihi lenta veto,
   ne tibi neglecti mittant mala somnia Manes,
    maestaque sopitae stet soror ante torum,
   qualis ab excelsa praeceps delapsa fenestra
40   venit ad infernos sanguinolenta lacus.
   desine, ne dominae luctus renoventur acerbi:
    non ego sum tanti, ploret ut illa semel.
   nec lacrimis oculos digna est foedare loquaces:
    lena nocet nobis, ipsa puella bona est.
45 lena necat miserum Phryne, furtimque tabellas
    occulto portans itque reditque sinu:
   saepe, ego cum dominae dulces a limine duro
    agnosco voces, haec negat esse domi,
   saepe, ubi nox mihi promissa est, languere puellam
50   nuntiat aut aliquas extimuisse minas.
   tunc morior curis, tunc mens mihi perdita fingit,
    quisve meam teneat, quot teneatve modis;
   tunc tibi, lena, precor diras: satis anxia vives,
    moverit e votis pars quotacumque deos.

ABBREVIATIONS

AAWW	*Anzeiger Akad. d. Wiss. Wien, phil.-hist. Kl.*
AJP	*American Journal of Philology*
A.P.	*Anthologia Palatina*
CB	*Classical Bulletin*
CJ	*Classical Journal*
CP	*Classical Philology*
CQ	*Classical Quarterly*
CRF	*Comicorum Romanorum Fragmenta*
HSCP	*Harvard Studies in Classical Philology*
JHI	*Journal of the History of Ideas*
JRS	*Journal of Roman Studies*
MH	*Museum Helveticum*
OCD	*Oxford Classical Dictionary*
OLD	*Oxford Latin Dictionary*
ORF	*Oratorum Romanorum Fragmenta*
Phil.	*Philologus*
RE	A. Pauly, G. Wissowa, and W. Kroll *Real-Encyclopädie d. klassichen Altertumswissenschaft*
REA	*Revue des études anciennes*
RELO	*Revue de l'Organisation internationale pour l'étude des langues anciennes par ordinateur*
RP	*Revue de philologie*
SIFC	*Studi italiani di filologia classica*
TAPA	*Transactions of the American Philological Association*
TLL	*Thesaurus Linguae Latinae*
WS	*Wiener Studien*
YCS	*Yale Classical Studies*

COMMENTARY 1. 1.

Let someone willing to bear the terrors and sleeplessness of military life rightly have the wealth of gold and lands, Tibullus prays. His wish is for contentment in a double sense—that his lot will both hold him back from wandering and give pleasure. Purification and offerings to Pales are now yearly events. As of old, the gods will happily receive libations from earthenware vessels (made of clay, not gold). Tibullus does not yearn for his ancestral riches, only for quiet protection with his mistress from winter wind and rain. Let him be rightly rich who can withstand the madness of the elements. Tibullus cannot even bear his girl's weeping. War's literal prizes befit Messalla. Tibullus, the poet as slave-doorkeeper, is the captive of his girl for life. Along with all youth she will mourn at his funeral. In the meantime while we are young let us make love. Soldiering and commercialism are for the greedy. Tibullus' philosophy of life and love will be moderate.

The poet weighs two styles of living in the balance, the ambitious, practical, acquisitive, political life of a Messalla and a poor, quiet, country existence toward which he aspires. Tibullus has clearly known and compared both and seen the difference between them in terms, for example, of motion versus rest, action versus passivity, ostentation and humility, exposure to the world and retreat out of life's glare, and even nature's menace, in winter to the fireside, in summer to the chill of shade and stream. Agriculture and viticulture have their gods, and religion requires ritual. But a georgic life and its humble offerings from earthenware dishes must be complemented by the enduring presence of love. And love conjures up the spectacle of the excluded lover, of doorposts broken, of old age creeping apace (so let's love), and of death—in other words a standard, imagined world of elegiac poetry different again from any literal activities centered on the soil or on war. Hence the ending leaves the poet (and his reader) poised not only half way between abundance and poverty, ancestral wealth and present limitation, war and peace, country and city but also at a moment in spiritual time between youth and age when Tibullus must pray away his own ambition (such phrases as *iam possim contentus, non ego requiro, non ego laudari curo* occur with enough frequency to be almost apotropaic) and at least claim to seek the security of mediocrity. One senses in this circular progress from *divitias* (1) to *dites* (78) a craving for lacking self-assurance which if gained, could lead from *paupertas* to an average means, to a compromise here and now between the clay goblets the rustic made of old (*antiquus agrestis*, 39) and the resources of his forebears (*antiquo avo*, 42). Yet, though Tibullus may progress in stature from planter of seedlings to purifier of his shepherd, we never lose sight of how much of his thoughts are couched in terms of future hope and how little describe a real present.

1–2   *divitias*: regularly associated by Tibullus with ambition and competition in love (the *dives amator*). Linguistically it has the same root as δῖος, "bright," "gleaming," anticipating *fulvo*. Riches are eyecatching and superficially attractive.

alius: however impersonal the statement, the singular rouses the suspicion that a special instance, perhaps even himself, is in the poet's mind.

congerat: the abstract for concrete object with *congerat* is a typical Tibullan device. *Auro* is the "concrete" aspect of *divitias*, and *fulvo* points up its reality. The row of subjunctives suggests prayer as much as command.

iugera: more specific than *divitias* and, like *auro*, another means of wealth. *Iugerum* is roughly equivalent to an acre, the amount a yoke of oxen could plough in a day. The soil is *culti*, "tamed," and the cattle who work the land submit to the *iugum*.

3–4   *labor assiduus*: the personification is vivid. *Assiduus* (from *assideo*) is chosen here for its quasi-military overtones. The enemy is near and continuous effort is by his side. The juxtaposition with *vicino* emphasizes the etymological pun.

somnos: the plural here (and often in Tibullus) signifies repetition of an action, and hence adds to the generality (cf. the use of *somnos* at 48).

pulsa: *pello* in connection with musical instruments is ordinarily applied to strings or percussion which one might "strike" (see 1.3.23–24). Here it continues the military metaphors in careful conjunction with *fugent* (and partially, *congerat*). The rich man may heap up and hold his money but the price is terror and the routing of his peace and quiet, a motif of the poem to which *pulsa* also contributes secondarily.

5–6   Though the personification of *paupertas* keeps up the pretense that the statement is generic, the triple *me, mea, meus* turns it toward Tibullus. The mention of hearth and home brings the sententious opening down to earth. The gleam of the flame serves as foil for the rich man's heap of gold. Fire, not *labor,* provides life's impetus and centrality. The *focus* and the family *arae* were the heart of a Roman home. Upon them the Lares received offerings.

traducat: the passivity (and hint of negativity) in the idea of betrayal (once more a martial notion) contrasts with the aggressively positive *congerat* (1) and the continuing, prayerful subjunctives.

vita inerti: the (assumed) leisurely life of the countryside. There is no *ars*, no complicated skill to rustic life though there is to writing poetry. The only thing that is *assiduus* is fire on the hearth, not *labor.* (Tibullus need not underscore the irony of his sentiment.)

dum: the poet is misled by *paupertas* and yet lays down conditions.

7–8   *ipse*: the implication is that such conduct, though demanded, might seem strange in Tibullus. (Because of social stature? Because he was an elegist?)

seram: either future or optative subjunctive, which only makes the prayer less definite.

teneras: an elegiac word, fitting an elegist's landscape and especially frequent in this poem.

maturo tempore: the "right," fulfilling time for the proper seeding of young plants. The contrast of *maturo* with *teneras* itself suggests growth as *assiduo* does continuity.

rusticus: *ipse* suggests divergence from social *mores. Rusticus* contrasts with the ordinary position of an "urbane" elegiac poet, which will appear occasionally in the poem's course.

facili manu: *facilis* is ordinarily a passive adjective, "without effort," a suitable detail in this easy *vita iners,* but perhaps strange for a *rusticus.*

poma: *pomus* is the more regular word for the fruit trees here meant. *Grandia* anticipates the productivity of his seedlings for which the next distich prays.

9–   Spes, the goddess of hope, had her chief Roman temple in the
10   Forum Holitorium. (See further 2.6.20 ff.)

destituat: continues the military metaphor in a new context.

The poet-farmer after all needs his allies, who furnish produce on a continuing basis.

frugum acervos: by contrast with the rich man's piles of wealth. The motif culminates at line 77.

musta: new wine, usually from the October vintage. The plural suggests a series of such events.

lacu: a large storage vat.

11–
12 *veneror*: the change of mood indicates that the focus of the wish has become more real but the object of devotion is still unstated. It might be Spes but no specific god is mentioned until line 14. *Stipes desertus* and *vetus lapis* may refer to Terminus, to other boundary gods, or to still more primitive superstitions. The adjectives transport the reader into a faraway, nostalgic world.

trivio: the crossroads where boundary lines met was a fit location for altars to the *Lares compitales* (see line 20). These would naturally be more frequented than a *stipes desertus* in the middle of the field.

florida serta: a common offering at shrines and at the houses of the mighty or magnetic (cf. 1.2.13, etc.).

13–
14 *novus annus*: each "new year," considered as the producer of crops from which an offering of first fruits is made.

educat: from *educo*, usually of people but Catullus refers to a flower *quem . . . educat imber* (62.41).

agricolae deo: purposefully vague. This adjectival use of *agricola* is the first in Latin.

ante: in front of the statue or shrine (not beforehand, of time).

15–
16 *flava*: the epithet is natural for the goddess of grain (as Vergil *Georg.* 1.96). There is an implicit contrast with *fulvo* (1)—acquired wealth.

sit . . . pendeat: the renewed chain of subjunctives takes the reader again into the world of wishful thinking.

nostro de rure: as with urban poets who claim to be *rustici* (8), we are reminded that Ceres' temple would as likely as not be in the city, whatever her rural connections.

spicea corona: a crown of grain spikes. According to Pliny (*Hist. Nat.* 18.6) this was the earliest type of garland to be used among the Romans.

17–
18 The fertility god Priapus was a chief Roman garden divinity (*custos furum atque avium*, Vergil *Georg.* 4.110). His cult seems to have centered originally at Lampsacus on the Helles-

pont. It reached importance during the Alexandrian period (see 1.4 *passim.*)

ruber: red was used to paint the statues of gods, especially on festive occasions (cf. 2.1.55–56 for its use as makeup by those on holiday).

custos: in other elegiac contexts (as 1.2.5) this word has quite a different ring.

saeva falce: irony (and humor) lies in connecting a wooden statue in a garden with a menacing weapon. What terror would his pruning hook offer birds save that of any scarecrow? The curved hook is primarily a literary attribute and not to be confused with his more prominent feature, the *phallus*, suggestive though both *ruber* and *falx* are. See H. Herter, *RE* 22 [1954], 1926).

19– The echo of Vergil *Ecl.* 1.74 (*felix quondam pecus*) is clear.
20   (There are others. Lines 31–32 refer obliquely to *Ecl.* 1.13–15.) Tibullus, unlike Vergil and his voices, is desperately attempting to recreate a dream, to shore up in his imagination the ruins of the past. For Tibullus it seems possible to be an unwilling warrior for a moment, then remake the land. This land is not wrenched from some defenseless shepherd, as in Vergil, but constitutes the poet's own ancestral acres, the refurbished dream based on a fragmented reality. Unlike the exiled shepherd Meliboeus in *Ecl.* 1, Tibullus comes from war into the country, however ravaged and impoverished it may be. The elegist's imagined fiction consorts with a very real Roman love for the land and its gods.

felicis: "rich," "productive," and then "well-omened," "fortunate," accordingly.

custodes Lares: these would be the *Lares compitales*, guardians of the *compita* (crossroads) and the land nearby, and celebrated at the Compitalia.

21– *tunc, nunc*: an elaboration of *quondam, nunc* (19). The size
22   of the offering (at the Ambarvalia, probably) depended on the richness of the land and its produce. With his worsened economic status, the poet can offer only a lamb in place of the cow of earlier days.

exigui soli: in line 2 the poet has wished the possession of large acreage (*culti iugera multa soli*) onto others. He will soon claim that a small crop is enough (43) and that he is content *vivere parvo* (25).

23– The gods have been listed with increasing directness and the
24   scene now becomes briefly dramatic. From the poet's own

apostrophes to Ceres and the Lares we pass to a moment where the ceremony of sacrifice is actually glimpsed.

The repetition of *agna* helps elaborate the thought of the preceding distich. The changes of tense and mood lessen the impact of the repeated *nunc* (19–22) and re-establish the sense of the earlier subjunctives (6 ff., 15 ff.). As cow was superseded by lamb, present vividness yields to future hope and distance.

circum: postposition is regular in Tibullus.

25– The reiteration of *iam modo iam* is particularly effective after
26   the progression of time contrasts in 19–25. Tibullus had not always been content (or forced) to live in straitened circumstances and his military ventures are symptomatic of the ambition which he is superficially decrying. Certainly there is an indirect connection between Tibullus' past behavior and his former possessions in a happier era. Is the exhortation in *possim* a reflection of positive desire or negative self-control?

deditus: the military terminology is carefully chosen. To "surrender" to long marches is to give oneself over to the enemy, perhaps here the ambition that has led to his present circumstances.

longae viae: a common Tibullan euphemism for travel, especially for military or commercial purposes (as 1.3.36; 1.4.41; 1.9.16; 2.6.3). The word *via* brings with it notions of separation, insecurity, desire, etc., common in all poetry and constant in elegy.

27– Avoiding the Dog Star's rising is a commonplace in Latin
28   poetry, often associated with the creative impulse and retreat from life's pressures (cf. e.g., Horace *Carm.* 1.17, 3.13; *Epist.* 1.10. 14–18). Here it is emblematic of the *vita iners*. The star rises, the river passes by, but the poet-farmer remains as constant as the tree in whose protective shade he sits. The soldier goes on long journeys; the poet can remain in one spot. *Contentus* (25) is a pun accordingly. The tension between motion and rest, search and restraint, has its spiritual counterpart in the earlier motif of satisfaction versus greed. The one operates in restlessness, the other is given to quiet. The poet, *contentus* with a little, is willingly "held in" by the confining shade of the tree.

rivos: as with *ortus* the plural makes the action habitual.

29– Suddenly there is active life, but of the farmer, not the soldier.
30   *Interdum* postulates only spurts of activity and *pudeat* hints at revulsion overcome. The abruptness of *nec tamen* and the row

of impersonal verbs, along with renewed subjunctives, alert the reader's imagination further, while keeping the thought less directly oriented to the poet. Has Tibullus ever done this before or is this a prayer for the ability to accept the labor as well as enjoy the relaxation of rural life?

stimulo . . . increpuisse: a typically challenging verbal usage. *Increpuisse* implies only use of words. *Stimulo* carries this into deeds, in the same phrase.

31– Compare the scene and intent with Vergil's description of the
32 dying landscape in *Ecl.* 1.13–15. There the shepherd does not pick up the baby goat because he is leaving the pastoral landscape entirely, not returning home. For Tibullus the mother has only forgotten her offspring. Vergil gives her the more deliberate, still more unnatural *reliquit*. (Cf. the use of *desertus* at line 11.)

33– *exiguo . . . magno*: the contrast goes back to the opening
34 lines.

furesque lupique: the real "enemy" to the rural retreat, both human and bestial.

35– With the menace of wolves and thieves gone by command, the
36 poet—now suddenly no longer completely *rusticus*—can take over the dutiful landowner's role of priest, and perform apotropaic and propitiatory rites. We are now in the vivid present.

hic: in this rural situation.

pastorem meum: The shepherd who pastures the poet's sheep.

quotannis: year after year.

placidam Palem: Pales was an early Italic pastoral divinity. Her feast was the Parilia celebrated on April 21, the traditional foundation day of Rome. Milk and oil, rather than wine, were the earliest ingredients of libation according to Pliny (*Hist. Nat.* 14.88). Only a goddess so "calmed" can willingly make the fields productive.

37– *adsitis, divi*: a regular, ritualistic invitation by summary
38 prayer.

paupere mensa: poor in wealth, not spirit. *Mensa* here is the sacrificial table.

puris fictilibus: *puris* is to be taken in a double sense, first "simple," "unelaborate" (parallel to *paupere*), then "clean," "pure." Both are a reflection of the poet and his way of life. *Fictilia* (from *fingo*) were earthenware vessels of little monetary value.

39– *fictilia*: Tibullus has a special fondness for verbal repetitions

40   (and especially for anaphora). The punning connection with
      fecit and *facili* (which sound enhances) is based on a false
      etymology.

      antiquus agrestis: Tibullus shows full awareness that reli-
      gious worship and rural society are two bastions of conser-
      vatism. Their combination virtually assures the stability of a
      custom.

      composuit luto: typically Tibullan wordplay: *lutum* from
      luo, "loosen," "relax"; *componere*, "put together." *Facili* is both
      active and passive, the mud both pliable and helpful. This dis-
      placement of *que* is another favorite device of Tibullus for em-
      phasis. Lines 40–44 are connected by homoioteleuton. Lines
      41–42 and 43–44 are therefore rhyming couplets (and lines 42
      and 44 closely associated by internal rhyme). The whole cen-
      ters on the impressive repetition in line 43, as the theme shifts.

41– *non ego*: by contrast with *hic ego* (35). For the first time
42   there is a connection between the generic riches of the opening
      lines and the particular wealth of Tibullus' forebears. He now
      takes on the *persona* of the knight we know he was. The reiter-
      ation of the poet's willingness to accept his present reduced
      status sounds occasionally like a despairing litany.

      fructus: produce, though the idea of income is clearly in
      the background. He repeats the pattern of *divitias* (1) and
      frugum acervos (9).

      requiro: "seek out" or simply "need"?

      condita: "put up," in this case of the harvest in storage
      barns (cf. Horace *Carm.* 1.1.9).

43– A beautiful expression of a poet's search for the quiet and the
44   customary which seems to echo Catullus' poem of return to
      Sirmio (with *requiescere lecto* cf. Catullus 31.10: *desideratoque
      acquiescimus lecto*).

      satis est: direct repetition, anastrophe and partial chiasmus
      at the caesura underline once more the litany of reconciliation
      with, or even desire for, *parva seges*.

      membra levare: the implication is that the soldier-wanderer
      had at last taken a great weight, literally as well as metaphor-
      ically, from his shoulders.

      solito toro: "customary," not out of the ordinary, as the bed
      of a wealthy man or a soldier might be to Tibullus.

45– As at 27–28 the nature symbolism is important. *Immites venti*
46   typify the violence of the world outside. Wind is associated
      by Tibullus with seafaring and hence with danger, with the
      greed of commercialism and the violence of military life (1.

3.38; 1.7.20), with the instability of love (1.4.21), of life's acquisitions (1.6.54), and of personal beauty (1.9.14).

immites: once in control the winds have no pity, like the *ars* of the person who invented the sword, or like death (1.3.48 and 55). Winds, like wolves and thieves, are a menace to paradise.

dominam: mistress, in the elegiac sense.

cubantem . . . continuisse: the stance is typically elegiac while revealing Tibullus' own yearning for love and quiet combined, another aspect of the poet *contentus* (25). *Quam iuvat*, however, is already compromised by *si licet*. (Frequent use of *teneo, pono*, and their compounds keeps the verbal texture of this poem especially taut.)

tenero sinu: compare this with the shepherd's position at line 31. Each has an element of wishful thinking.

47–48 Water is a second symbol of instability (see line 28). The added characteristic is coldness. The house gives protection from wind, rain, and winter chill. Though there are similarities between lines 27–28 and 45–48, we have moved from hot to cold, dry to wet, summer to winter, as the menace changes. Inner fire counteracts outside chill. (There is no need to alter the reading of the codices, *igne*, to *imbre*. Cf. Ovid *Rem. Am.* 188, *igne levatur hiems*.)

fuderit: characteristic Tibullan play on words. It is unusual for anyone, not to say a wind, to pour something frozen.

somnos sequi: as often, Tibullus actively pursues what is passive.

49–50 Announced by the strong verbal reminiscence in line 49 of lines 1–6, the opening theme is now recapitulated, this time leading to an elegiac, not a pastoral interlude. Riches come rightly to him who can bear the elements' uncontrollable madness.

hoc mihi contingat: again wishful thinking. There is the latent implication of reaching one's own goal through effort (as, e.g., Horace *Ars Poet.* 412, *optatam cursu contingere metam*).

tristes pluvias: cf. *pluvias Hyadas* (Vergil *Aen.* 1.744; 3.516). *Tristes* means sad and saddening as well.

51–52 "O, may as much gold and emeralds as exist perish rather than . . ."

quantum est auri: genitive with *quantum* is a construction found in Tibullus only here. The addition of *smaragdus* (any bright precious stone, emerald, malachite, etc.), emphasized by the position of *-que*, to the more common *aurum* makes the reader journey linguistically as well as geographically east.

nostras vias: the poet's journeys by land and sea (see 25–26). Does the plural also foreshadow the entrance of Messalla? We would expect *nostra* to be attached to *puella*. Instead the vague *ulla* only nebulously anticipates the apostrophe to Delia (57).

53– *te . . . Messalla*: this is the first direct mention in the poem of
54   Tibullus' friend and patron. The only excuse for warfare, and the travel it entails, is military necessity, not greed, etc. Messalla, who can put up with danger, is justly rich.

hostiles exuvias: enemy spoils were often placed in the *vestibulum* of a Roman house in recognition of achievement.

praeferat: the house "sports" the booty in front of itself, as if it were leading the triumphal procession. (Delia's house, as the next couplet shows, presents only Tibullus on the threshold, spoils of another sort.)

55– Variations on a stock elegiac situation (see further 1.2.5–6).
56   As the "captive" of a beautiful girl, he has no freedom to wander afield. She is the *domina* in a double sense, he the slave, prize of love's warfare (both *retinent* and *vinctum* are regular amatory ambiguities, the latter, of course, anticipating *vincla*).

ianitor: the lover is the slave-doorkeeper, chained helplessly to his post but without the power to open the door. The hardness of the door complements its mistress, *dura*.

ante fores: an echo of line 16. We have completed the transition from rural dream to more hardened elegiac "realities."

57– *non ego*: compare the denial of riches at line 41.
58   *laudari*: to gain the *laudes* bestowed on a successful soldier.

mea Delia: her first mention by name though her presence is intimated as early as 46. The reader of Tibullus is often forced to remark on the appropriateness of an epithet of the virgin goddess Artemis-Diana as pseudonym for the poet's mistress.

dum: the poem abounds in clauses of proviso (6, 58, 69, 73). We are taken back into the subjunctives of hope, away from the indicatives of (assumed) fulfillment. Love of home and love of Delia both obviate ambition, but there is a hedging clause attached to each sentiment.

segnis inersque: for *iners* see line 5 (but country living and the *segnitia* of city life and a lover's *otium* are far apart).

vocer: in prose we would expect *ut* following *quaeso*.

59– The combination of love and death is an elegiac common-

60 place. But even this continuity of affection and the presence of Delia at the poet's death is expressed as a wish. There is a resemblance to two of Vergil's most beautiful lines as Orpheus sings of his lost Eurydice (*Georg.* 4.465–66):

> te, dulcis coniunx, te solo in litore secum,
> te veniente die, te decedente canebat.

61– The vivid moment of burning becomes real, though future.
62 The attributes of love (*lectum, oscula*) are transferred to the instant of cremation. (Compare the fires at lines 6 and 48.)

The lines are an admirable example of the artistic possibilities of the elegiac couplet: unity (*flebis . . . dabis*) amid diversity (chiastic order in 61; AABB and chiastic order in 62).

63– *praecordia*: literally muscles which protect the heart but poet-
64 ically often for the heart itself as seat of the emotions. Here there is a play on the word. The *prae-cordia* which is "in front of" her heart is not hard, like the *duras fores* before which the enslaved lover sits, not *vinctum* like the poet (55). And once one penetrates the outer defenses, there is no hardness at the heart itself either. The analogy of the heart to *silex* is proverbial (cf. 1.10. 59–60).

65– Youths and maidens are those who would most appreciate
66 Tibullus as poet, all amatory implications apart.

illo funere: the distancing effect is purposeful.

referre domum: the same phrase is used at line 32 of the poet-shepherd carrying home a deserted lamb. The repetition (like that of *ante fores* in 16 and 56) shows the ease with which Tibullus moves in his thoughts between pastoral and elegiac themes, as well as between life and death, but may point up a certain confused insecurity as well.

67– Tears would ordinarily please the dead, but for Delia to tear
68 her loosened hair and scratch her cheeks would only hurt his ghost, which he assumes to be still sensate after death.

solutis crinibus: a common sign of mourning (as 1.3.8) and the first of several references to Delia's hair.

69– *iungamus amores*: again a wish (cf. Catullus 64.372: *optatos*
70 *. . . coniungite amores*; Propertius 2.15.20).

tenebris: the grammar is ambiguous. The word may be taken as a moment in time, as an implement time uses, or as the darkness around the head of death. The latter seems specially fitting.

Mors adoperta: there is no ancient parallel for this effective description. Death is shrouded perhaps because it cannot be seen or anticipated. For the elegist night is the time of love. Death puts a stop to this with unending darkness.

iam veniet: the phrase leads directly to the more specific *iam subrepet* (71) and suggests an urgency to living in the present which challenges the inevitable pace of age and advent of death.

71– Passing age, being *iners*, can only creep along (even then a
72   slight contradiction). There is also the implication that, like death itself, it comes upon one with stealth. The poem's three instances of *iners*, like the mentions of fire, connect it first with country life, then love, and finally death. Age may have no *ars*, but also there is no *ars* against it.

cano capite: poverbial for old age (as 1.2.94, 1.6.86, etc.) and here verbally linked with death (*caput*, 70). The contrast of *tenebris* with *cano* accents the connection.

73– *nunc*: a slightly ironic continuation of *iam . . . iam* (70–71)
74   into the present.

levis Venus: here "light," "buoyant," as opposed to *iners aetas*, though the more pejorative amatory sense, "fickle," is not far away.

tractanda: the (erotic) violence inherent in the verb ("take in hand") is made explicit in the instances which follow. Door-crashing and brawling are regular elegiac events.

pudet: we may compare the elegist-agriculturist at work earlier (line 29).

inseruisse: "introduce," here in the sense of start.

75– Instead of the elegist retreating from real warfare we now
76   have the poet partaking in the "battles" he knows well. The metaphor is elaborated at some length by Ovid in *Am.* 1.9.

signa tubaeque: a reference to line 4 as *cupidis* is to the opening couplet. War brings wounds along with wealth to the greedy.

cupidis vulnera: elegiac commonplaces, too.

77– For all his attacks on the acquisition of wealth, Tibullus has his
78   own "heap" stored away. He is in a position to compromise between luxury and starvation. Or, if we consider the distich within the preceding amatory framework, the poet claims to be the master of love and arbiter of his involvements. He will have neither surfeit nor famine. The iteration of *despiciam* asserts that the poet's *modus vivendi* is loftier than any other, though his actual pile of money might not be as high as that of

someone more ambitious. The thought as well as the image brings the poem full circle.

securus: cf. the situation of line 48 and the prayer of 57.

COMMENTARY 1. 2.

Tibullus orders more wine to bring upon himself soothing slumber while Love in turn sleeps. Delia is under harsh guard. The house door is to blame, yet may it open for him alone. Do not shine torches on the waiting lover or inquire his name. Venus takes revenge on the gossip. The witch has promised that Delia's *coniunx* will not believe in their affair, but can she be trusted? She did not succeed in ridding Tibullus of his passion by her magic. What he truly wants is mutual love. Military campaigning may bring rich gains; Tibullus would rather be a rustic and sleep on rough ground, again provided Delia were with him. What good is wealth without happy love? Vengeance will strike whoever laughs at his misfortunes. Nothing is more ridiculous than an older man lately come to love. But Venus, spare your servant. Why in bitterness burn your own harvests?

Technically the poem is a *paraklausithyron*, song of the excluded lover before his mistress' closed door. The posture lends itself to emotional extremes, and the poet's fluctuations of mood and the visual impact of his gestures throughout the poem are moving and effective. Wine and sleep are only momentary distractions from what the initial apostrophe to the door portends—that we will watch the poet struggling with contradictions, love and hate, pride and humility, daring and helplessness, as curse alternates with prayer. Delia should have courage because Venus teaches and protects brave lovers (yet Delia could take the initiative whenever she wanted). Tibullus boasts that he is sacrosanct and immune to harm from any quarter with the notable exception of Delia. This means, of course, that actually he is more open to suffering than not. He has magic on his side but even the most potent sorceress cannot help him any more than do wine, Venus, and poetry. And this help he does not want anyway. Whoever goes off to war when he could have Delia deserves the unhappiness that only wealth without love can bring—though this is vicariously a probable curse on himself. He will make amends for any unintentional act of sacrilege against Venus, yet this means that she is now a potential enemy. And the ending is a prayer like the beginning, this time taking the form of a curse against those who laugh at him and a supplication to Venus to spare the deserving poet from anxiety and humiliation.

1–2 *adde . . . compesce*: the poet commands himself (or perhaps a servant) to pour some pure wine and put him out of his misery. There is a simultaneous effect of action and passivity, distance and involvement, control and passion. Nothing is directly personal until line 5.

merum: wine unmixed with water.

compesce: "keep in check," by contrast with *adde* which suggests that lack of control against which he claims to be fighting.

occupet . . . victa: sleep is the victor over the poet's exhausted eyes. The defender craves immediate defeat. Military metaphors predominate in the first distichs. *Requiescit* (4) brilliantly makes the transition to a new picture.

fessi: as a result of drink, but grief (and perhaps even love) would be a remoter cause.

3–4 *Percussum* (we might expect a verb like *fundo*, as 1.7.50) continues the military metaphor. The word fits the half-personification of wine-Bacchus who strikes with his thyrsus.

tempora: Greek internal accusative.

excitet: "wake up."

infelix amor: though it is the poet who is asleep, the phrase personifies his unhappy love and makes quiet depend on Amor's indulgence. It is thus an external cause of *novi dolores*, yet part of them as well. The positioning of *amor* is effective. Only now are we sure the poem deals with love.

5–6 The distich serves as transition to the παρακλαυσίθυρον itself, the song of the excluded lover before his mistress' door. The idea is at least as old as Aristophanes and becomes a stock subject of the elegists. For a detailed discussion see F. O. Copley, *Exclusus Amator, A Study in Latin Love Poetry* (Am. Phil. Assoc., 1956).

We are now assured of the extensive difference from the preceding elegy, as we move from the breadth and tension of a poem which holds country and city in solution to a distinctly urban, quite specific setting.

custodia: the military language switches to the poet's girl whose bastion is under seige.

saeva, dura: characteristics of the opposing door and the coldhearted mistress alike.

sera: bar which bolted the door shut.

7–8 The poet now addresses the door itself. The sudden play within play suggests an intellectual game, as if the poet, occupying himself with the external frame of a literary genre, thought of format as a meaningful exercise in spiritual delusion. Escape into wine and sleep becomes—is already—escape into literary form. And yet the poet implies his ability to remain aloof and consider both!

domini: the master of the house, Delia's father or *coniunx*, either of whom might be unyielding or annoying to the poet.

te verberet: traditional curse of the door, exposure to the elements at their harshest.

fulmina: the thunderbolts of Jove would not only hurt the door—the poet's primary concern—but stand as a sign of the god's displeasure. Jupiter's *imperium* is pitted against the *dominatio* of the owner; rain and lightning are on the side of the poet (literally and figuratively).

9–
10 The repetition of *ianua* connects 9–10 with the preceding distich, but Tibullus mitigates his tone from curse on door and master to prayer and then changes nearly to command (no noise, please, in the process of opening). All the door need do is open, yielding to the poet's complaints. Any creaking, of course, would have given away the entering lover's presence. (This is assuming inability on the part of the *dominus* to hear the preliminary *querelae!*)

pateas, sones: subjunctives used as imperatives.

victa: the echo from line 2 is ironic. (If the poet is overcome how can he conquer the door?)

11–
12 In his drunkenness Tibullus over-apologizes, at the same time concluding his abrupt changes of mood with a curse on himself. The metonymy of *dementia* humorously divorces the poet from the curse his madness has uttered.

ignoscas: there is a probable pun on the etymology of the verb in relation to *dementia*. The door should ideally pretend "not to know" what the poet's "lack of mind" has uttered.

capiti: the head, often a symbol of a person's life, is a common object of a curse in antiquity. See, e.g., Pliny *Epist.* 2.20.6. Dido (*Aen.* 4.613) speaks of Aeneas' *infandum caput.*

13–
14 Tibullus' mood in the past was less violent when he offered suppliant vows, not curses, and placed his own garlands on the doorposts. The gesture, as a poetic theme, is already common among the Alexandrians (e.g., *A.P.* 5.92, 145, etc.). It seems to appear first in Latin with Catullus (63.66) or Lucretius (4.1177f.).

voce supplice: "with the voice of a suppliant" (unlike his present grumbling).

florida serta: wreaths of flowers (cf. 1.1.12).

15–   The anaphora *te . . . tu* helps make the transition from the
16   poet to Delia on the other side of the door. The "e" and "de" sounds prepare grandly for her entrance.

custodes: the *custodia* of line 5, whether outside or in.

fortes adiuvat ipsa Venus: an elegiac variation of the adage *fortis fortuna adiuvat* (Terence *Phorm.* 203, et al.). The aphorism introduces a depersonalized description of Venus' role in helping new lovers play out the stock scenes of erotic elegy (lines 17–24).

17–   Outdoors and indoors, *iuvenis* and *puella*, new lovers come
18   together with the help of Venus.

reserat: from *sera*. She is to undo the bar that kept the door from opening outward.

dente: for *clavis*, by synecdoche—the "teeth" of the key for the key itself (the only parallel in Latin is Germanicus *Arat.* 196). Since both *dens* (1.8.38) and *temptare* (e.g., 1.3.73) appear in amatory contexts elsewhere, they help make easy the transition to the next stanza. The threshold and the bar alone prevent love. Their undoing is all that stands in the way.

19–   Venus as *magistra amorum*. The need for quiet in such mo-
20   ments is a common elegiac sentiment. Both lines seem meant to be soundful and soundless; plosives are carefully interwoven with liquids and sibilants. (It may not be necessary to change *decedere* of the manuscripts to *derepere*. That lover need not slink away who has Venus' aid).

furtim: cf. line 10.

posse: the ability is as important as the deed (see 65–66).

21–   Undetected lovemaking in the presence of the girl's husband
22   or settled lover is another mark of elegiac accomplishment.

nutus loquaces: nods that speak what mouths cannot.

blanda verba: a lover's "soothing" words.

compositis notis: "with signals agreed upon" (among them *nutus*).

23–   *Inertia* (in spite of 1.1.5 and 58) and *timor* do not befit a
24   lover nor deserve Venus' help.

obscura nocte: the phrase is Ennian (*dram. frag.* 257 Jocelyn) and used by Vergil in connection with night fighting (*Aen.* 2.420).

25–   *en*: the exclamation suggests the poet's own amazement at
(26)   how his sacredness is made manifest (the missing pentameter

clearly contained some statement such as "I still remain safe").
The word *vagor* is used by Horace in another instance of the
poet-lover's invulnerability to harm (*Carm.* 1.22.11). The
fearless, elegiac lover is here, as often, a humorous contradiction in terms. The same theme is elaborated by Propertius
(3.16) and Ovid (*Am.* 1.6). See S. Commager, *The Odes of
Horace* (New Haven, 1962), 130ff.

ego: back strongly to the personal.

tota vagor . . . urbe: the phrase parallels Vergil's description
of Dido at *Aen.* 4.68–69: *totaque vagatur/ urbe furens*. The
lovesick poet, like Vergil's distraught heroine, cannot stay in
one spot.

The juxtaposition of *vagor* and *anxius* is a typically Tibullan
wordplay. *Vagor* means to "wander about" while *anxius* is related to *ango*, "bind" or "choke."

tenebris: "after nightfall."

27– The *locus classicus* for showing the dangers of any nocturnal
28   wanderings in Rome is Juvenal *Sat.* 3.302 ff.

occurrat: the final subjunctive without *ut* after forms of
sino is more common following the imperative.

praemia: those who snatched garments in the night as "re-
wards" were called *praemiatores* from the time of Naevius (*CRF*
20 Ribbeck [p. 9] [Leipzig, 1897–98]).

29– The sacred bard is "held" by love but "goes" at the same time.
30   Venus uses the same phrase (*magno . . . teneatur amore*: *Aen.*
1.675) of Dido's future love from which she is unbound only
by death.

sacer: sacred and therefore unharmable, because a devotee
of Venus.

timuisse: fear is not a proper emotion for a lover (see 24
but note other contexts such as 1.6.59; 2.1.77).

31– The holy lover is invulnerable to nature's power. These trials
32   are also typical of the sufferings of the *exclusus amator*. Happiness, as the next distich more realistically shows, depends on
Delia's whim.

pigra: both numb and numbing.

nocent . . . noctis: Tibullus is utilizing the ancient (false)
etymology of *noceo* from *nox* (first used by Plautus, *Curc.*
2.3.73). See Isidorus *Orig.* 5.31.1.

33– The whole operation really is *labor* after all. Following Ti-
34   bullus' engaging volatility, we are back before the door, ready
to suffer Delia's fancy.

vocet: the striking interplay of sound and silence recalls lines 19–22.

35– *parcite luminibus*: i.e. "avert your glance" (as Propertius
36 4.9.53: *parce oculis*). It is a bold alteration to have *lumina* mean "eyes" in 35 and "torches" in 38. The transfer is perhaps intimated in *celari* (to be hidden from sight or from the light).

furta: the "thefts" of love.

obvia: an etymological pun—to meet, here directly on the street.

37– We have to imagine the apprehensive poet waiting for Delia
38 to open the door and yet retreating from the approach of other nocturnal wanderers. The lover is not quite as immune as he would hope, from either direction.

strepitu . . . pedum: a good thing only if announcing the poet's tread (as 1.6.62). The sound of the phrase is onomatopoetic.

prope: with *ferte*, "close to hand."

lumina: "torches" (as 1.9.42).

face: poetic singular for plural.

39– *imprudens*: "in ignorance," not knowing the sacred quality of
40 the situation.

aspexerit: a verb used often of an omen in Vergil (e.g., *Ecl.* 4.50, 52; 8.105) and hence to be taken closely with *imprudens*. His glance should have automatically been averted from such a sight!

occulat: "let him keep secret" what he has seen. Compare line 13.

41– The allusion is to the birth of Venus out of the sea where the
42 blood of the emasculated Uranus fell. Venus will take revenge on the gossip through blood and the sea, a regular symbol in ancient poetry for violence and death's imminence (e.g., 1. 1.50: *furorem maris*).

rapido: "grasping" as well as "rushing" (cf. line 46 below and 1.9.49).

sentiet: he will feel as well as comprehend and see (45).

43– The *saga* is a stock figure in elegy, serving as a go-between and
44 purveyor of charms and potions. At 1.5.59, when Delia is under her spell, the witch is called *rapax*. (For these and the lines which follow see also 1.8.17–18, 21–22; 1.9.49–50).

huic: the person who is *loquax* (41). Even if he did talk, Delia's husband would not believe him.

verax: "truthful." A rare word, occurring only here in Tibullus, perhaps under the influence of *loquax* (21 and 41).

    magico ministerio: "by her employment of magic."

45– The "drawing down" of the moon (stars are an unusual vari-
46   ation) was a famous charm of the ancient sorceress, mentioned
    frequently from Aristophanes (*Clouds*, 749) on. It was a
    specialty of Thessaly. References are collected by A. S. Pease
    (on Vergil *Aen.* 4.489 [Cambridge, Mass., 1935]) to this and
    to the turning back of rivers.

    Use of anaphora is particularly prominent in 45–56. It re-
flects, among other things, the heightened intensity of ritual as
Tibullus, through his own song, conveys the power of the
witch's *carmen*.

    vidi: how much has the poet himself been mesmerized into
believing the impossible?

    carmine: here with overtones of its original Latin sense,
"charm," as in the XII Tables (*qui malum carmen incan-
tasset . . .*).

    vertit iter: the order of the letters partially mirrors the
river's reversal. Note change to present tense for more direct
evidence of her power.

47– The reference is to *necyomantea,* summoning spirits from the
48   tomb to prophesy. The classical literary tradition goes back to
Odyssey 11. Parting of the earth is a necessary preliminary to
the escape of ghosts from the underworld.

    Manes: either ghosts or corpses, here probably the latter
(for the distinction see Pease on *Aen.* 4.427; H. J. Rose,
"Ancient Italian Beliefs Concerning the Soul," *CQ* 24 [1930],
129–35).

    elicit: "conjure up"—the usual religious term.

    devocat: for her own magic purposes she busily calls down
bones from the pyre before the fire has died. The distich
changes from underworld and tombs to the still warm pyre, and
from inhumation to cremation. (The existence of both is attested in Rome as early as the XII Tables [Cicero *De Leg.* 2.23].
See H. J. Rose, *OCD*, 314–15).

49– Intensity grows as she controls the crowds she has "evoked."
50   *magico stridore*: the magic shrieking of the witch (Ovid,
Fast. 5.139, draws an explicit connection between *stridere* and
striga, "witch").

    catervas: "crowds," as also in 69 (and cf. 97).

    aspersas lacte: milk can be used to allure (Seneca *Oed.*
562ff.) as well as dispel (Statius *Theb.* 4.544ff.) spirits.

    referre pedem: "return" where they came from.

51– Anaphora of two distinct words is especially rare and comes

52   at the height of her exacting ritual. (We have been only par-
     tially prepared by the preceding distich). The challenge be-
     tween *depellit* and *convocat*, showing the strength of her con-
     trol over the elements, is central to the antinomies in the distich
     —the one of light and dark, happiness and sadness, the other
     of hot and cold, summer and winter. The clouds and snows
     are treated like the crowds in the preceding lines.

     aestivo orbe: "from the summer sky."

53– Medea was the sorceress *par excellence* in ancient literature
54   (for her connection with herbs see A.S.F. Gow on Theocritus
     Idyl 2.14–16). Hecate is the underworld aspect of the *Dea
     Triformis* (Luna in heaven, Artemis-Diana on earth). She is
     often called Trivia for her worship at crossroads, and was
     regularly accompanied by dogs (see Gow on Theocritus *Idyl*
     2.35). By controlling Medea's herbs and taming Hecate's
     hounds, the witch would gain control over these powerful
     beings themselves.

     tenere: "regulate" as well as literally "hold." It helps estab-
     lish a theme of the poem (29, 49).

55– *Haec* completes the emotional circle by reference to 45–47. Ti-
56   bullus draws these fantastic powers to himself, but for the use
     of Delia!

     composuit: as in the case of the lover (22 and 93), it is
     important for the magician to put the right words together for
     casting a spell. The boundary line between the two spheres
     starts to grow dim.

     ter: the magic value of the number three, here used twice,
     is of time immemorial (1.3.11; 1.5.14). On the apotropaic
     effect of spitting see F. Nicolson, "The Saliva Superstition in
     Classical Literature," *HSCP* 8 (1897), 39.

57– Tibullus' wishful thinking reaches its height, not without a
58   touch of humor, as the traditional theme of the *coniunx in-
     cautus* is combined with that of magic. The husband actually
     sees what is going on rather than being deceived behind his
     back (as at lines 19 ff.) but has no comprehension. *Viderit*
     need have no expressed object to convey the sense intended.
     (Cf. the similar situation at 39 ff.).

     ille: the *coniunx* of line 43. The repetition of *credere* makes
     the connection explicit.

     nihil: accusative of inner object.

     molli toro: cf. the context of *molli lecto* (19).

59– The distich qualifies the thought of the preceding lines. The

60 magic will work in the case of the poet alone. The husband will see everything and everyone else.

The lines are constructed with noteworthy care. Line 59 moves chunkily in alliterative pairs; line 60 has a verbal unity running from *omnia* to *uno* to *nihil*. *Omnia* has special force because it ends its own clause yet begins a new line while at the same time contrasting with *nihil*. *Nihil*, in turn, carefully picks up the second word in the preceding distich and points the difference between *credere* (belief from intellectual perception) and *viderit*, *cernet*, and *sentiet*. The echo of *viderit ipse* in *sentiet ipse* gives further, final stress to *nihil* which in turn highlights the change from *ille* (57) to *ipse*.

me uno: the poet's confidence seems to have grown greatly since the first use of the phrase at line 9.

61– The tension between believing and nonbelieving is given a
62 more realistic turn as the poet looks to his own love. For him all these magic powers have produced only words, not deeds (*cantibus* is echoed from 47 and 55, *herbis* from 53). The poet reveals throughout the poem a continuing fascination with words and their potential (or lack of it).

solvere: the usual word for release from the binding effects of a spell (see Pease on *Aen.* 4.479 and 487). The grammar suggests a secondary ambiguity, however. If *meos amores* refers to Delia, *solvere* could look to her release from an observant *coniunx* or a barred door.

63– For the purifying effect of lustration with the sulphur that
64 would come from torches, see 1.5.11–12.

nocte serena: a proper time and occasion for ritual and sometimes even work (see commentators on Ennius *Ann.* 396 and Lucretius 1.142). Perhaps also the moon must shine clearly for the release as well as the binding of love. Contrast the clandestine *obscura nocte* of line 24. The idea of darkness is subtly recurrent through the poem.

hostia pulla: a dark victim is apt for *magicos deos*, who would be classified as gods of the underworld.

65– In focusing on *amor*, line 65 suggests a difference between *totus*
66 *abesset* and *mutuus esset*. The poet desires to be rid, not of love but of the torture of *infelix amor*. *Mutuus* anticipates the prayer for *amor secundus* (77), a love that is given and taken equally by both partners (the metaphor comes from lending). Hitherto the power of magic has been important. The poet now disclaims any desire for power, at least to rid himself of Delia.

His desire is for her, which does not necessarily mean being without *dolores*.

    abesset . . . esset: in prose we would expect *ut* following *orabam*.

67– In spite of the impersonal tone, the reference in these lines may
68   well be to the poet himself, another victim of the *ferrea saecula* he describes at 2.3.35. Somewhat the same guilt feelings may be lurking that came to the surface through 1.1 (especially lines 51–52). What is a love poet doing off campaigning with the ambitious! Yet, if the reference is to Tibullus, he is now assuming at least the ability to be ironhearted as well as to possess Delia, two points whose validity seems dubious.

    Both *ferreus* and *stultus* appear elsewhere in amatory contexts. For the former, see, e.g., Propertius 2.8.12; for *stultus* cf. 1.9.45 and 65. (Is the poet *stultus* in the sense that during such an absence another lover might take his place?) At 1.4.34 *stultos dies* refers to a time when the lover did not take advantage of his situation.

    habere: "possess" in a sexual sense.

69– The allusion could well be to Messalla's eastern campaign (see
70   also 1.7.16 and cf. the similarity of the language at 1.7.3 ff.).

    catervas: "crowds," either of soldiers in rout or of captives ready for slavery.

    Martia castra: *Martia* looks specifically to the victory of Italy over barbarian lands.

71– He who had a character of iron is now said to be manufactured
72   completely of gold and silver (the participle *contextus* comes neatly between the materials it interweaves). Hyperbole and the use of the adjective *totus* for an adverb stress the poet's dislike. The victor is no person at all but an object "woven" of costly metals, if such is metaphorically possible. The man and his trappings are one, suggesting an equestrian statue rather than a human being. The fact that *conspiciendus* can be taken in an unfavorable as well as a favorable sense suggests a pejorative tone to *insideat* also. Nemesis, in love with riches, is described in a similar way at 2.3.49–54.

73– The change from *equo* to *boves* and from *ille* (69) to *ipse* takes
74   us again into a rustic world which embraces both georgic (yoking of cattle) and pastoral (herding of sheep) elements. The only other necessity is Delia whose presence is left in doubt (adding a touch of irony to *mea* and *tecum*, as at 1.1. 57). Cf. the use of *modo Delia* at line 33.

75– Line 75 is a virtuoso piece of construction in sound. *"Te"* per-

76 meates the line; the letters of *liceat* all reappear in *lacertis* and
retinere echoes *teneris*. The ideas of Delia, permission and possession, are interwoven verbally and sonically.

liceat: the poet's hopes, unlike the soldier's (69), are insecure.

inculta: ambiguous. Either "uncared for" (because Delia is
distracting or because the setting looks to a golden age?) or
"unkempt" (which contrasts with the warrior's booty and
anticipates the next lines). In either case there is a challenge
between *inculta* and *mollis* which is only partially mitigated by
the preceding *teneris* (the elegist's tender arms compensate for
any roughness in the terrain; sleep with Delia is smooth, no
matter where). Subtly we are back to the opening theme. *Humo*
is used in amusing contrast to *lecto* (19) and *toro* (58). One
wonders how far Delia will play such a rustic game.

77– The thought is Lucretian (2.34–36) and recurs at 1.8.39–40
78 (cf. also Propertius 1.14.22). It anticipates return to the original theme of the poet as *exclusus amator*.

Tyrio toro: clothes dyed in the famous Tyrian purple, perhaps a further reference to wealth gained in such deeds as
Messalla's eastern campaigns (see 1.7.20 and 47).

vigilanda venit: replacement of the more usual *est* or *fit* by
venit suggests the horror of the impending loveless night.

79– *Plumae* (pillows of down) and *stragula picta* (ornate spreads)
80 are further traditional emblems of luxury.

placidae: both "calm" and "calming." (The abundance of
liquids and sibilants in the distich enhances the soporific effect
of the objects described. Wine alone might work for the poet.)

81– Possible reasons for the poet's misfortunes have been in the
82 back of his mind all along. As often in Tibullus his thoughts
take a religious turn. One word uttered in a rash moment of
blasphemy would be sufficient to bring down the wrath of
Venus.

violavi numina: "did I violate the majesty of Venus . . .?"
The phrase is Lucretian (see commentators on Lucretius 2.614
and Catullus 76.4).

83– *feror*: "am I said . . . ?"
84 *incestus*: either physically or morally unfit to worship.

serta: see line 14 (Delia is now associated with Venus).

focis: here altars, decorated by garlands which the lover
might steal to offer to his mistress (if we follow the pattern
of 2.4.23 where, however, votive offerings, not garlands specifically, are involved).

85– The excess of such prostration and kissing of thresholds was
86 more common in a woman (as at Propertius 3.8.11) than in
a man, though the pose (ungainly and therefore humorous?)
is regular enough for an *exclusus amator* (cf., e.g., Lucretius
4.1179; Propertius 1.16.42). He is excluded from Venus, his
divine protectress as well as Delia, his mortal love.

templis: locative ablative or poetic dative for *ad* with accusative. Whether of Delia or Venus, the shrines are personified.

87– These forms of self-torture were common in antiquity, though
88 disapproved by Cicero (*Tusc. Disp.* 3.62: *muliebres lacerationes genarum*). The posture once more mirrors that of the
exclusus amator (cf. the use of *postis* at 14 and 33). Tibullus,
not without a touch of self-parodic humor, offers the cry of a
suppliant before Delia's door at line 14. Repetitions of *supplex*
(14 and 87) and *serta* (14 and 84) tighten the connection. The
preceding elegy offers examples of the same alternation of religious with amatory poses (cf. 1.1.15–16 with 55–56).

89– The *deus* is some generalized form of Venus' revenge or of
90 Nemesis. We may compare Catullus' warning to Calvus (50.
18–21):

> nunc audax cave sis precesque nostras
> oramus, cave despuas, ocelle,
> ne poenas Nemesis reposcat a te.
> est vemens dea: laedere hanc caveto.

laetus: either from *Schadenfreude* or because he is momentarily happy. In either case the poet's revenge will be harsh.
91– The aging lover has already appeared in the first elegy of the
92 book and is a favorite butt of writers of comedy.

vidi ego: Tibullus uses the same phrase at line 45 watching
his witch at work. It lays claim to an authority patently absent.

lusisset: "to make fun of" with no amatory connotations.

vinclis subdere colla: a mixture of two traditional elegiac
poses, the lover as tamed animal (as 1.4.16) and prisoner of
Venus or his girl (as 1.1.55). *Vinclis* merges both ideas. *Colla*
is poetic plural (the action occurred on several occasions).

senem: note the emphatic position.

93– The phraseology of line 93 reflects that of line 22 with the
94 addition of *tremula voce* (which again recalls the picture of
1.1.71f. where white also symbolizes age).

fingere: "arrange." He is so powerless that this can be only
a desire.

95– The ultimate shame of the old man (who should have others'

96 respect instead of performing disreputable acts himself) is to accost the girl's maid where all can see, *medio foro*. In comedy and elegy the maid often serves as go-between in such illicit situations.

  stare: to stand abjectly and not even walk around (cf. 1.5. 71–74).

97– *circumterit*: a neologism of Tibullus. The crowd is so jostling,
98 so "tight" around him, that it rubs him on all sides. (There are sexual implications). The repetition of *hunc*, with the variation *puer* and *iuvenis*, stresses the disparity between youth and age.

  despuit: here, as possibly at 56, spitting (probably in this instance on one's self) is apotropaic, to ward off the curse which such a foolish creature might bring.

  molle: because still youthful, and capable of love (unlike the old man).

99– Venus, who, though abstract, seems to exert a greater spell
100 over the poet than Delia, should spare her slave but instead "burns her harvest" (Tibullus instinctively combines pastoral and elegiac metaphors). As a loyal servant Tibullus is part of her "holdings." But she does not fulfill the commitment made earlier (*illa favet . . .*) and serves more as an example of fickleness than loyalty. She is elegiac love, after all.

COMMENTARY 1. 3.

Tibullus announces the departure of Messalla, who has left him sick on the island of Phaeacia (Corfu). Messalla will leave, but Death, do you hold off your hands. Tibullus has no family here to mourn him, no Delia who had found the omens propitious at the time of his departure from Rome. But there were also bad omens. Love was unwilling. Perhaps Delia's worship of Isis can help him now to recover and return home. In the golden age of Saturn there was no seafaring, no competition, no unnatural boundary lines, only spontaneous productivity in nature. Now, under Jupiter, war brings death. Should he die, however, Venus will lead him to an Elysium of happy landscape and love. In another part of the underworld deep night enshrouds and dark rivers roar around those who, like Ixion, have misvalued Love. Let Delia remain chaste in the poet's absence, for suddenly he will return like a vision become real, at the dawn of a happy new day.

Tibullus, love elegist caught in a military career, Roman far from Rome, imagines himself on an island which to Homer was a never-never land, neither wholly a part of, nor completely removed from, ordinary humanity. He is sick, alive and yet, as he projects the moment, near to death. This ambivalent position, which can be seen in temporal, geographical, physical, or even spiritual terms, sparks a meditation on death which leads his thoughts (and as often in Tibullus reversal of time leads closer to perfection) to Rome, Delia, his own household gods and the pastoral heaven of Saturn's golden age. But, via the idea of war, Saturn leads to Jupiter, imagined ideal to actual real, to a tombstone announcing fidelity to Messalla at the cost of life. Life alters and contradicts itself and the realm of death, in the poet's dream of mortality, has set divisions where just and impetuous lovers suffer happiness or punishment (and poets are continually surrounded by gaiety, song, and dance). But the more potent dream leads from Phaeacia back to Rome, as death gives place to life, and darkness to a light and colored dawn. Yet there is a dream within a dream. Tibullus, an Odysseus returned to his version of Ithaca, imagines Delia as Penelope become Roman *matrona* with all the trappings of enduring fidelity (a spectacle more humorous than wistful). In addition he sees himself as a portent in her eyes. Maybe his return was as unexpected to Delia as his portrait of her is fictional.

1–2 *ibitis*: plural, though Messalla, the most important member of the party, is singled out here and in the next line (*ipse*). Tibullus imagines in the same instant their future departure and their (hoped for) remembrance thereafter.

Aegaeas . . . per undas: Messalla's trip will lead from the Adriatic through the stormy Aegean to parts unmentioned.

sine me: cf. the poet's boast to Messalla at 1.7.9 (*non sine me*). The sound "me" connects the poet himself (*me . . . mei*) with Messalla and *memores* and emphasizes the interlocking word order.

utinam: used elliptically, "I trust." This is the first occurrence in Latin reinforced by *"o."*

cohors: usually the staff of a proconsul or propraetor during his provincial tour of duty. We think of Catullus as part of Memmius' retinue (see commentators on Catullus 10.10). About the specific situation of Messalla, historians remain uncertain.

3–4 Tibullus has become ill on the island of Corfu. He chooses to remind us directly of its Homeric name rather than of Corcyra or Drepane, the name given it by Callimachus (Pliny *Hist. Nat.* 4.52; Call. *Aet* frag. 14Pf.). The reader must choose for himself how far a parallel with the wandering Odysseus can be pressed, but the reference here and the concluding *nostos* leave little doubt that this was in the poet's mind.

me tenet: the verb contrasts with the motion of *ibitis* as the dream world Phaeacia, *ignotis terris*, challenges the specificity of *Aegaeas undas*. There is also a punning connection with the repeated *abstineas*. To be "held" by Phaeacia is bad enough, provided death itself "holds off" its hands. (Cf. *contentus,* 1.1.25).

ignotis terris: death in an unknown spot was terrifying to the ancients (Vergil *Aen.* 9.485 and R. D. Williams on *Aen.* 5.871 [Oxford, 1960]).

avidas manus: by hypallage from *Mors* itself. The greed of death is proverbial (cf. *rapax Mors*, 65).

Mors nigra: blackness is associated with Tartarus later in the poem (68, 71, 76). *Atra* is the most common epithet of *Mors* in Latin; *nigra* and *rapax* (65) are unique (see J. Carter, *Epitheta Deorum*, 73).

5–6 *non . . . mater*: a catalogue of appropriate mourners commences that extends to *non soror* and culminates in *Delia non usquam* (9). Family relationships are very real to Tibullus.

hic: i.e. Phaeacia.

maestos sinus: again hypallage (a figure of speech Tibullus favors).

ossa perusta: bones burnt through and through on the pyre. (The sound of line 6 is noteworthy, suggesting weeping or hissing or both.)

7–8 Climax of the (imagined) funeral scene: the bones and ashes are collected and both placed in the *sepulcrum*.

Assyrios odores: Syrian perfumes were specially prized (Syria is regularly confounded with Assyria by the poets). It was common practice (reasons for the gesture would be obvious) to throw perfumes on the burning pyre (Propertius 2. 13.30) or on the cooling ashes. The sound of line 7 continues the effect of 6.

effusis comis: cf. 1.1.67–68, *solutis crinibus*. By using a verb suitable to tears (*effundere*) to describe hair, Tibullus adds to the effect of *fleat*. (Tibullus is fascinated by hair in this poem. Witness lines 31, 66, 69, 91.)

9– Delia's late entrance into the poem is a dramatic moment. It

10   serves to transfer the mise en scène to Rome, to the thought of leaving the city rather than of yearning in absence, to Delia seeking counsel at all the shrines instead of the poet's sister unable to mourn *ante sepulcra*.

    mitteret: the sense here is "let go" (cf. Catullus 64.221, 66.29). *Urbe* without *ab* is rare.

    dicitur: Tibullus knows of her action only by hearsay.

    ante: the shrines stand for the gods from whom Delia sought advice. *Omnes* adds a hyperbolic note that fits with the poet's (humorously?) exaggerated self-pity.

    consuluisse: technical term: "seek a response from."

11– The past tenses continue a vivid glance back at Tibullus' de-
12   parture from Rome.

    In divination by *sortes* diverse lots were placed in an urn whence they were drawn out by an assistant (*puer*) and interpreted by the *sortilegus*. The apparent meaning of line 11 is that Delia did the drawing herself, three times for good and lucky measure, while the *puer* served as prophet.

    In line 12 the Ambrosianus reads *e triviis* which Muretus, followed by some later editors, changed to *trinis,* as balance for *ter*. But that soothsayers took their place in the crowded parts of the city we can see from Horace *Sat*. 1.6.113–14.

13– In weeping and above all "looking back," it is Delia herself
14   who delivers, unwittingly and somewhat peculiarly, the bad omens of Tibullus' departure. For instances of prohibition against the latter see Vergil *Ecl*. 8.102, *Georg*. 4.491, and the comments of Gow on Theocritus *Idyl* 24.96; J. G. Frazer on Ovid *Fast*. 6. 164 (London, 1929): ". . . on setting out on a journey from home you should not look back because the Furies are following you. Failure to observe the rule inevitably results in disaster."

    reditus: poetic plural for singular. The noun is anticipated by *rettulit* (12).

    dabant: "gave" in the sense of "promised," "foretold."

    est deterrita . . . quin: the construction is patterned on that of *prohibeo*. The extent of her fright did not inhibit weeping.

15– *solator*: though the formation of agent nouns like *solator* is
16   common enough, the word itself is very rare.

    mandata: "my (final) injunctions."

    tardas moras: delays, slow and slowing (cf. Vergil *Aen*. 1.746).

    anxius: an etymological pun, as at 1.2.25.

    usque: here adverbial, equivalent to *semper* (1.2.90).

17– In spite of the earlier *omina certa* Tibullus now presents the
18 pretext that birds, regular vehicle of auguries, had presented
     omina dira, ill-boding omens (see Cicero *De Leg.* 2.21).

 sum causatus: "offered as an excuse." The order of words
is curious and emphatic, while the text of line 18 remains
still open to doubt. Should *sacrum* be read instead of *sacram*?

 Saturni diem: the earliest surviving literary reference to our
Saturday. For prohibitions against traveling on that day, see
Ovid *Ars Amat.* 1.413ff., *Rem. Am.* 219–20, etc.

 me tenuisse: for *retinuisse*, out of contrast with *me tenet* (3)
and to preserve the simplicity of legal-ritualistic language.

 sacram: an echo of *sacras sortes* (11).

19– These lines balance 9–14 as his reaction to departure comple-
20 ments hers. She consults the gods and draws the lots, but causes
     a bad omen. He appeals, as pretext, to birds, to the day itself,
     and finally to a bad omen of his own doing. Stumbling on a
     threshold or at a gate was a particularly bad sign (see Servius'
     comment on *Ecl.* 8.29; C. J. Fordyce on Catullus 61.161 [Ox-
     ford, 1961]; Austin on *Aen.* 2.242 [Oxford, 1964]). The meta-
     phorical use begins as early as Plautus *Cas.* 815ff.: "sensim
     super attolle limen pedes, nova nupta; sospes iter incipe hoc
     . . ." (Cf. line 92).

 o quotiens: the poet is now thoroughly involved in his
recollection, transferring the emotion of *o utinam* (2) to the
past.

 tristia signa: synonymous with *omina dira* (17).

21– Tibullus should have looked to Amor, not Saturn, for signs
22 concerning departure. A generalized warning to all lovers. For
     Tibullus it is more the emotion, *amor*, that held him back.

 sciat: know as a mental fact, before the physical effects
strike him.

 se: position allows easy connection with both *egressum* and
prohibente.

23– The worship of the Egyptian fertility goddess Isis, an occa-
24 sional subject in elegy because of its restriction to women
     (hence *tua*), came into Rome early in the first century B.C. and
     remained popular well into the Christian era. Herodotus iden-
     tifies her with Demeter and there are undoubted parallels
     between the two. Her life—the murder of her brother-husband
     Osiris, her lamentations and wanderings, and his final resur-
     rection (triumphing with the help of their child, the sun-god
     Horus, over Seth, the god of war)—formed the basis of her
     ritual worship. The cult's exotic nature made it an easy object

of suspicion. Delia is depicted as worshiping the Egyptian goddess on the poet's behalf, a reason for the alternation *tua mihi, mihi tua.*

aera: by metonymy, the *sistrum* or rattle associated with the cult of Isis and with Egypt in general (see commentators on Propertius 3.11.43; Vergil *Aen.* 8.696). It consists usually of a "u" shaped piece of bronze attached to a long handle. Wires were stretched between the two sides and bits of metal of various shapes were attached to them which rattled when shaken. This reverberation may be the reason for the word *repulsa* which would ordinarily be applied to cymbals as would *aera*, and they may possibly be meant here. On the clash of metal as apotropaic see 1.8.21–22; Gow on Theocritus *Idyl* 2.36.

25–
26 The periods of chastity prescribed by the cult of Isis would have been especially annoying to the elegist. Hence the parenthetical *memini.*

pure . . . puro: the initial meaning ("cleanly") leads directly into the elegiac sense ("chastely").

27–
28 The repetition of *nunc* underscores the urgency of the poet's appeal now to the goddess herself, his own thoughts returning for a moment to Phaeacia.

picta tabella: wooden slabs illustrating cures, hung on her temple wall. (For the location of shrines to Isis in ancient Rome see S. Platner and T. Ashby, *A Topographical Dictionary of Ancient Rome*, 283–86; E. Nash, *Pictorial Dictionary of Ancient Rome*, 510-11).

29–
30 The worshiper was provided with seats outside from which to contemplate her image inside the *fores*. Linen is associated with the cult's purity. (Delia is momentarily in the position of an *exclusus amator*.)

ut: purposive.

votivas voces: we would ordinarily expect *vota*, not *voces*, after *persolvens*. Instead of writing "fulfilling the vows which she had uttered" Tibullus has "fulfilling the utterances which served as vows."

31–
32 *resoluta comas*: nothing should be bound during religious ceremonies (see Servius on Vergil *Aen.* 4.518).

dicere laudes: "sing the deeds of" as well as "hymn."

insignis: because she is dressed in white and because of her beauty. She is a "stand-out" from the rest of the crowd.

Pharia: Alexandrian (then Egyptian), from the island first mentioned by Homer (*Od.* 4.355), on which Ptolemy II built his famous lighthouse. The substitution is common (as Propertius 3.7.5; Ovid *Ars Amat.* 3.635).

33–
34 *At* initiates a contrast between Delia, Isis (*tibi,* 31) and Tibullus (*mihi,* 33). Though couched in the form of a prayer apparently still to Isis, Tibullus contemplates his own household gods, his from time immemorial, and not any foreign divinities, however responsive. (The contrast is subtly abetted by the echo of *turba Pharia* in *tura Lari*). The Lares and Penates make no more poignant appearance in Tibullus' verses than here.

antiquo: comparison with 1.7.58 and 2.1.60 shows the importance of such traditions to Tibullus.

35–
36 With smooth transition from hallowed, inherited gods, Tibullus turns to the long past golden age of Kronos-Saturn when journeying on land and sea was unnecessary. He would have been well advised to follow the instincts he expressed in line 18. Like most Latin authors, Tibullus is fond of the theme of a golden age, first expressed in Classical literature by Hesiod (*Works and Days* 109 ff. See K. J. Reckford, "Some Appearances of the Golden Age," *CJ* 54 [1958], 79–87).

Saturno rege: Saturn, ancient Italic divinity and father of Jupiter, hence easily identified with Greek Kronos, was expelled along with his fellow Titans by the future Olympians (cf. 2.5.9: *Saturno rege fugato*). In the Roman myth which Vergil expounds in books 7 and 8 of the *Aeneid,* he came to Italy and established an era of unprecedented peace and natural prosperity.

longas vias: the generality has specific reference to Tibullus himself and his fear of change (see line 14 above and 1.1.26 and 52).

est patefacta: the image is a common one (e.g., Cicero *De Nat. Deor.* 2.141; *Phil.* 5.49, 10.7). It may come from the opening of the starting gates at a race (as Lucretius 2.263–64; 4.990) or of a city gate or house door (as Livy 2.15 or Propertius 1.16.1). Though the reference is general, it may look back specifically to lines 14–20.

37–
38 The beginning of seafaring, like the discovery of fire, helped to initiate what to many ancient thinkers was a decline from the golden age (the word *contempserat,* a unique usage by Tibullus, is emphatic). The Argo is the traditional symbol for this event. It is often said to be made of pine (Catullus 64.1; Horace *Epode* 16.57 and the more generalized statement of Vergil *Ecl.* 4.38).

pinus: for ship, by synedoche, underscoring the personification.

effusum sinum: "billowed sail." In such a context *effundo* is ordinarily applied to the sea itself (as, e.g., Velleius Paterculus 2.43; Horace *Epist*. 1.11.26)), but further enhancement of the personification is not out of the question.

39–   *vagus navita*: Tibullus regularly frowns on wandering (2.3.39;
40   2.6.3). *Navita* is used elsewhere by Tibullus only of Charon (1.10.36).

ignotis terris: the same phrase occurs in the same metrical position in line 3. Since *undas* ends both lines 1 and 37, it is likely that these two couplets are a generic homily against those like Messalla (and his poet, too) who, for motives of greed or ambition, destroy the possibility of a golden age.

repetens compendia: "seeking gain." Cf. 1.9.9–10: *lucra petituras . . . instabiles . . . rates*.

externa: trade with a foreign country is in question.

41–   There was no need for agriculture in the golden age. The
42   motif of subjugation, introduced in the preceding couplet, is expanded to embrace the bull and the horse. In Tibullus' present way of thinking loss of the golden age means a combination of labor and slavery. Alliteration is prominent in this and the following couplet.

frenos: "bit" and reins, to the horse what *iuga* are to the bull.

43–   In those days of liberty houses had no need for doors (there
44   were no locked-out lovers) nor fields for fixed bounds. *Fores* recalls not only the temple doors of line 28 but the habitual posture of the *exclusus amator*.

regeret finibus arva: the ordinary expression would be *regere* (for *dirigere*) *fines*. The language is archaic—"measure off the fields with boundary lines." There are examples of simple verb for compound in lines 9 and 18.

For *fines* and *arva* in a context that illustrates the contrast between the golden age and a more realistic present, see Vergil *Ecl*. 1.3 f.

45–   The quintessence of the golden age is seen in nature's spon-
46   taneity (*ipsae, ultro*) as she performs the ordinarily impossible. There will be no need for either georgic (bee-keeping) or pastoral (shepherding) labor. The production of honey from oaks is a common golden age motif (as Vergil *Ecl*. 4.30; Horace *Epode* 16.47). Cattle or sheep, udders swollen with milk, with no menace from nature either to them or their guardians, also constitute a common picture (e.g., *Ecl*. 4.21 ff.).

obvia: i.e. up to meet their keepers, rather than *vice versa*.
securis: cf. 1.1.48 and 77.

47–
48   Anger is the emotion which causes battle lines to be formed and swords to be forged. The couplet forms the transition from the age of Saturn to the present decadent dominion of Jupiter, via the mention of war. Swordmaking especially was singled out as a symbol for this change (as, e.g., Vergil *Georg.* 2.540). The whole is topical for Tibullus' present situation.

   duxerat: *ducere* here means "mould," "forge" as Vergil *Aen.* 7.634) but the military overtones are undeniable. The artisan is considered *saevus*, his workmanship *immitis*, because of the destruction he causes. He would be held vicariously responsible for the death of Tibullus *immiti consumptus morte* (55). The use of *immitis* here reverberates with some irony through the next five couplets.

49–
50   With a threefold *nunc* we are back in the present. Saturn had been a *rex* (35) under whom there had been no need to set off boundaries (*regeret*, 44) or tame horses (*domito ore*, 42). Under the tyranny of *dominus* Jupiter all this is changed. For the distinction between *rex* and *dominus* see Cicero on Tarquin (*de Rep.* 2.47): "Videtisne igitur, ut de rege dominus extiterit . . . ."

   Though again generalized, war, the sea and *leti viae* have particular bearing on Tibullus' own situation. *Viae* links this general passage with lines 35–36 while *leti,* supporting the most negative side of *viae,* prepares for the theme of 53 ff. The placement of *repente* is emphatic.

51–
52   A direct appeal to Jupiter as *pater*, partially to mitigate the implied slur of *dominus*. Tibullus protests that he has performed no impiety to provoke Jupiter's wrath, especially something drastic enough to cause his death. The connection between impiety and heaven's revenge through disease or death is a common notion in antiquity (the plague in Lucretius 6 is a notable example).

   The chiastic order of *sanctos impia verba deos* abets the friction between *sanctos* and *impia*.

   timidum: not cautious so much as fearful (of divine indignation).

53–
54   The connection between the generalization of 49–50 and Tibullus' present state becomes explicit.

   fatales: the years allotted by fate.

   explevimus: see 1.4.69.

   fac stet: suppression of *ut* after an imperative form of *facio* is a matter of choice. Presumably we are to imagine that Messalla is being addressed. The shift is abrupt.

lapis: an unfortunate kind of marker (line 44).

inscriptis notis: epitaphs made occasional appearances at more gloomy moments of elegy (e.g., Propertius 2.13.35–36; 4.7.85–86). *Notae* are first "letters," then "writing."

55– Tibullus exploits the position of the names to stress the con-
56 nection between himself and Messalla and the contrast between *iacet* and *sequitur*. Though the phrase *terra marique* is trite, the words individually recall lines 3, 39, and 50. (Cf. 1.1.53: *te bellare decet terra, Messalla, marique*.)

This and the dedication at 1.9.83 are the only occasions where Tibullus mentions his own name.

hic: the tomb, with special reference to Corfu (3).

immiti: "pitiless," but possibly also "unripe," "immature," because it came early. It is intimately connected with the swordmaker's *immiti arte* (48).

consumptus: the conception, which also appears in *Carm. Epig.* 1064.1, seems to be that of death as a devouring beast. (Cf. Lucretius 1.852; Catullus 3.13–14. Vergil at *Aen.* 6.201, 241, 273 uses *fauces* ambiguously as the jaws of a beast or entranceway into the house of death. See E. Norden, *Vergil, Aen.* 6 [Leipzig, 1926], *ad loc.*).

57– Faithful as he has been to Messalla in life, it is his accomplish-
58 ment as love-poet that will serve him after death. Venus herself, arrogating the role ordinarily given to Hermes, is the poet's *dux* into the underworld.

facilis: with dative it has the meaning "suitable to," "proper for."

tenero Amori: cf. 2.6.1. The epithet is frequent for Love and his followers.

campos Elysios: the Elysian fields provided an eternal paradise for the saints and heroes of love, as befits elegy. The alternative was Tartarus. We may sense an echo in the opening lines of the epigram (probably by Domitius Marsus) prefixed to the ancient *vita*:

> Te quoque Vergilio comitem non aequa, Tibullus,
> mors iuvenem campos misit ad Elysios . . . .

Tibullus provides the first surviving description of the Elysian fields in Roman literature which cannot be traced as a whole to any particular Greek source (see H. Eisenberger, *Hermes* 88 [1960], 193.)

59– We are now in the underworld. The couplet presents an ex-

60 cellent example of sound complementing sense.

choreae: dances. The word is poetic and appears in Latin first in Lucretius (2.635) and Catullus (64.287). (It need not necessarily have the meaning "dancing-floor" at *Aen.* 6.644, as Norden says.) *Chorus* and *cantus* are among the pleasures of Osiris at 1.7.44.

vigent: striking in a passage dealing with the dead.

passim vagantes: though *vagor* is unusual in this sense, Cicero (*De Div.* 2.80) speaks of birds *huc et illuc passim vagantis*. The ability to wander freely is a mark of the golden age (Vergil *Ecl.* 4.19: *errantis hederas passim*). There is a wry contrast with the use of *vagus* at line 39.

tenui gutture: size of the throat is a metaphor for the delicate quality of voice. (The phrase is borrowed by Ovid, *Am.* 1.13.8). There is much about elegists and elegy that is "slender."

61–
62 *casiam*: "an aromatic shrub, perh. mezereon or marjoram" (*OLD*).

non culta: there is no labor in Elysium any more than there had been in the golden age (cf. lines 41–46).

seges: here "field."

odoratis rosis: sweet-smelling and appropriate for Elysium as symbols for love, youth, and beauty.

63–
64 *iuvenum series*: groups of youths holding hands while dancing. The etymology of *series* (from *sero*, "plait," "interweave") makes a punning connection with *immixta*. They form *serta*, garlands of dancers.

ludit: to play, write love poetry, make love or any combination thereof.

assidue: the adverb and its metaphoric context recall 1.1.3–4.

proelia miscet: amatory battles far different from those of a Messalla.

65–
66 Tibullus makes a similar change from love to death at 1.1. 69–70.

illic: though equivalent to *hic* (59) because Tibullus is describing himself, it prepares the way for the altered perspective of 67 ff.

rapax: "grasping," "plundering" (see lines 4–5 and cf. Horace Carm. 2.18.30: *rapacis Orci*).

myrtea: made of myrtle, a shrub sacred to Venus. In Vergil's underworld a myrtle wood protects those whom the cares of love had wasted in life. Among them was Dido (*Aen.* 6.440 ff.).

insigni coma: "Remarkable" because distinguished by the token of Venus' approbation.

67– *scelerata sedes*: the resting place of those who have committed
68   *scelera. Iacet* and *sedes* contrast with the dancing *series* as
      deep night with the reds and greens of the preceding descrip-
      tion. *Iacet* comes too close to the poet's own epitaph (55) for
      us to dismiss possible reference to the poet's illness (and con-
      templated death).

      flumina nigra: these were usually Cocytus and Phlegethon.
      To suit the poet's present purpose they are black rather than
      fiery. Nevertheless *sonant* may suggest the hissing of flames,
      sounds which contrast with the birdsong in Elysium (60). The
      attribute was given to *Mors* at line 4.

      nocte profunda: at *Aen.* 4.26 Vergil uses the same expression
      (see Pease, Vergil *Aen.* 4, *ad loc.*, for further parallels).

69– Tisiphone, chief of the tormenting Furies, rules here as Venus
70   in Elysium. Snakes are the traditional hair of the Furies and
      raging their characteristic role.

      impexa: "uncombed." In the subsequent accusative of spe-
      cification which follows, *angues* replaces the expected *crines*.

      impia turba: the darting, uncertain motion *huc illuc* implies
      contrasts with the regular scheme of the *choreae* in Elysium.
      The origins for the various impieties are recounted below.
      Tibullus in line 52 has made sure we do not include him in
      such a group.

71– *niger Cerberus*: cf. the other uses of the adjective at 4 and 68.
72   *in porta*: Cerberus, monstrous dog with neck or tail of a
      snake, guards the entrance to Tartarus. Though on occasion
      he has fifty or a hundred heads, ordinarily he is the possessor
      of three mouths (Hesiod *Theog.* 311–12; Cicero *Tusc. Disp.*
      1.10; Vergil *Georg.* 4.483, *Aen.* 6.417; Propertius 3.5.43).
      Usually his heads are canine (hence *latratu trifauci*: *Aen.*
      6.417). The hissing, important for the context, would issue
      from the snakes not the heads (*ore* is poetic singular for
      plural).

      aeratas fores: the Homeric tradition calls for gates of iron
      (*Iliad* 8.15), portals of bronze (*ibid.*; Hesiod *Theog.* 811).
      Vergil is noncommittal (*Aen.* 6.552, 573). (Cf. lines 30 and
      43 for other *fores*).

      excubat: the guardian, more forbidding than the usual elegiac
      custos, lies before his door.

73– The first *sceleratus* is Ixion who tried to seduce Juno (the
74   tradition is preserved from Pindar *Pyth.* 2.21 ff. on). He is the
      passive sufferer of a swift torture. At *Georg.* 4.484 his wheel
      is stayed by the singing of Orpheus. At *Georg.* 3.38 snakes

are an added torture, but in *Aen.* 6.601 f. Vergil changes the story.

noxia: "guilty."

75– Tityos, who attempted to violate Latona, was another tradi-
76   tional figure in Tartarus (cf. Homer *Od.* 11.576). The punishment is the same in Homer with whom the figure of nine
acres and the vultures—in his description only one—originate.
The first Latin reference is Lucretius 3.984–94, and he appears
also in Vergil's underworld (*Aen.* 6.595–600). Most of the
words in Tibullus' description are chosen for their reference
to Elysium. Here, too, the victim is passive, his torture filled
with motion.

assiduas: an etymological pun (as 1.1.3).

atro viscere: bile secreted by the liver (the meaning of *viscus*
here) was black, but *atro* may be seen as well in the sense of
accursed, unfortunate.

pascit aves: a macabre variant of the pastoral *pascit oves.*

77– Tantalus, son of Jupiter and father of Pelops, was relegated
78   to Hades for revealing the secrets of the gods and not, apparently, for any sin against Amor, as the context might suggest,
though gossip is naturally frowned upon by the elegists. He
is surrounded by water, yet he cannot reach it to drink (again
stability and motion are in conflict). The *stagna* are part of
the *flumina nigra* which encompass him and Tartarus in general. Both *unda*, which performs the torture, and *sitis*, its
vehicle, are personified. *Acer*, therefore, has a double meaning,
"severe" and "zealous." However intense the thirst, the wave
gives up like a coward and fails the eagerness of the prospec-
tive drinker.

iam iam: the repetition conveys the immediacy of something
which seems almost to have happened (see Austin on *Aen.*
2.530).

79– With the daughters of Danaus we have an example of a crime
80   against Venus. With the exception of Hypermnestra, all mur-
dered their husbands, sons of Aegyptus, on their wedding night.
This punishment also involves water with which they vainly attempted to fill storage vats from leaky jars. The phrase *numen
laedere* makes its first Latin appearance at Horace *Epode* 15.3
(cf. also *Aen.* 1.8; 2.183).

cava dolia: because of their hollow shape or porous texture
the vessels are always empty (the opposite of *cavus* here is
plenus).

81– A transitional distich which the preceding lines anticipate.

82 *Illic* picks up lines 73 and 77 (Ixion and Tantalus in Tartarus). From dream we turn to wish. Whoever has treated Delia the way Ixion did Juno deserves comparable punishment. There is no mention of Tibullus' death, only his absence.

meos amores: Delia. For *violare* in this sense cf. 1.9.19. The curse implies that the event has already occurred.

lentas militias: a slow journey away from love is as painful as "slow" love itself (1.4.81; 1.10.57–58).

83– The first address to Delia since line 23. The last use of *precor*
84 (4 and 5) was against his death. His absence is now assumed, her fidelity in doubt. Delia's *pudor* is treated like a shrine. The *anus*, traditional butt of the excluded lover's wrath, fulfills a positive role, to guard the temple against hazard, a good Cerberus.

assideat: there is a pun on the word which the sound of the line enhances—*assideat, sedula, semper*. The primary meaning is "watch over," "take care of." The pun centers around *sedula* (and its implications of *assidua*).

85– We are now inside the "shrine," as Delia becomes, with un-
86 derstated irony, a chaste Roman Penelope waiting for her wandering warrior-poet. The old woman purveys only stories, nothing more. Storytelling and spinning or weaving are stock pastimes in such a situation, often depicted, for obvious reasons, going on well into the night. (Hence *posita lucerna*, on which see W. T. Avery, "Tibullus 1.3.65," *CJ* 49 [1953–54], 165–66.) Cynthia makes such a claim of chastity for herself in one of Propertius' most charming elegies (1.3.41). (Cf. also Vergil *Aen.* 8.408 ff., but the tradition of the chaste Roman matron, staying at home usually spinning, goes back in literature at least as early as Terence *Heaut.* 275. For further discussion see Ogilvie on Livy 1.57.9, the tale of Lucretia.) Both *plena* and *longa* are chosen to attest Delia's endurance. *Referat* and *deducat*, however, might well be meant to recall another role of the *lena*, less conducive to the maintenance of discipline. For the technical sense of *deduco* here, see Fordyce on Catullus 64.311 ff.

stamina . . . colu: threads drawn down from the distaff.

87– *circa*: around about her (the *anus* or Delia).
88 *gravibus pensis*: the words complement each other. *Pensum* means first something of weighty importance, then, in particular, a weight of wool to spin. *Affixa* is well chosen to illustrate Delia's involvement as well as her steadfastness. It is reversed in *remittat*.

    puella: perhaps singular for plural, but Delia herself is probably meant.

    fessa: the context recalls Propertius 1.3.42, a poem with which Tibullus 1.3 has much in common. (Is the placement in the book coincidental?)

89– Instead of death's advent we have the epiphanic return of
90   Tibullus unannounced from near death to imagined reality and of her lover to Delia.

    subito: suddenly, with the unexpected quickness of a dream or omen.

    videar: of a dream, this time on Delia's part.

    caelo missus: proverbial for something supernatural (see A. Otto, *Die Sprichwörter der Römer,* 62). A good omen, obviously, as opposed to those manifested on the day of his departure (17f.).

91– The dream language continues with the phrase *qualis eris*. With
92   the language of both distichs we may compare the manner in which Vergil describes the appearance of Hector to Aeneas in *Aen.* 2: *Hector / visus adesse mihi* . . . (270–71); *ei mihi, qualis erat* . . . (274). (Cf. Ennius *Ann.* 6V[3] and the references in D. R. Shackleton Bailey, *Propertiana,* 296). The language proves that Delia was as much a dream become real to Tibullus as he to her (and all this, to be sure, still in the poet's fancy, especially the spectacle of Delia as *matrona*). Moreover the phrase *longos turbata capillos* tells something of the emotional state in which he hopes to find Delia, in deep distress, perhaps even mourning for the dead (line 8 and 3.2.11, *longos incompta capillos*). Perhaps she was only sad (cf. Ovid *Met.* 4.261 of Clytie, *humo nuda, nudis incompta capillis*). Perhaps a deeper ritual meaning is present (cf. Ovid *Met.* 7.183 of Medea, *nuda pedem, nudos umeris infusa capillos*).

    nudato pede: bareness of foot connotes haste which here, because it arises from eager affection, portends change and renewal. At least she is not dressed for other lovers.

    Delia.: the sudden vocative and its placement are striking.
93– *precor*: all this is still only a prayer (cf. 4, 5, 83). The parallel
94   with Odysseus breaks down in the poet's wishful thinking. His return, from imagined death and adventuring, is greeted by none of the tests Penelope gives her husband.

    hunc illum: "this very day, the one I have been telling about" (Tibullus is still ambivalent).

    Aurora . . . Luciferum: suddenly all is clarity—day after night, light after darkness, life from death.

roseis candida: the juxtaposition of red and white is a favorite Roman color contrast (see Fordyce on Catullus 61.9f.), though both adjectives are ordinary attributes of dawn in antiquity. (Cf. *rota Luciferi*: 1.9.62). By allusion to line 62, Tibullus conjures up a paradise on earth.

COMMENTARY 1. 4.

"May shade protect you from the elements, Priapus: What is the reason for your success with youth? It is certainly not handsomeness." To the poet the rustic child of Bacchus replies: "Whether it be for beauty or boldness, each youth has a reason to be loved. Resistance is gradually worn down, like seasonal change. Even perjury is defensible in love. Do not be slow in pursuit; beauty soon fades in the passing of time. Only Bacchus and Apollo have eternal youth. Yielding sometimes wins in love, though it may mean long journeying by land and sea, or undergoing hard trials, hunting or fencing. Though he be adamant at first, soon he will ask for kisses. Now the times are corrupt and young love demands gifts. A curse on him who first taught the selling of love! Love creative, immortalizing poets, not gifts. Let the person who sells love become a eunuch priest of the Magna Mater. Venus enjoys a lover's blandishing supplications." Tibullus sang what the god pronounced to Titius but his wife forbade remembrance. Tibullus boasts of being teacher to those whom a clever youth has caught. But, alas, Marathus now twists him, and his knowledge is useless when put to a practical test. He will become a laughingstock unless Marathus relents.

Priapus initially appears in Latin elegy in poem 1 and here, where he first assumes the role of *magister amorum*. (Hellenistic writers often style him helper of the lovesick as well as garden and harbor god. For details see H. Herter, *De Priapo*; V. Buchheit, *Studien zum Corpus Priapeorum*; Gow on Theocritus *Idyl* 1.21 and *Epig.* 3.) It is a mock-didactic poem (in a firm tradition whose most famous exemplar is probably the *parabasis* of Aristophanes' *Birds*), enriched by parody of both hymn and epic, particularly Ennius and Lucretius. Heroic language abounds, wordplays are especially common, catalogue is piled on catalogue, example on example, aphorism on aphorism, to illustrate wittily a light theme. Placement between two generally serious poems emphasizes humor still further. We are to imagine the statue of an ugly (and undoubtedly ithyphallic) Priapus, static, exposed to the elements, yet oracular in the most cogent manner. He even tells us that poets and poetry are to be preferred to love bought by riches, and the poet, too, for a moment takes the same aloof, magisterial pose. But in an engaging twist at the end—undercutting and a touch bitter—we learn that precepts have little control over realities; words, even a poet's words, yield before the hard facts of life. Tibullus cannot put into action Priapus' preachings which he repeats so well. The dream, an amusing spectacle in itself of a double teacher-student relationship, is shattered.

1–2   In the first three distichs Tibullus himself addresses Priapus. The *do ut des* formula, expanded upon here, is common in Roman ritual petitions (in poetry see, e.g., Vergil *Ecl.* 9.30–31). The postulant makes an offering and the god is expected to grant his request in return. Here it is first positive, then apotropaic (*ne* with negative wish clause). Ironically—he is a garden god—sun and rain, heat and chill, are the elemental hazards to which Priapus must be resigned (5–6), and to which the lover must submit by his command (41–44). The formulaic prayer, by its very impossibility, suggests a similar outcome for the poet's request.

     contingant: "be your lot," but, given theme and assonance, a physical effect is just beneath the surface.

     capiti . . . noceant: the phrase has a legalistic ring which adds to the mock solemnity (see Livy 3.55.5: *capitalis noxa*).

3–4   Priapus himself is so *informis* that he must have some hidden talent to produce the effects he does. The threefold use of anaphora in these six lines is effective in such a ritual address. The repeated *tibi* suggests a humorous parody of the ritual *tu* form of hymnic invocation (see E. Norden, *Agnostos Theos*, 143–63).

     nitet: "be shiny," and hence beautiful. The phrase *barba nitet* is apparently a Tibullan coinage (cf. Ovid. *Tr.* 3.10.22 and Seneca *Epist.* 115.2). The beard is a symbol of handsomeness (Catullus 37.19 but cf. R.G. Austin on Cicero *Pro Cael.* 33.25 [Oxford, 1960]). The beauty of hair is a recurrent motif in the poem (26, 30, 38, 63).

5–6   *producis*: unique in Tibullus and in an unusual intransitive ("endure") rather than transitive ("produce") sense. Again it is hard to avoid the notion of witty parody. How can the garden god aid a lover if all he brings upon himself is rain and heat? And at the same time he is dependent on someone else to evoke the shade he needs as protection against the elements. Moreover, and in spite of *nudus*, *frigora* often typify a loveless state (as 1.8.39) and *siccitas* may also have similar connotations (cf. Catullus 23.12). Mention of the seasons anticipates the theme of time's passage, basic to the poem's development.

   nudus . . . nudus: the ancient reader would have recalled Hesiod's injunction to "sow nude, reap nude" (*Works and Days* 391), adapted by Vergil (*Georg.* 1.299: *nudus ara, sere nudus*). Priapus only stands helplessly exposed to the weather.

7–8 The language is that of seeking and granting an oracle. Tibullus later (78) puts himself in the same position only to admit his inadequacy. In keeping with the hymnic tradition, but without much elevation of tone, we hear of the god's ancestry (he is usually considered the child of Dionysus and Aphrodite) and of one of his chief attributes, the pruning hook.

   rustica proles: a common designation of Priapus (see H. Herter, *De Priapo*, 203 f.).

9–   "As befits the immense importance and value of his theme
10   Priapus soars into it from the upper realms of poetry" (K. F. Smith, *The Elegies of Albius Tibullus*). He is portrayed, ironically and amusingly, as the ideal *praeceptor amoris*, professor of expertise in love. The ridiculous statue is given the reverence due the highest authority and responds with suitably lofty language. We may compare *o fuge*, for instance, with Hector's command to Aeneas *heu fuge* (*Aen.* 2.289).

   fuge: the construction with a prolate infinitive is Latin, not Greek, and is strictly poetic. The first recorded use is at Lucretius 1.1052 (see C. Bailey on Lucretius 1.102 [Oxford, 1947]).

   tenerae: a commonplace (also in 14, 58), by hypallage from *puerorum*.

   credere: "entrust."

   causam . . . habent: the idiom first appears in Plautus (*Asin.* 789) and is attested in Cicero (*De Off.* 3.31) and Livy (2.4.3). The hypallage of *iusti*, ordinarily expected with *causam*, stresses the meaning of the latter as "pretext" not true "reason," fake rather than true cause. The line is a burlesque of ordinary judicial phraseology.

11–   A catalogue of four types of youths that please, in two con-
12   contrasting pairs. The first is the rider and the swimmer. There is parallelism (*hic placet* to *hic placidam*) and yet the main order is chiastic. The first exemplifies energy curbed, the second calm destroyed.

compescit: the horse is first bridled (*compes*=fetter, bond) and then held in by tight reins. *Placidus* is an attribute of fresh water (Ovid *Ars Amat.* 3.386) or salt water (Catullus 64.269; Lucretius 2.559, etc.). *Niveus* is ordinarily a feminine attribute but Catullus speaks of the *niveis manibus* of the emasculated Attis (63.8).

pectore pellit: Ennian (*Ann.* 230V³), lending an epic touch of subtle irony.

13– The second pair (which may be associated with the first)
14 juxtaposes bravery with modesty.

adest: "be present" to lend aid if necessary (as Vergil *Aen.* 2.701; 4.578). Hence *cepit* is "take by storm," bravery being a characteristic of the attacker.

stat . . . ante: it seems easiest to personify *pudor* and treat *ante* as a preposition: "Modesty keeps watch over his tender cheeks." The courageous youth seizes, the other is guarded against seizure. There is a metaphorical similarity with the more literal situation at 1.2.95: *stare nec ante fores puduit.*

15– A variation of the "capturing" motif. *Taedia* are the last thing
16 that should win out.

negabit . . . dabit: an erotic truism in ancient literature as early as Sappho (frag. 1, E. Lobel and D. Page [Oxford, 1955]).

sub iuga: another regular amatory metaphor. See 1.2.92 (and Callimachus in *A. P.* 12.149. 3; E. Baehrens on Catullus 68.118 [Leipzig, 1893]).

17– Lines 17–38 center on the idea of time's passing, for good
18 (17–26) as well as bad (27–38).

longa dies: the phrase is also epic (Vergil *Aen.* 5.783, the length of Juno's wrath; 6.745, the time needed to purify a soul). Again anaphora and heightened diction turn serious to comic. Informal merely sounds formal.

leones: perhaps chosen amusingly, because at least in recent times lion taming was an art of the Galli, emasculated priests of Cybele (see commentators on Catullus 63.76; Lucretius 2.614).

saxa peredit: proverbial, unlike the previous example (Otto, *Sprichwörter*, 156–57, and Bailey on Lucretius 4.1286–87), but infrequent in connection with love. The phrase is Lucretian (1.326: *vesco sale saxa peresa*). The latent oxymoron between *molli* and *saxa* stretches the time involved (like taming lions).

19– Time, passing in a set pattern, brings even love to maturity.
20 The first line is a verbal bow to Vergil *Ecl.* 9.49 (*duceret*

apricis in collibus uva colorem), but the sentiment is closer
to Horace *Carm.* 2.5.9–12.

   certa vice: the assurance of time changing will become a
negative aspect of the poem after line 27.

   lucida signa: Lucretian (5.518).

21–   Winds (and waves) scattering the oaths of lovers form an
22   ancient erotic platitude (Otto, *Sprichwörter*, 17–18, 364–65).
In Catullus alone there are three examples (30.10, 64.59, 142).
(The language prepares for lines 45–46.)

   nec time: the substitution of *nec* (or *non*) for the regular
ne plus imperative is rare (see M. Leumann, J. Hofmann, and
A. Szantyr, *Lateinische Grammatik*, 2.340).

23–   The high tone is belied by the context (compare the mock
24   legality of line 10). Thanks are due Jupiter only for the freedom to be perjurious (Jupiter lied to Juno about his liaison
with Io). The sentiments of lines 21–24 are borrowed from
Catullus (70.3–4).

25–   It is part of the wit that two virgin goddesses—straight and
26   somewhat stuffy—should be addressed. Arrows are one of
the stock symbols of the huntress Diana. Dictynna was a
Cretan nymph whose cult was assimilated to that of Artemis.
Minerva, as the story of Medusa proves, was especially proud
of her hair. (For details see Servius on Vergil *Aen.* 6.289.)

   sinit: though common with the imperative, use of a finite
form of *sino* plus subjunctive without *ut* is rare.

27–   Gnomic acknowledgment of time's passing is depicted by a
28   series of examples (which sound also illustrates). No single
day stands still or returns. There is a purposeful look back at
lines 17–18. Time may gradually bring love; it also takes it
away.

   transiet: rare example of substitution for *transibit*, on analogy with the fourth conjugation.

   non segnis: *non* goes with *segnis* (a litotes, further to stress
cito) and with both verbs.

29–   Loss of color and dropping of leaves in autumn are universal
30   examples of time's advance.

   colores: compare Corydon to Alexis (Vergil *Ecl.* 2.17):
o formose puer, nimium ne crede colori.

   comas: the context personifies the tree and associates it with
other instances, here and elsewhere, of the whitening or loss
of hair as equivalent to old age. Cf. line 63.

   populus: traditionally a tree of death.

31– Ennius in his old age had already compared himself to a brave
32 racehorse whose career was over (*Ann.* 374–75V³; cf. Horace
Epist. 1.1.7–9). The figure of heroism past (a sly reference
to line 11?) is more amusing than pathetic here. What is the
horse, prime symbol of virility, doing in such a flaccid context?

iacet: lifeless (as, e.g., 1.3.55). The image follows directly
on that of the preceding couplet.

prior: a poeticism for the adverb *prius*.

Eleo: Olympia, seat of Greece's most famous games, was
in Elis.

carcere: the starting gate, and the barricades around it.

33– Probably the image of a race (with time the winner) is meant
34 to be continued.

premeret: in connection with charioteering, cf. Ovid *Ibis* 364.

serior: only use of the comparative in Tibullus (the unique
occurrence in Horace, *Carm.* 2.3.26, is associated with the in-
evitability of death).

stultos: emphasized through hypallage.

35– The snake shuffling off his coil was a common symbol in antiq-
36 uity for youth renewed (as Lucretius 4.60 ff.; Vergil *Georg.*
3.437 f.; *Aen.* 2. 471 ff.).

crudeles divi: a rhetorical climax of mock profanity. So
empathic has Priapus become while contemplating youth's
transcience that he apparently has forgotten his own divinity.

37– From Diana and Minerva we pass to Bacchus and Phoebus
38 Apollo who, unlike mortals, remain eternally youthful. The
hair of Roman youths was usually cut when they assumed the
toga virilis at age 16. These immortal gods submit to no such
human gesture.

39– Grant whatever will tempt your beloved. Be subdued in order
40 to subdue. Love gains its ends often by attentive devotion.

obsequio . . . amor: the jingle resembles Vergil's famous
omnia vincit amor (*Ecl.* 10.69). *Obsequium* means "obedience," "compliance," but its literal meaning, "a following
after," leads directly into the next distich. There is an oxymoron
between "yielding" and "conquering."

41– Accompany him, whether the journey be lengthy, hot, rainy
42 (43–44), or by ship (45–46).

via longa: at 1.1.26 this connotes a military life. It is also
connected there with the heat of the Dog Star whose rising is
avoided by fountain and shade. Here, especially in view of the
usual amatory associations of *via*, the advice may be ironical.

Perhaps we are meant to smile at an unmilitary *miles amans*. In any case the time would be summer; the orientation away from the countryside.

43–
44
"Though the rain-bringing bow, fringing the heavens with embroidered black, shroud the coming storm." Density of metaphor combines with textual uncertainty to make these lines particularly difficult. The chief problem is *amiciat* which would ordinarily contain four short syllables; many substitute readings have been proposed. Though the use of *amicio* in the sense of shrouding water is unique, it is typical of Tibullus at his most evocative, fitting perfectly with the pattern established by *praetexens* and *picta*.

ferrugine: the ancient sources connect the color with a very deep purple (see Servius on Vergil *Georg.* 1.467; *Aen.* 9.582).

imbrifer: the rainbow is a harbinger and bringer of rain. The epithet may be a coinage (re. Vergil *Georg.* 1.313).

45–
46
Again there is a contrast between the elevated epic-heroic phraseology and the actual context. Compare an Ennian description of the sea (*Ann.* 385V[3]):

caeruleum spumat sale conferta rate pulsum.

caeruleas undas: also apparently a rich purple color. Cf. Cicero *Acad.* 2 (frag. 7): "quid? mare nonne caeruleum? at eius unda, cum est pulsa remis, purpurascit" (the same passage from which the Ennius fragment comes).

puppi: first, synecdoche for the ship as a whole, second, perhaps the literal position of the boy as he watches his lover row.

pelle: the ordinary sense would be "strike," here strike the waves with oars (cf. line 12). It has the special sense of push or hurl like a weapon (which *levem* complements).

47–
48
The lover's submission to labors is an elegiac commonplace (as, e.g., Propertius 1.1.9 ff.).

nec te paeniteat: the phrase comes from Vergil *Ecl.* 10.17, a poem which also mixes elegiac with "practical" matters.

insuetas: the irregular absolute use is best viewed as an hypallage. The *opera* is as unusual as the hands are unaccustomed to it.

atteruisse: the unique example of the old perfect of *attero* before its revival by Apuleius.

49–
50
The dutiful lover carrying nets for hunting is another occasional erotic theme (Vergil *Ecl.* 3.75).

insidiis: ambushes for the animals, created by closing off the end of the valley.

umeri: that part of the body which does the hard work personified.

51– Finally fencing as a lover's amusement. The words imply a
52 close connection with lines 39–40 and are almost without exception erotic enough to make an easy transition to what follows.

levi dextra: "with a light hand," i.e., nothing serious involved.

temptabis: the future with imperative quality reminds us that a didactic god is still at work.

nudum latus: i.e., open for an easy hit (but naked as well, of course).

53– After endurance, happiness; violence and calm combine.
54 *mitis*: gentle but, perhaps, ready, ripe, as well.

apta: the absolute use of the participle of *apo*: "fitting" in a double sense.

55– The sentiment as well as the verbal pattern (*rapias, apta dabit,*
56 *rapta dabit, volet*) follows directly on the preceding distich. Line 56 presents a rare example of elision within the caesura of the pentameter's second hemistich. As often, prosody enriches meaning.

implicuisse: for the sexual overtones cf. Catullus 61.35, 103–104.

57– Sudden change of theme to more abstract thoughts on the
58 present age. *Nunc, iam,* and *haec* imply that once there was a happier time.

heu: the empathic Priapus again.

artes miseras: negatively, schemes that cause lovers trouble.

tractant: "deal in," often, as here, in a pejorative sense (cf., e.g., Horace *Epode* 3.8; *Carm.* 2.13.10).

59– A serio-comic variation on the common Tibullan subject of
60 initial discoveries by Osiris, Prometheus, first sailor, etc. (as, e.g., 1.7.29 ff; 1.10.1 ff.). It makes use of a traditional form of *devotio* with *quisquis es* covering for a name not known (the negative equivalent of the hymnic *quocumque nomine*). The actual words of the prayer, *infelix . . . lapis*, are a reversal of the traditional sepulchral dedication *sit terra tibi levis* (cf. also 2.4.50). We may compare the curse put on the *lena* at 1.5.49 ff.

61– Specific command for boys to love poets (i.e., Tibullus) and
62 allow spiritual to triumph over material (i.e., poems over more tangible gifts, poor over rich).

Pieridas: Muses of Pieria, an area of Thessaly, from the eponymous Pierus. Zeus is regularly the father of the nine sisters. The word first appears in extant Latin in Cicero (*De Nat. Deor.* 3.54).

doctos: epithet of poets and poetry from Catullus on (35.16–17; 65.2).

aurea munera: literally "golden," metaphorically, "enticing," "alluring."

superent: "surpass," "win the day over."

63–   Two contemporary poetic subjects. The tragic story of Nisus
64   and his daughter Scylla was treated by Callimachus (see Pfeiffer on frag. 113 and 288 [Oxford, 1949–53]) and Parthenius (*Met.* frag. 20 Martini). It is the theme of the pseudo-Vergilian *Ciris* and is recounted by Ovid (*Met.* 8.1–151).

The story of Pelops and his ivory shoulder, replacement of one mistakenly eaten by Demeter, is first preserved in Pindar *Ol.* 1. By the time Vergil comes to write *Georg.* 3.7 the topic is already hackneyed. Tibullus may be poking fun at himself again by having Priapus base poetic immortality on banal themes and on a type of poem (the epyllion) which he himself appears to have avoided.

For the change of tense from *sint* to *nituisset*, see 1.8.21–22. In terms of sound, the tale of Nisus depends on *ni sint*.

purpurea coma: the parallel with 29–30 is curious.

65–   Those treated by the Muses will remain as immortal as the
66   universe (the corollary being that love for a poet provides eternal fame). Nature's continuity is of special importance again. For other examples of a series of proviso clauses as part of a strong assertion, see Vergil *Ecl.* 5.76–78; *Aen.* 1.607–10.

referent: "tell of" (but unusual with a personal object).

vehet: the verb goes with the two preceding phrases by zeugma but the sense is stretched.

67–   Back in theme to lines 59–60. Ops, Roman goddess of plenty,
68   wife of Saturn, was linked with Rhea whose cult, in turn, was connected with the Phrygian goddess Cybele. Cybele, the Great Mother from Phrygian Mt. Ida, makes two famous appearances in Latin poetry before Tibullus, in Lucretius (2.600ff.) and Catullus (63 *passim*). The former offers a brisk description of her chariot and those who follow in its wake.

69–   The boy will become a maddened Gallus, like Catullus' Attis,
70   castrating himself to the sound of the *tibia*.

erroribus: "wanderings," both physical and mental.

expleat: the only other instance of *expleo* in the sense of "fill the tale of" (except 1.3.53 above) is at Vergil *Aen.* 12.763: *quinque orbis explent cursu*. We would expect *complere* or *implere.* Ordinarily *expleo* means fill up with plenty, which would have been the role of the Latin Ops. The Magna Mater only fills up cities with wandering and reaps the harvest of castration.

Phrygios modos: cf. Lucretius 2.620 (*Phrygio numero*) and Propertius 2.22.16.

vilia membra: "worthless parts" (for different reasons, before or after castration). He has not much to sell (line 67).

71–72 A capsule description of the love-elegy, which battens on the correct form of "lament." Venus sides with the elegiac lover, favoring *miseris fletibus* rather than the *artes miseras* (57) practiced nowadays. Since the *tibia* is the traditional ancient instrument associated with lament, and with the Phrygian mode, there is a direct connection between this and the preceding distich. The constructive purposes for sad sounds are ordinary *querelis* and *fletibus*, not cursed emasculation.

73–74 The Titius in question is unknown.

edidit ore: the phrase (which balances *respondit*, 7) is common of an oracle (e.g., Vergil *Aen.* 7.194; cf. Ennius *frag. sc.* 43V³).

meminisse: apt both for didactic sentiments and the poet's oral delivery (*canerem*).

75–76 Tibullus assumes Priapus' role. Taking advantage of his newly acquired expertise, he becomes a *magister amoris* for those who can listen and (momentarily, at least) for himself.

celebrate: in a double sense, "throng around," then, "sing the praises of."

magistrum: part of the humor is that a *magister* is ordinarily a teacher of *pueri* (note the strategic placing of each). Here, ironically, he must instruct those duped by a boy who is already *multa callidus arte.*

male habet: a virtually colloquial expression, unique in elegy.

callidus: "adroit," here with implications of artful slyness.

77–78 Tibullus' proud boast is to be a *iuris consultus*, a teacher-adviser to distraught lovers.

gloria cuique sua est: the expression has a proverbial ring (cf. Catullus 22.20; Vergil *Aen.* 10.467). The boast and the stance are of short duration (compare Horace's thoughts on *gloria* at *Carm.* 1.18.15 ff.). The phrase prepares the reader for the beginning of the next poem (1.5.2).

ianua: the threshold of the poet in his oracular temple (Cicero *De Nat. Deor.* 2.67: *foresque in liminibus profanarum aedium ianuae nominantur*). Part of the wit is that in ordinary

elegiac parlance (and circumstances) the *ianua* is the door of
the haughty mistress, rarely opened (as 1.2.9, 1.5.68, etc.).

79– The most mock-solemn moment in the poem. Tibullus looks
80   to his future role as an aging *praeceptor amoris*, aloof from
love himself, no doubt, but celebrating its potency to his crowd
of young admirers.

tempus erit cum: an epic phrase, usually in the past (as
Vergil *Aen.* 2.268: *tempus erat quo . . .*), here prophetic.
References to time's passage and old age, common enough at
the conclusion of Tibullus' elegies, are particularly crucial here.

deducat: a technical term for escorting distinguished citi-
zens home or to work but also with erotic overtones.

turba: a careful echo of line 9.

81– In a typical ending, Tibullus shatters his dream (and comic-
82   epic tone) with the double cry of a rude awakening into the
present. We turn from his contemplated power to Marathus'
actual torture, from the imagined acclamation of an eager mob
to the slow love against which neither *artes* nor *doli* avail.
Marathus will reappear in poem 8.

lento amore: cf. Horace *Carm.* 1.13.8 (and C. L. Babcock,
"Si certus intrarit dolor: A Reconsideration of Horace's Fifteenth Epode," *AJP* 87 [1966], 408, n.14).

torquet: the slow turning of one tortured on a rack (cf.
1.5.5, etc.).

artes: see lines 57 and 76. It is Marathus after all who
knows "art," not Tibullus. Again we think ahead to 1.5.4.

83– Tibullus, in reality, must entreat, not command. Ironically the
84   poet makes people immortal but does not wish to become a
"story" himself.

turpis fabula: a scandal (Horace *Epode* 11.7–8).

vana magisteria: the ultimate irony, reversing the poet's own
magisterial stance of 75–76 and turning the tables on himself.

COMMENTARY 1. 5.

Tibullus was harsh and spoke lightly of separation. Boasting
is a thing of the past while the poet is now like a top, controlled
at a child's whim. Delia, spare your slave. Though another now
enjoys your love, Tibullus once (was said to have) saved you
from death by incantation and prayer. At that time he had
fancies of a perfected rural life with Delia playing the role of
country wife, watching the harvest, numbering the sheep,
playing with slaves, ordering the house. Messalla would also

participate in this idyl and Delia be his dutiful slave. Once the dream was shattered, Tibullus tried forgetting through wine and other women but he was bewitched, as Peleus by Thetis. Present troubles are caused by a rich lover but the harm was really done by a clever procuress: May she drink poison, go mad and run naked through cities, chased by dogs. So wills the rage of Venus. Delia should forego gifts and *lena* alike. The poor poet offers better allegiance. All in vain; only riches open doors. He whom she loves now, the one pacing before her door, should expect the poet's own turn of fortune. Love hides his plans; seize the opportunity to sail while the water is calm.

A poem of happiness and sadness, past, present, and future, dream and reality interchanging with each other. The opening couplets establish the main tensions as deeds vie with mere words and a former active, controlled position gives way to passive acceptance of someone else's power. The symbol which interpenetrates these thoughts is of life as constant change, motion, flexibility. The poet was once "rough": now he is a top sent whirling over level ground at another's command. He once boasted bravely; now he is a slave twisted on the rack. But Fortune turns her wheel quickly, finding fit vehicle in the new lover, stopping and pacing before Delia's door (one of many variations on the *paraclausithyron* throughout the poem). He directs his skiff in calm water but Love, Fortune's minion, has hidden plans. Tibullus, too, had had hope and attempted to structure his life. He had saved Delia from death only to find her unfaithful (*ille ego . . . ipse ego . . . nunc*). He had conceived the ideal of country, Delia, and Messalla amazingly combined only to find it impossible (*felicem vitam fingebam . . . haec mihi fingebam . . . nunc*). The only present activity (wine and new love have failed) is to curse the *lena* with madness (as surrogate for his own suffering?), while she is driven wailing through cities by a "rough" crowd of dogs. One final attempt at charm: The poor man is faithful, steadfast, a shield from the crowd, a trusting slave. He would undo the "bonds" of Delia's shoes. But the charm fails. Words alone, here at least, have no power to conquer a closed door.

1–2   The opening distich succinctly contrasts past and present, vainglory and humility, positive action and passive endurance, motifs that run through the poem.

    asper eram: the adjective is applied to Amor (1.6.2) and Venus (1.9.20), whose prerogatives Tibullus once took into his own hands. Love's victories inspire *gloria* at 1.6.3 and 1.8.49. As with *loquebar,* the tense denotes continued past action. The vocabulary of the opening distichs recalls closely the conclusion of 1.4.

discidium: "separation" (also a technical term for divorce).

ferre loquebar: already an element of doubt is introduced. The poet's roughness involved words, not deeds, endurance, not positive action. *Bene* could go with either word. With the first the sense would be "easily"; with the second, more idiomatic but less plausible, it would be "ably."

longe abest: spatial distance subtly yields to temporal separation.

3–4　The theme now changes fully from positive to negative, from control to its lack. A top, mentioned in Greek literature as early as Aristophanes (*Birds,* 1461), is also used effectively by Vergil (*Aen.* 7.378–83). The change from active to passive, begun by *agor,* is carried throughout the simile. *Citus,* "quick," really means "put in motion," while the boy is *celer. Turben* (the form, replacing the more usual *turbo,* is vouched for by Charisius, *Gram. Lat.* 1.145.8K) means first whirlwind, then a top, made to spin.

per plana sola: it spins smoothly from place to place (*plana* by contrast with *asper*).

verbere: literally the "blow" of the lash, it looks to the twists given by the youth (*versat*). It also anticipates lines 5–6 by suggesting the lashes endured by the slave of love. A *puer* would more regularly be a slave, subject to such blows. Here, as Cupid or surrogate for Delia, his *ars* rules the top.

adsueta: "customary," for the boy and poet as well.

5–6　*ure et torque*: punishments to which the lover-slave must now submit, especially when he has been unruly (*ferum*). They are often mentioned by Tibullus (e.g., 1.4.81; 1.8.5–6, 49; 1.9.21–22). On the *topos* in general see F. O. Copley *"Servitium Amoris* in the Roman Elegists," *TAPA* 78 (1947), 285–300. "Turning" is a motif of the poem.

There is a direct line from *asper* to *ferum* and *horrida,* from *gloria* to *magnificum,* from free lover to slave deserving torture, the animal who must be tamed (*doma*). There is also a punning contrast between *libeat,* with its associations of freedom, and *doma.* Tibullus' ordinary wildness has apparently been shown in words alone (*loquebar, dicere, verba*). This focusses attention on the chiastic unity of the distich, from *ure ferum* to *verba doma.*

magnificum: in a bad sense: bragging, pretentious, pompous.

doma: with *hcrrida*, it raises the specter of "bestial" conduct.

7–8 Delia becomes the direct subject of a prayer such as a slave would address to his master. This type of oath appears already in Homer (*Iliad* 15.39), with the addition here of the elegiac *furtivus*.

te: the lengthy displacement of *te* (especially when it is juxtaposed to *per* with which it first seems to belong) lends special emphasis.

furtivi: the epithet is transferred to *lecti* by hypallage.

venerem: their love or the goddess herself.

compositum caput: her hair is arranged while she, presumably, lies on the bed.

9– As we change to the past, from bed of love to bed of illness,
10 the poet, as priest, modestly claims to have saved Delia from a dread disease by his prayers (which seem scarcely to be distinguished from a lover's desires). Lucretius uses the phrase *defessa iacebant corpora* (6.1178) for victims of the plague while *iaceas* is common in epitaphs. *Defessa* therefore means "moribund." (Compare the context of Catullus 50.14–15). As at 1.3.55 death is thought of as a beast from whose jaws a potential victim must be snatched.

eripuisse: "to have snatched" you (away from death).

11– The rite of lustration here combines elements of both religion
12 and magic. Judging from the tense of *praecinuisset*, the witch (traditionally an old woman) first sang her magic song. Then Tibullus walked around Delia with (smoking) sulphur. The latter is a traditional purifying material from Homer on (*Iliad* 16.228; *Od.* 22.481). It is suggested by Vergil (*Georg.* 3.449) as a remedy for the plague.

puro: "pure" and "purifying."

carmine: as often, song with a magic effect.

13– *procuravi*: in a religious sense *procuro* is kindred to *lustro*,
14 i.e., "expiate," "atone for," then "gain by prayer" (see A. S. Pease on Cicero *De Div.* 1.3 [Urbana, 1920–23]).

saeva somnia: the harsh nightmares of a feverish person, here personified.

ter: regular magic number.

sancta mola: holy, salted meal, a regular accompaniment of a sacrific since Numa (Pliny *Hist. Nat.* 18.7).

deveneranda: a rare word, used only here in Latin with the meaning "avert," by prayer or offering (with clear contrast to the earlier, positive *procuravi*).

102 TIBULLUS: *A Commentary*

15–
16 Roman priests traditionally wore a fillet. Nothing should be bound or knotted during a religious service. Hence *tunicis solutis* (see also 1.3.31).

novem: an odd multiple of three would, he hopes, be efficacious. Are the vows those of line 10?

Triviae: Diana of the Crossroads, i.e., Hecate, underworld divinity associated with magic, into whose hands Delia almost fell (see also 1.2.53–54).

nocte silente: akin to *nocte serena* (1.2.63) as the proper time and setting for sacrifice, especially when a moon goddess is involved (though there may also be a need for darkness to perform a magic ritual and silence is essential for several reasons).

17–
18 *omnia persolvi*: back to present reality: "I rendered all that was due." Asyndeton draws attention to the change into present time with *fruitur*.

utitur: the rival lover takes the advantage gained by the poet's prayers. Once cured, Delia transfers her affections. The use in adjacent lines of two verbs that take the ablative presses the point.

felix: "fortunate" as well as "happy."

19–
20 *felicem vitam*: a life blessed by the gods. The repetition of the adjective from line 18 adds force to the change into a dream now past.

fingebam: repetition of the verb at line 35 gives the bounds of the poet's imagined dream of the future, experienced while Delia was possibly suffering *saeva somnia* of her own.

renuente deo: "nodding up" is tantamount to denial, as *sed* implies.

21–
22 The future tense transfers us immediately into the dream. The details have a quasi-religious ring.

colam: "dwell in," "till," "care for." The implication remains, whether pretense or not, that the idea is new to Tibullus.

frugum custos: Tibullus fancies Delia as country chatelaine whereas in reality she has *custodes* of another sort in the city.

aderit: cf. *abest* (line 2).

area: threshing floor and sun do the work in this idyllic spot.

messes: "harvests." The plural implies summer after summer.

teret: "rub" grains out of the ears (as Horace *Sat.* 1.1.45; Vergil *Georg.* 1.192).

23–
24 Grain and wine are the staples of a farm society. Again Delia need only stand guard.

lintribus: vats to hold the grapes prior to pressing.

musta: fresh, unfermented wine before bottling. As with *messes* (22), the plural may be poetic for singular or may look to a prolongation of the idyl into many years (harvests for summers, vintages for autumns).

pede: the foot of whoever treads the grapes, perhaps Delia herself.

25– *consuescet*: the repetition is typical of Tibullus (we grow
26 accustomed to the verb as its subjects do to their actions), but the switch to a second subject lends variety. The phraseology is more fitting for elegiac than rustic living. (With similar ambiguity Catullus describes Lesbia's sparrow *quicum ludere, quem in sinu tenere* / . . . *solet*: 2.2–4.)

verna: a (usually young) house-born slave of either sex.

27– Delia will become a central figure in bringing the blessing of
28 divinity upon the vines, crops, and flocks over which she already presides. *Deo agricolae* is vague enough to cover any vegetation god (for the adjective see 1.1.14).

spicas: ears of grain (connected with Ceres at 1.1.16; 2.1.4; 2.5.84).

dapem: a sacrificial meal ("ubi daps profanata comestaque erit, verno arare incipito": Cato *De Agr.* 50.2).

29– It is Tibullus' desire that Delia be everything (*cunctos, omnia,*
30 *tota*), himself nothing (which is to anticipate being a dream). (Line 29 reflects Damoetas' description of the power of Jupiter at Vergil *Ecl.* 3.60–61).

illi . . . *curae*: one of the two instances in Tibullus of a double dative (the other is 2.3.43).

nihil esse: to be of no use or value (the opposite is *aliquid esse*).

31– *Messala meus* is almost as necessary an ingredient in the idyl
32 as *mea Delia*. Delia's gesture suggests that his heroic presence is necessary for the land. Even the trees are carefully chosen for the "hero." (Compare Vergil *Ecl.* 1.37–38, where fruit remains on the trees in the absence of the land's "hero.")

poma: often a lover's gift.

33– Though Delia is treated as divine, Messalla is a still loftier
34 divinity with Delia for slave (*ministra*) and worshiper (*venerata*).

virum hunc: the words draw particular emphasis. Lengthening of a final vowel at the caesura is rare; hiatus with a syllable in "m" rarer still.

sedula curet: for the sentiment compare Horace *Carm.* 1.38.
5–7: "simplici myrto nihil allabores / sedulus curo: neque te
ministrum / dedecet myrtus . . . ."

epulas: the object of both *paret* and *gerat*.

35– *Fingebam* closes the dream and *nunc* returns to the present.
36   Eurus (the southeast wind) and Notus (the south wind) are
chosen for their violence, not any specific directional power.
Such a method of scattering lovers' vows is proverbial (see
1.4.21).

odoratos Armenios: *Armenios* for the more usual *Assyrios*
(for which see 1.3.7). Exotic sound more than inexactitude of
locale conveys the vagueness of distance.

37– Though dream has given way to reality, we are still in past
38   time. Recourse to wine is the poet's remedy at 1.2.1 ff. (and
figures in Ovid's list of possible cures for lovesickness: *Rem.
Am.* 809–10; cf. the striking parallel in Horace *Carm.* 1.7.31).

The conceit of line 38 is not paralleled elsewhere. Beginning
with lines 3–4 "turning" is a recurrent motif. No witch is
needed to accomplish this unhappy metamorphosis. *Dolor* has
sufficient power.

39– This remedy for lovesickness is also prescribed by Ovid (*Rem.
40   Am.* 441; cf. *Am.* 3.7).

gaudia: with *adirem*, a type of metonymy.

admonuit: omission of *me* as object is rare.

41– *devotum*: "bewitched," overcome by someone else's *vota*, a
42   prey to magic.

et pudet et narrat: with *pudet* supply *eam*. Though an unusual phrase, it need not be altered. The manuscript reading is
supported by a series of parallels in Ovid (*Rem. Am.* 407; *Met.*
14.279; *Ex Pont.* 4.15.29). The clash between *narrat* and
nefanda suggests that the tone may not be all in deadly earnest.

meam: i.e., Delia, the subject of *scire* which has *nefanda*
as object.

43– Delia's "sorcery," bewitching Tibullus, is accomplished not by
44   words but by physical grace (the *figura etymologica* between
facit and *facie* marks the distinction as well as the connection).

teneris lacertis: regular elegiac attribute for beauty (as, e.g.,
Propertius 3.6.13; 4.3.23).

flavis comis: blonde hair, if only for its rarity, was considered by the ancients a mark of special beauty.

45– Such mythological comparisons are a trademark of Propertius,
46   rare in Tibullus. The analogy projects once more a wish in
past time. Delia is envisioned as the sea-goddess Thetis, daugh-

ter of Nereus, come to visit her mortal lover, Peleus, and apparently drawn by (or riding on) a dolphin (this version of the legend is recounted at greater length by Ovid in *Met.* 11.221–65). The exotic note serves to heighten the spectacle of her beauty while the very ornateness of the description removes it from reality.

Haemonium: i.e., Thessalian.

caerula: the color of the eyes and other attributes of water divinities is often given as blue, if only by association. Tibullus seems fond of the contrast between *flavus* and *caerulus* (1. 7.12).

47– The *dives amator* is a stock figure of comedy and then elegy,
48   often the butt of jokes. For the elegist he was to be feared as well as cursed. The clever *lena*, procuress and go-between, is in much the same position (cf. the imprecations at 2.6.44ff.). The punning connection between *venit* (and cf. *veniet*, line 31) and *exitium* calls into question the seriousness of the tone, however, and the excess of the curse that follows confirms the impression.

huic: i.e., Delia.

49– Blood and gall are time-honored causes of madness. The *lena*
50   is cursed with a fate akin to that of Thyestes and Tereus. (Could the feast in question be human?) She will become like Vergil's *Furor impius* who roars also *ore cruento* (*Aen.* 1.296). Just as the poet's wine turns to tears, so for the *lena* ordinary food and drink become maddening, not festive.

tristia: first because gall puckers the mouth, then for the long-range effects.

51– Spirits (of lovers she has ruined?) will return to haunt her,
52   and an owl, symbol of death and doom, will sing unceasingly of her (and theirs?) fate. The owl is *violenta* not in itself nor even for its screech but for the violence its presence portends. If the roof in question is her own, the omen is the more worrisome. (For further details see Pease on Vergil *Aen.* 4.462).

53– The double curse, what she brings on herself and what the
54   ghosts and owl presage from outside, has accomplished its effect. She is now *furens*. To eat plants is madness enough. To devour those on tombs combines desperation with sacrilege. Moreover in seeking out bones left over by wolves, she becomes wilder than they, a victim of lycanthropy.

55– Her wildness grows as the curse intensifies. She becomes a
56   creature of Hecate, a divinity regularly connected with crossroads. Compare Dido's invocation of the witch goddess of night

(*Aen.* 4.609): "nocturnisque Hecate triviis ululata per urbes." (For further connections of howling dogs with Hecate see 1.2. 53–54 and Norden on *Aen.* 6.255 ff.).

There is an overtone in these lines of sexual desire run amuck. *Lupis* (54) is ambiguous, *inguinibus nudis* and *triviis* suggestive. She will be the victim of the despair to which she drives others. (With *aspera*, cf. *asper eram*, line 1.)

post: "from behind" or, perhaps, "afterwards."

57– Intensity gives way to a breathless style as the poet proclaims
58 with assurance that the curse will be fulfilled.

eveniet: a usual word in such circumstances (1.7.5; 2. 1. 25).

dat signa deus: the same idiom occurs at 1.3.20 and 2.5.83.

iniusta lege: the "law" (procedure) was "unjust" (unfair) because it was abused by only one of the two people involved. Venus takes the side of the injured party (i.e., of the poet, in this roundabout homily to Delia).

59– Once more a desired future is fabricated.
60 *sagae rapacis*: a further reference to the *lena* (who would easily fulfill the roles of both witch and go-between) just as line 60 alludes again to the *dives amator*.

vincitur omnis amor: a variation—and reversal—of the Vergilian *omnia vincit amor*, in which love itself is overcome, here by gifts. (Ovid takes another tack, *Rem. Am.* 462: *successore novo vincitur omnis amor*.)

61– The devoted behavior of the poor lover by contrast to that
62 of the *dives amator* (as 1.4.57–64). Line 62 may imply that such constant companionship has an erotic as well as a servile purpose. Compare, e.g., the use of *latus* at Catullus 21.6 (*haerens ad latus omnia experiris*).

63– Again the lover's posture is that of a slave, helping clear a
64 path for his mistress through a dense crowd, though *subiciet* remains ambiguous. Propertius (1.10.27–28) uses similar phraseology to describe the happy results which follow humility.

65– *occultos amicos*: her, or possibly his, friends are sly about
66 their doings and Delia sly about slipping away to meet them. The context is usually taken to be a dinner party where one's shoes would be removed, but the erotic potential is clear as well.

niveo pede: the epithet is feminine (though used of Hymen by Catullus, 61.9–10, of Attis at 63.8, of a *puer* by Tibullus at 1.4.12). This is a secret (elegiac) *deductio*, no real marriage. The role of slave is as strange for the poet as it is for Delia (34), despite his offers of servile attention.

67– The cry brings reality out of dream. We have been reading
68   (hearing) another *paraclausithyron.* The "charm" of the poet's
     words works no better here than at 1.2.9.
         plena manu: the phrase recurs at 1.9.52 and is proverbial
     for generosity (see Otto, *Sprichwörter, s.v. manus,* n. 17). The
     full hand of the rich lover has more force to break down the
     door than a poor lover's empty palm.
69– The first reference to the wheel of fortune in extant Latin is
70   Cicero *in Pis.* 22 (for further references see R. G. M. Nisbet,
     [Oxford, 1961] *ad loc.*).The twists of fate add a more extensive
     and universal turn to the initial symbolism of Tibullus as top,
     which is echoed here.   ,
         at tu: the same words addressed to Delia at 59 are thrown
     at his rival here.
         potior: the lover who is at the moment the object of Delia's
     affections (cf. Horace *Epode* 15.13).
         furta: the rival lover, who is now having his turn at *furta*
     ("thieving" is a minor motif of the poem) should learn from
     Tibullus' example, perhaps even to the extent of fearing Ti-
     bullus' attempts to steal her back. The manuscript reading is
     often changed, perhaps rightly, to *fata.*
71– The drama becomes intense and complicated, and not without
72   a touch of humor. Tibullus, undoubtedly not far off, watches
     in his imagination a new lover pacing before the house within
     which we can only assume Delia and her present suitor are
     enclosed.
         A number of verbal plays lighten the tone. Fortune's wheel
     turns easily but now a new lover stands persistently on the
     threshold. (Yet for how long?) There is also a punning con-
     nection between *perstat* and *sedulus.* He "stands enduringly"
     yet "sedulously" (see 1.3.83–84).
         non frustra: the observing poet realizes that the new arrival
     will have better luck than he (*frustra,* 67).
         refugit: he is in motion after all (out of fright, as Vergil
     Aen. 2.380).
73– Activity continues (the wheel of fortune once more in motion?)
74   as the new lover pretends to pass by, runs back and then
     coughs before the door itself, as if he were now determined
     on a direct course of action. Passing by and returning are both
     used elsewhere by Tibullus, of time rather than place, and may
     well subtly imply here love's fickleness as well as fortune's
     changeability.
         excreat: on coughing as a signal see Terence *Heaut.* 373;
     Ovid *Her.* 21.24.

75– *Nescio quid* is deliberately vague. Will it be good or bad things
76 that sly love has in store? The analogy of love to a sea and
lovers to a boat or boats thereon is proverbial. The tension between change and stability, motion and calm which runs
through the preceding distichs is finally resolved. The new
lover's skiff (Tibullus, for a change, urges him to take advantage of his situation) is swimming in clear, and therefore calm,
water. The implications are obvious for the future, however.

COMMENTARY 1. 6.

Love is seductive, then harshly bitter. What glory in a god's
ferocity against a man? Though she denies it, Delia cherishes
a new lover in secret. She learned her tricks from the poet
himself. Her husband should now be on guard: "Why do you
need a gentle wife if you cannot watch her and she thinks only
of someone else? If you entrust her to me I will be her faithful
slave (in every sense)." Whoever comes upon them should
stand far off lest he be guilty of crime. This was predicted by
the priestess of Bellona: "If you touch a girl love guards, your
wealth will disappear like ashes in wind." The poet will spare
you, Delia, because of your mother who brought them together.
Yet, should he sin or strike her, may he be dragged through
the streets or lack hands. Be faithful from love, not fear. As
sign of Venus' bitterness toward infidelity the unfaithful mistress, grown old, spins on a rented loom. These are curses for
others. Let us, Delia, as our hair whitens, serve as an example
of love.

The last poem to Delia and in many respects the most ironic.
It is intimately connected verbally with the preceding poem
and brings full circle many ideas first raised in 1.2. Delia has
been unfaithful now both to her husband and to Tibullus. Her
punishment is a motif of the poem, now hoped for, now wished
away as present and future, reality and desire interweave. The
whole is a curse which is not a curse. It ends in a prayer to
avert what the poet seems to pray for, retribution on Delia,
the imposition of poverty on the aging courtesan who has all
her life absorbed riches yet scorned the poor poet. Tibullus
takes to himself the power of the priestess of Bellona (the tortures she suffers make her words the more potent) and then
nullifies it by saying that Bellona's threats have no value if
Delia lets him in the house. He loves her for her mother. We

would think this an example of the poet's genuine affection for the family life (as seen in 1.10, for instance) until we notice that the mother is really her daughter's procuress. And everything he passively endures (*inducar, premor, ducar, proripiar*). Instead of behaving like Bellona he abhors violence and is as subject to Amor as beast to hunter. Instead of inflicting harsh fear on Delia (*saevo metu*, 75), he is the victim of Love's harshness (*saevitiae*, 3). Occasional touches of humor lighten the spectacle of a poet torn between love and hate, devotion and bitterness, hope and despair, prayer and imprecation, who boasts of his former prowess as teacher and deceiving lover and now suffers fortune's negative turns. The calm of the ending is deceptive.

1–2   *semper*: the last of the Delia poems begins with an emphatic acknowledgment of love's instability. *Semper* goes with *offers* but by proximity to *inducar* suggests a more general, ominous constancy of change.

    inducar: "be deluded," "cajoled." Tibullus is love's pawn for his continuing game (cf. 1.5.3: *agor*).

    blandos vultus: "alluring looks." The contrast between past happiness and present suffering, love's superficial false charms and true hardness is echoed in the change from *offers* to *es*.

    Amor: the apparent naïveté of such an intimate and reproachful address by a mortal to a deity scarcely masks its sophistication. With love *asper* here we should compare the poet *asper* at 1.5.1.

3–4   *saevitiae*: love's harshness is proverbial in Latin at least as early as Ennius (*frag. sc.* 254V^3). The construction *quid . . . saevitiae* is unique in Tibullus (and the manuscript reading open to doubt).

    gloria: love is proverbially a soldier or huntsman. He has taken over the role which was a proud boast of the poet at 1.5.1–2.

    insidias composuisse: the expression is used by Cicero for the guileful deception of a well-planned oration (*Or.* 61.208: *compositae orationis insidiis*).

5–6   *casses*: snares of any sort, here a hunter's net. Tibullus is being "trapped" by Delia's infidelity.

    Delia: the context of her nocturnal doings makes the pseudonym of the chaste moon goddess Diana—born on the island of Delos—especially ironic here.

    furtim . . . fovet: the piling up of words of slyness and ignor-

ance in such a setting may owe something to Catullus 7.7–8.
A Roman might have heard a punning connection between
callida and *calida* because of the proximity of *fovet*.

7–8   *tam multa*: if the manuscript reading is to be retained (the
usual change is *iurata*), the phrase must be treated adverbially,
"so many times," "so often." C. G. Heyne reads *iurata* by
analogy with Ovid *Tr.* 2.447 which refers to Tibullus.

negat: the echo in *pernegat* and the continuing present tenses
undercut the seriousness of the poet's own situation and look
ironically ahead to his apostrophe of the *coniunx*.

sic etiam: the rhetoric piles up in this succinct scene between
Delia and her *vir*.

viro: possibly the *coniunx* of line 15 and 1.2.43, though in
elegy *vir* may simply denote the lover in favor at the moment.

9–   *miser*: ambiguously applicable to both past and present.

10   *ludere custodes*: cf. 1.2.15. The poet as *praeceptor amoris*
is deceived by his own teachings. Reflection of the ordinary
elegiac meaning of *ludere* gives the word a bitter twist.

premor arte mea: there is a possible aural pun on *ars-artus*,
the poet caught in the meshes of his artifice as well as lured
and trapped by Amor and Delia. (Cf. once again 1.5.1–4.)

11–   *fingere*: the metaphor, from moulding or modeling a statue,

12   particularizes the poet's *ars* at work in his capable pupil.

nunc: the repetition of *nunc* (10, 11, and 12) highlights the
transition into the past.

sola cubaret: cf. 1.3.26.

cardine tacito: cf. 1.2.10 (*neu furtim verso cardine aperta
sones*) and the teachings of Venus at 1.2.17–18.

13–   *sucos herbasque*: to be taken closely together, "juice from

14   herbs." The use of lotions or poultices made from a variety of
plants is common in antiquity for this purpose. See, e.g., Pliny
Hist. Nat. 13.125, 20.24, etc.

quis: old ablative for *quibus*, revived by the Augustan poets.
impresso dente: see 1.8.37–38.

venus: here primarily sex in a physical sense, though the
juxtaposition with *dente* tends to personify. Note the interlocking word order. *Mutua* (the metaphor concerns lending)
adds to the statement's force.

15–   *at tu*: back to the present. The poet had taught Delia to be

16   deceiving. She practiced her new knowledge on Tibullus and
will now do the same on her *coniunx*. (The word order and
ponderous sound imply that he is caught all around.)

     me servato: the solemn, juridical future imperative in a most unsolemn occasion: "take an example from me" or, better, "watch out for me" in a double sense. From line 37 we can assume that "entrust her to me" is also a hoped for command.

     peccet: the usual elegiac sense of sexual misbehavior.

17– *celebret*: "sing the praises of" (abstractly); "frequent the com-
18 pany of" in conversation (more realistically).

     caveto: another mock-solemn injunction addressed with apparent futility to someone who is already *incautus*.

     cubet: Tibullus replaces the usual *accumbo* with the more explicit *cubo*, with the meaning "recline at table," though we are not far from the suggestiveness of line 11.

     laxo sinu: with garments loose and perhaps arms unfolded.

     pectus: accusative of respect.

19– For such means of communication between wife and secret
20 lover at the husband's dinner table, see 1.2.21–22. At 1.10.32 spilled wine is used for a different purpose.

     mensae in orbe: "on the round table top."

21– *seu*: here the equivalent of *et si*, "even if." The use of *seu* with-
22 out a correlative is rare (only once elsewhere in Tibullus, 2.4.43 and once in Propertius, 2.26.29). Tibullus never uses the form *sive*. Likewise he prefers *neu* (12 instances) to *neve* (one example).

     Bonae Deae: Roman goddess of fertility, allied to the ancient Italic Fauna. Men were not admitted to her rites. This fact, coupled with their common use as trysting spots, would make temples doubly suspicious. Doubts are already cast on Delia's reliability with the word *dicet*.

23– If the husband entrusts Delia to Tibullus, let him be assured
24 that no other possible rival will follow them both. Tibullus, by making fun of the husband's lack of *cautio* in believing him trustworthy, prepares for the subsequent couplets which discuss his past subtleties.

     ad aras: Tibullus will go only to the altar, which would therefore be outside the temple itself, and avoid risk of the blindness which supposedly threatened those who profaned the rites of the *Bona Dea* (Propertius 4.9.53ff.). (Perhaps Tibullus is implying that they will not be going to any rites at all. In any case he need not fear seeing her with someone else.)

     timuisse: infinitive subject of *sit,* with no definite temporal value.

25– Ovid (*Tr.* 2.451–52) quotes this distich with only minor

26 changes.

> *signum*: signet ring.
>
> *probarem*: "put to the test"; then "approve."
>
> *velut*: introduction to a comparative clause that is never expressed.
>
> *per causam*: "as a pretext."

27– In Ovid (*Am.* 1.4.51–52) this particular piece of deception
28 is left up to the mistress. The sigmatism is noteworthy, especially given the setting, while anaphora points up the poet's almost insulting boast.

> *sobria*: hypallage, ordinarily applied to *aqua*.
>
> *supposita aqua*: *suppono* is the verb ordinarily used for the substitution of one child for another. The metaphor therefore takes *peperi* one stage further. He "begets" sleep for the husband. His own "child" is water, adroitly substituted for wine.
>
> *victor*: wine and sleep are creative (or destructive) allies in any "military" operation (cf. Vergil *Aen.* 2.265; 9.189, 236, 316).

29– In his specious reasoning Tibullus makes use of what the
30 rhetoricians called a *concessio per purgationem* (for details see [Cicero] *Ad Her.* 2.23). Each stage in the logic is deliberately faulty. The preceding couplet proves him quite *prudens* (i.e., *pro-videns*) and boasting of his role as *victor* whereas now the blame is placed on love's orders, though the poet can still command pardon. The lover-poet does bear love's arms and so presumably does the *coniunx*. We cannot help but recall Tibullus' concept of Amor in lines 1–5. (For another pun on *ignosce* see 1.2.12.)

31– The dog is an ordinary *ianitor* in elegy (as, e.g., 2.4.32) and
32 elsewhere. The boastful tone—and admission that in this case the truth is not shameful—is scarcely matched by the exploit itself.

> *instabat*: the dog menaces with bite as well as bark (cf. Vergil *Aen.* 12.751).

33– A similar point is made by Catullus (17.12ff.) of an old man
34 with a young wife. A careless husband has no need for a beautiful wife.

> *servare*: a motif of the poem as are the doors whose guarding is in question. (The long final letter, which gives the word special stress, is a rare example of vowel lengthening in the thesis of a foot before two consonants the second of which is a liquid. Many editors add a monosyllabic word, such as *heu* or *et*, not sanctioned by the major manuscripts.)

35– *te tenet*: Tibullus has experienced similar emotions himself
36 (1.5.39).

 suspirat: with accusative of the person yearned for.

 amores: a lover (as 1.3.81 and often in Catullus and Propertius).

 condoluisse caput: the excuse is as old as Plautus who
couches it in the same terms.

37– Tibullus now assumes that the request implied in lines 15–16
38 and reiterated at 23 has been granted and that he is now the slave-
guardian of Delia. The lashes and bonds are only for a moment
literal. They are the happy tortures the slave of love endures
(*vincla*: 1.1.55, 1.2.92; *verbera*: 1.8.6, 1.9.22; and cf., especially, 1.5.3ff.). You cannot very well guard something fickle
while in chains yourself, so the elegiac assumption of Delia as
domina and Venus is immediately operative. (But there is an
ambiguity: should not Delia, as the person under guard, also
suffer tortures?)

39– As the fantasy continues, the wishful lover, ever bent on re-
40 forming his wayward mistress, announces that the presence of
Roman dandies will not be tolerated by mistress and slave. Both
curled hair and overample, loose togas were considered signs
of effeminacy in men. For the first compare the prayer of
Turnus at Vergil *Aen.* 12.97–100 and Ovid's portrait at *Ars
Amat.* 1.505 ff. There is an example of a *laxa toga* at 2.3.82.
Cf. Delia at line 18, *laxo sinu*.

 effuso sinu: describes a billowing sail at 1.3.38.

41– Line 42 is usually considered corrupt and obelized. But the
42 repetitions (within 42 and of *procul* three times in four lines)
may be ritualistic—and hence parodic—to dramatize the sacrosanct quality of the couple. If anyone comes too near he will
be guilty of *crimen*. He should either keep his distance or take
another street.

43– *ipse deus*: probably Amor, if we may judge from line 30.
44 *magna sacerdos*: priestess of the goddess Bellona hence appropriate for the *miles amans* to consult—a combination of the
old Italic goddess of war and the Cappadocian goddess Ma
whose worship was introduced into Rome by Sulla in 92 B.C.
It was an orgiastic cult whose priests (Tibullus alone mentions
a priestess), the *bellonarii*, slashed their arms and body in their
ecstasy. (For further details see R. J. Getty on Lucan *Phars.*
1.565 [Cambridge, 1955].)

45– The priestess in her madness does not fear physical pain. The
46 torture of fire and whip are traditional for slaves (see 37–38

above and 1.5.3–4) and are regularly associated by Tibullus with devotion to love. There are several suggestive links between Bellona and the poet himself.

motu agitata: the phrase suggests physical movement as well as mental emotion (the double result of the goddess' inspiration). The words are combined by Cicero (*De Nat. Deor.* 3.27) in a discussion of Nature at work.

47– *bipenne*: the double bladed axe is a common instrument of
48 ritual and war from Minoan times on. The rare ablative replaces the regular *bipenni* for metrical reasons.

sanguine effuso: the blood from her wounds is used as a libation on the statue of the goddess.

inulta: without doing any harm to herself. The goddess approves.

49– *latus*: accusative of respect.
50 *praefixa*: a unique use of *praefigo* in the sense of "pierce." The word ordinarily means "fasten in front of," "tip with," either of which might go well with *veru* (a dart or short spear) but not with a person. There is a double notion, that the wound is superficial and that she now remains in one spot. In the passage as a whole, and in this distich particularly, the vocabulary has erotic overtones.

saucia pectus: see below 53–54 and cf. Vergil *Aen.* 12.5.
monet: "foretell," here with a special admonitory sense.

51– Her warning when it has come is a calculated letdown.
52 *parcite*: for the more usual *nolite* which Tibullus never writes (cf. *fuge* at 1.4.9).

ne pigeat: the proverb that fools learn only from experience is as old as Homer (*Iliad* 17.32). The knowledge in this case is only that Delia is under the guardianship of Amor.

53– The transition is brisk and oracular.
54 *attigerit*: In a sexual sense (as Catullus 67.20). The omission of the conditional sign gives a colloquial briskness to the curse.

opes: the curse is apropos, against the resources necessary for the *dives amator* to maintain his position. The analogies of *sanguis* and *cinis* carry the implied threat one stage further.

For *cinis* in a ritual curse see commentators on Theocritus *Idyl* 24.91 ff. and Vergil *Ecl.* 8.101.

55– Delia's possible punishments are vaguely enumerated.
56 *admittas*: "agree" that you have been unfaithful, yet with the elegiac overtones of "admit" a lover into her presence (as, e.g., Propertius 1.16.19) or even to "take in" lovers.

levis: here "gentle" though the sense in elegy is often "fickle."
illa: Bellona.

57– Tibullus imagines himself in a position of power, ready to avert
58 the punishments from Delia. The implications of his remarks could scarcely please her, however.

propter: postposition of *propter* with pronouns is invariable in Tibullus.

tua mater: Delia's mother takes the place of—or, more realistically, plays the role of—the *callida lena* who helps or obstructs the lover's progress. She is her daughter's procuress. The preceding iteration of the second person stresses the pronominal adjective here.

me movet: "arouses my concern."

aurea: often of seductive feminine beauty, here of supposed moral fiber.

59– Her mother brings—the present is striking—Delia to the poet's
60 house, an unusual situation in elegy where the lover's trials before his mistress' door are *de rigueur*.

adducit: the specific connotation is the procuring of a courtesan (as Terence *Adelph.* 965, Nepos *Dion* 5, etc.). The couplet implies a type of "marriage," in which ceremony the *manus* played an important part (see *OCD s.v.*).

timore: fear that the husband would observe her departure or that some prejudiced witness would take note.

61– The scene changes to Delia's house and to another service of
62 the cooperative mother, to recognize the sound of the poet's approach and open the door. Darkness, silence, and secrecy are common Tibullan allies.

63– *mihi*: dative of reference.
64 *dulcis*: equivalent to the English "dear" in addressing friends.

cum contribuisse: the construction is unique in Latin, emphasizing the prefix in the compound.

tecum: "to" rather than "with" you.

sit modo fas: "provided it is right," i.e., in this case, as long as it does not contravene the laws of nature.

annos: sound hints a punning connection with *anus*.

65– As at 58–59, the reiteration of the second person pronoun is
66 pointed. Tibullus claims to love Delia (and love her always) because of affection for her mother!

sanguis: the unusual lengthening has two possible causes: position at the caesura or descent from an original *sanguins* (or both). (Is this very stress meant to force recollection of line 48?)

67– The *vitta* (hair fillet) and *stola* (long gown) were distinctive
68   and, in the latter case, exclusive features of a Roman matron's
     garb from as early as the second Punic war. The fact that
     Delia possesses neither seems to place her in the class of
     libertinae whose sexual license was notorious (see, e.g., Ovid *Ars
     Amat.* 1.31–34). *Quamvis* is therefore well chosen. Tibullus
     prays that she remain *casta* even though the chances of falling
     through temptation are great.

   doce: her precepts (and the poet's own words) ironically
   reverse the situation of line 9 (*docui*).

   ligatos: a startling transfer from *vitta* (and of active to
   passive) since her hair must actually be *solutos* as she did not
   use a fillet. There is a punning link between *impediat* and *pedes*
   and consequent suggestion that the trappings of a matron would
   only get in Delia's way. Would this result in a greater or lesser
   degree of *castitas*, however?

69– Tibullus too has laws to balance his demands of Delia.
70   *durae*: the metaphor draws out a possible origin of *leges* as
     statutes which bind.

   ullam: i.e., *puellam*. The same substantival use occurs at
   2.1.9.

   quin oculos appetat: "without her attacking my eyes." Regular manifestation of feminine wrath (Propertius 3.8.5ff.).

71– Such punishments, to be inflicted after only a thought on
72   Delia's part, would typify the sacking of a city and are as such
     a deliberate exaggeration in the context.

   immerito: "unjustly."

   proripiar: unique example in Latin of *proripio* with an
   accusative of motion without a preposition. The double pas-
   sives recall *inducar* (1) and reiterate the power that Amor has
   over his helpless subject, now through Delia.

73– For such quarrels, where violence (willing or otherwise) is
74   provoked, see 1.1.74, 1.3.64, et al. The gentle Tibullus wishes
     none of it, but were such madness to seize him he prays not
     to have the physical means to behave disgracefully. The cou-
     plet is a study in complex emotions: I wish never to strike you.
     But if madness creates such desire may I have the sanity to
     arouse another desire, to lack hands. (The wish of a madman!)

   iste: second person demonstrative would ordinarily mean
   "that frenzy of yours." Here "that frenzy instilled by you" is
   a better paraphrase.

   optarim: perfect subjunctive used as a potential.

75– *sis casta*: picks up the motif from line 67.

76 *saevo metu*: out of fear of any *saevitia* on Tibullus' part.
A positive statement, by contrast with lines 3 and 37.

mutuus amor: cf. *mutua venus,* 14. Love will no longer take
sides. (For the metaphor see 1.2.65–66.)

absenti te: whatever the specific occasion, the desperate in-
quiry into Delia's *castitas* and *fidelitas* is further clarified by
the phrase.

77– Picture of the aging courtesan who gets her punishment after
78 the passage of time. Spinning is ordinarily a symbol of chastity
(see 1.3.85–86). Here the chastity is enforced upon a faithless
Penelope who must spin on and on. The faithless mistress
will have to earn her meager living now (since she can take
in no more lovers, the implication is). Trembling hand and
twisted thread support the picture of age. The subsurface
oxymoron between *tremula* and *stamina* suggests that such
tasks remain constant; the quivering of old age, however, means
a life soon to pass.

inops: most authors (e.g., Horace *Carm.* 1.25, 4.13) limit
the aged courtesan's torture to loss of beauty combined with
heightened desire. Here, suitably enough, poverty is to be her
lot.

79– *firma licia*: the steadiness of the web's threads is another con-
80 trast to her trembling hand.

conductis telis: the loom she uses is rented, further proof of
her poverty.

tracta: three stages of wool preparation in a nutshell: drawing wool from the pile to be cleaned (*putat*). The simple directness of these two couplets, with their abundance of past par-
ticiples, iteration of words with similar roots and, above all,
uncomplicated physical action, provokes a contrast with the
elegist's complex emotional world.

81– *animo gaudente*: the crowds of youth symbolize all those who
82 rejoice in her demise.

commemorant: first recall, then call to others' attention. The
alliteration of *merito* connects recollection with righteous results.

merito: contrasts with *immerito* (72).

senem: unique feminine adjectival use of *senex.*

83– Venus flaunts Delia as a negative object lesson (with the phrase-
84 ology, cf. Vergil *Georg.* 1.95–96 of Ceres rewarding a man
who works hard at his farming).

acerba: of Venus also at 1.2.100.

monet: cf. Bellona, line 50.

85–   A prayer to avert the curse inherent in such words. *Nos* unites
86   the lovers but in spite of the hope expressed this is the last
      appearance of Delia in Tibullus' extant poetry.

      cadant: often of a curse but here looking to Venus *sublimis*
      on her Olympian height.

      cana coma: cf. 1.2.94. Once more we end on the theme of
      old age with one of its commonest symbols.

COMMENTARY 1. 7.

The Fates once sang of Aquitania's defeat and now Messalla
celebrates his victorious triumph. Tibullus witnesses the Gallic
campaigns. He will sing also of the east, of the Cydnus River
and Mt. Taurus in Cilicia, of Syrian doves and Tyre, founder
of seafaring, and of the fertile, ever-flowing Nile. The people
hymn Osiris, the Nile god, and his incarnation, the bull (Apis).
Osiris invented the plough and the planting of seedlings; he
taught viticulture and invented wine which moves men to dance
and relieves the sufferings of farmer and slave. Not cares, but
song and love, colorful vestments, and flowers are fitting for
Osiris. Join the celebration for Messalla's birthday spirit which
should be present today to receive the honors of incense and
honeycake. Messalla, may your family grow and the farmer, as
he returns to his dwelling in the Alban hills, sing that you refurbished the Via Latina. Come, birthday spirit, to be feted for
many long years.

Tibullus honors his patron, M. Valerius Messalla Corvinus,
on the occasion of his triumph, celebrated September 25, 27
B.C. (see introduction, page 4). The poem combines within an
elegy elements of other major poetic genres: birthday song,
heroic ode, and religious hymn. It begins with an imagined
quotation from a song of the Fates which could well have called
to a Roman reader's mind similar moments in Catullus 64
(which praises the courage and indicts the morality of Achilles)
and Vergil's fourth *Eclogue*, seeking a visionary existence
where pastoral escape and political involvement could be combined. The poem begins with Roman triumph and moves first
to Aquitania (where poet and warrior were together), then
east to the nourishing Taurus and inventive Tyre. Finally we
reach Egypt, the Nile, Osiris, and his discovery of agriculture
and wine, promoter of song and easer of suffering. The youth
of Egypt praise Osiris and the Roman young hail Messalla,
allowing us to compare the two. And when we return to Rome

we have Messalla's work of renewal there, the repaired Via Latina which takes the farmer out of the mighty city back to his land. This journey, from city to country, parallels the poet's own mental progress, first taming Gallic rivers, moving east to fertile Cydnus, and ending at the source of productivity, the mysterious Nile-Osiris. And at the same time we follow changes in poetic genre from heroic ode to birthday poem. Messalla, as Roman Osiris, conquers and restores. Tibullus retreats into more "poetic" thoughts of water, wine, and rural living. Yet the poem begins and ends with the theme of birth and generation, and much of what intervenes varies the notion of masculine creativity and didactic achievement: rivers as sources of life and strength, Messalla and Osiris as men of positive force, conquering, inventing, repairing.

1–2   The *Parcae*, Fates (Roman equivalent of the Greek *Moirai*), whose words are not subject to divine alteration, traditionally spin the threads of a man's life from the moment of his birth. Here their song comes in easy combination with a birthday hymn and eulogy. Elsewhere in Latin literature it is associated with the actual birth of a child (Vergil *Ecl.* 4) or with a wedding (Catullus 64, a poem this line itself echoes—cf. 64.383).

   Hunc diem: the date of birth which need not necessarily be the same as the date of either Messalla's victory or his subsequent triumph. Since its verb appears only in the next distich, *dies* is given particular force.

   stamina: either threads hanging from the distaff (as 1.3.86) or the warp of life's web. *Dissoluenda* is apt in either case. Spinning figured prominently at 1.6.77ff., suggesting an easy transition from poem to poem.

3–4   The repetition of *hunc* at the beginning of the initial distichs and the end rhyme of lines 1 and 3 enhance the hymnic solemnity.

   Aquitanas gentes: Aquitania corresponds to the southwestern quarter of Transalpine Gaul (modern France), bounded roughly by the Pyrenees on the south, bay of Biscay on the west and the Garonne on the east. The *Atax*, modern Aude, rises in the Pyrenees and enters the Mediterranean near modern Narbonne. The strength or weakness of a landscape as well as its major outlines was often seen by the Romans in terms of its rivers. Here the (personified) Atax trembles at defeat.

   posset: power is given to the day itself.

   fundere: "rout," but the root idea of pouring connects the verb with the sound of *Aquitanas*, and the meaning of *dissolvenda* (2).

quem: accusative of inner object.

5-6 *evenere*: the language and material of prophecy continues (cf. 1.5.57).

pubes Romana: populace, with special overtones of youth growing to maturity (cf. Horace *Carm.* 4.4.46).

triumphos: poetic plural perhaps because involving a series of places.

evinctos . . . capta: the double hypallage is rare even in Tibullus. Tying of arms is a universal sign of bondage.

7-8 The description shifts dramatically to Messalla the *triumphator*, wearing the victor's laurels, standing in a chariot adorned with ivory (and gold) and drawn by white horses. The actual ceremony concluded on the top of the Capitoline at the temple of Jupiter Optimus Maximus. (For further details see R. D. Williams on Vergil *Aen.* 3.537 [Oxford, 1962]). Cf. the spectacle of the *dives amator* at 1.2.71.

9–
10 Tibullus witnessed the events which brought the present honor. The place names that follow (through line 12), though all located in transalpine Gaul, are not listed according to a set geographical pattern and therefore are apparently not the stages of a particular journey.

non sine me: rare example of litotes in Tibullus, adding emphasis to the poet's boast and contrasting with *sine me* (1.3.1).

Tarbella Pyrene: the western part of the Pyrenees. The name derives from the Tarbellians, an Aquitanian people living in the valley of the Adour whose name lives on in the modern Tarbes.

Santonici: the Santones lived in modern Santonge, near the mouth of the Garonne.

11–
12 *Arar*: modern Saône which joins the Rhone (*Rhodanus*) at Lyons. *Garunna* (masc.) is the modern Garonne.

caerula lympha: in apposition to the *Liger* (Loire). The adjective or its variant *caeruleus* (as line 14) is a common attribute of rivers in Latin. The juxtaposition of *flavus* and *caerulus* appealed to Tibullus (see 1.5.45–46). Its origin may be Ennian (see J. P. Elder, "Tibullus, Ennius and the Blue Loire," *TAPA* 96 [1965], 97–105).

Carnutis: native of the modern Chartres.

13–
14 As the milieu switches to Cilicia, Syria, Phoenicia, and Egypt, the high tone remains but there is no longer any assurance that the poet actually journeyed to the places he mentions. It does seem likely, though as yet unprovable, that these are note-

worthy stops on Messalla's eastern campaigns which followed on the battle of Actium.

Cydne: the Cydnus (modern Tersus-Chai) is the chief river of ancient Cilicia. The abundance of epithets suggests the quiet meander of a river's delta. (Cf. Vergil's description of the Tiber at *Aen.* 8.87–89).

15– The sudden change of construction to indirect question (still
16 dependent on *canam*) calls attention to the hyperbole, unusual in Tibullus. (With the epic diction cf. Vergil *Aen.* 4.441–46 and 12.701–703).

Taurus: modern Bulgar Dagh, though 11,000 feet in height, was cultivated to its summit, according to Strabo (12.570). Hence *alat*. There is a tension in the language between animate and inanimate—a bull that is a mountain, nourishment from what is cold.

intonsos Cilicas: bearded, with the implication of unculti- vated roughness.

17– The device of *praeteritio* introduces a new series of names,
18 culminating in the Nile.

crebras urbes: cities both frequent and densely populated.

alba columba: white doves were sacred, and for this reason *intacta*, to the Syrian-Phoenician goddess Astarte as they were· to her Greek equivalent Aphrodite. Catullus (29.8) calls the debauched Mamurra *albulus columbus* with an irony which we may also sense in any connection between Aphrodite and vir- ginity.

Palaestino Syro: Palestine merely specifies an area within ancient Syria.

19– Tibullus is fond of the theme of the *heuretes* or first discoverer.
20 This particular honor, the invention of seafaring, was more often ascribed to the Egyptians, though the Phoenicians were the most famous seafarers and merchantmen in antiquity. In Latin letters the first sailor is given more blame than praise (as, e.g., Horace *Carm.* 1.3.9 ff.; Propertius 1.17.13–14). The change of *venue* from the city looking out from its lofty build- ings (*turribus*) to the boat preyed on by the winds pinpoints the emotions of those participating in the actual moment of dis- covery.

credere docta: the idea of "teaching" runs through the sub- sequent lines. The infinitive with an adjective or participle is a Greek construction, common to all the Augustan poets. (Tibullus' other examples with *doctus* are line 28 below and 1.9.37.)

21– The mysteries of the Nile, its source and abundance in a desert
22   land and during the driest of seasons, challenged writers in
antiquity from Herodotus on (2.19).

  Sirius: the Dog Star whose rising betokened the most intense summer heat (see 1.1.27–28 and 1.4.41–42; Horace
Carm. 1.17.17–18; etc.).

  findit: usually of ploughing, here pejorative, "cracks open"
from the heat (as Vergil *Georg.* 2.353).

  fertilis: active ("fertilizing") as well as passive.

  abundet: a pun on the etymology of the word in a context
illustrating the bounty of water, not land!

23– *pater*: common epithet for river gods.
24   *quibus in terris*: Vergil uses the phrase twice (*Ecl.* 3.104
and 106) of a riddle. Here Tibullus asks the meaning of a geographical puzzle which was not solved until the nineteenth
century.

25– *propter*: for the position see 1.6.57–58.
26   *pluvio Iovi*: Tibullus is the first author (and one of the few)
to give Jupiter what is usually considered a regular designation.
He is translating the Greek Zeus Ὑέτιος to replace the more
common Latin *Imbricator*.

27– ·Osiris is the Egyptian Nile god, both brother and husband of
28   Isis. He was another *heuretes*, a god of vegetation and was said
to have taught men to use wheat and grapes. Because of the
latter he is the Egyptian equivalent of Dionysus-Bacchus. His
incarnation was Apis, the bull god, whose death was the object
of annual mourning. He had a magnificent temple at Memphis.

  pubes barbara: cf. line 5, *pubes Romana*, which helps unify
the poem around Messalla.

29– As inventor of the plough and teacher of agriculture, Osiris
30   plays a role assigned in Greece to Byzyges, Demeter, or Trip-
tolemus.

  manu sollerti: cf. 1.1.8, *facili manu*.

  sollicitavit: "stir" the soil, but "disturb" it as well (the experience was new).

  teneram humum: this is usually taken as a literal description
of Egypt's alluvial soil. Emotionally, however, it reflects the
violence done the unsuspecting virginal earth by the iron's first
onslaught.

31– *inexpertae*: passive, "untried." The seeds are given over to an
32   untested charge.

  non notis: "not yet known." As the developer of grafting,

Osiris would have shown how fruits could be plucked from trees that were not their own.

33– Two important vineyard events in brief, *alligatio* and *ampu-*
34 *tatio*, binding of the vine to a support and pruning.

teneram vitem: tender because both young and unused to such treatment but timely for education.

palis: it was the ancient practice, still followed in much of the Mediterranean basin, to bind vines either to stakes, as here, or more usually to trees.

viridem comam: the "hair" (foliage) of plants or trees is a common image in Latin poetry. As in line 30, the personification arouses the reader's sympathy as nature, in her prime, is (attacked and) cut by the hard pruning fork. *Caedere* is used elsewhere by Tibullus only of slaughter (1.1.21; 1.6.47) while Cicero employs the phrase *ad palum alligati* of condemned criminals ready to pay the penalty (*In Verr.* 2.5.5.11).

35– After the growing up of the grapes comes the moment of wine
36 making. Nature, still under duress, now yields her fruits to the attacker.

sapores: metonomy for the sweet wine itself.

incultis pedibus: both physical ("uncouth," "barbaric") and mental ("ignorant," "untutored"). The context is apt for both.

37– By intensifying the personification, Tibullus has moved from
38 *hic docuit* (33) to *ille liquor docuit*, from Osiris the inventor to the inherent power his great discovery has to urge men to sing and dance. (The passage owes much to one of Lucretius' descriptions of the origin of song: 5.1379 ff.)

inflectere: the metaphor goes equally well with words or music.

certos modos: fixed rhythms. Taking *certus* in its original sense (as past participle of *cerno*), there is a virtual oxymoron between *certos* and *nescia*. Wine bridges the gap between certain knowledge and ignorance.

39– There is nothing novel about the power of wine (Bacchus-
40 Osiris) to release men from care. But the sudden realistic note (and the momentary change to the god's Roman title) in the reference to the tired farmer and slave in bondage is impressive. Ironically to produce one of the specific benefits of the culture-hero Bacchus demands labor from (and creates *tristitia* for) the farmer. Only the result, wine, brings (momentary) relief. (Compare Horace's advice to Plancus, *Carm.* 1.7.17–19.)

tristitiae: genitive of separation. Used by Plautus and revived by the Augustan poets by analogy with the Greek.

dissoluenda: gerundive after *dare* with the idea more of intention than necessity. But compare line 2 where release is impossible.

41–
42   *requiem*: a momentary relief from the cares that dash men down, even for a slave.

crura sonent: the sentiment is paralleled at 2.6.25–26, where the goddess Spes brings the slave help. Note the heavy alliteration.

43–
44   Grief and cares are unfitting for laughter-loving Osiris (Diodorus Siculus 1.18). Cf. 1.3.59 (*choreae cantusque*).

levis amor: cf. 1.1.73 (*levis Venus*). Here love is so "light" as to bring no cares with it. (It is from *tristis curas* that Catullus prays for relief at 2.10.)

45–
46   The external attributes of Bacchus-Osiris in festive contrast to sad cares.

varii flores: flowers of different colors.

corymbis: ivy is a stock emblem of Bacchus. His forehead is regularly wreathed with clusters of its berries.

lutea palla: ordinarily the long garment of Roman women, it is also worn by tragic actors and by divinities. Yellow is a festive color, often, for instance, of a bride's veil. Pliny (*Hist. Nat.* 21ʼ.46) calls it a feminine color. Here it is in easy association with *palla* and *teneros pedes* to stress Osiris' femininity.

47–
48   *Tyriae vestes*: garments dyed in Tyrian purple, fitting for a festive occasion, conventionally costly.

tibia: a flute, apparently originally made from a shin bone. Though often associated with Bacchus and hence with happy moments (as Vergil *Aen.* 11.737) its sound is not always considered *dulcis* (cf. Catullus 64.264).

cista: a wickerwork (hence *levis*) basket containing mystic objects of the god's rites, unknown (*occultis*) to the public. *Conscius* with the dative is first used here or at Vergil *Aen.* 4.167.

49–
50   A prayer to Osiris to join in the celebration of Messalla's Genius, the spirit born to a man at birth. Sacrifice to him would be particularly apt on one's birthday. Osiris will himself do homage.

concelebra: an initial use by Tibullus in Latin with the meaning "join in honoring."

tempora funde: for the hoped for effect of such a gesture cf. 1.2.3–4. Cf. the uses of the verb at lines 3 and 46.

51–
52   *illius*: i.e., of the Genius. (Or its statue?) The crowning with garlands links the Genius with the triumphant Messalla and

splendidly attired Osiris. (Cf. the similar description of the Genius of Cornutus at 2.2.6–7).

53– Prayer to the Genius to attend the celebration and receive the
54 traditional offerings of incense and cakes dipped in honey.

hodierne: a Greek construction frequently witnessed in the Augustan poets where an adjective is attracted into the case of a vocative noun to which it is attached, even when the noun is unexpressed.

Mopsopio: the renowned Attic honey from Mt. Hymettus. Mopsopia is the name given Attica by Callimachus (frag. 709Pf.) whence Tibullus may have derived the epithet.

55– Prayer that Messalla's family might flourish. By his first wife,
56 Calpurnia, he had M. Valerius Messalla Messallinus (born 39) whose elevation to the board of *quindecimviri sacris faciundis* is celebrated in 2.5. A second son, M. Aurelius Cotta Maximus, consul A.D. 20 was born (date unknown) to his second wife Aurelia who also had a daughter, Valeria Messallina.

succrescat: the image is that of a smaller plant growing beside its parent.

facta parentis: the phrase is used by Vergil (*Ecl.* 4.26) of the epic deeds of a newborn boy's father. The compliment is to Messalla's sons. They further enhance the deeds of their father and are themselves worthy of admiration.

57– At the end of the civil wars Augustus undertook a program of
58 road repairs and apportioned to himself and his generals various stretches which they were to renew with monies accumulated from the spoils of their campaigns. Messalla was assigned part of the Via Latina which leaves Rome by the Porta Capena in a southeasterly direction, and passes over the Alban hills between Tusculum and Alba Longa. Thence it continues paralleling the Via Appia inland which it joins finally at Beneventum. (For further details see G. McCraken, "Tibullus, Messala, and the Via Latina," *AJP* 53 [1932], 344–52.)

The scene shifts to the countryside where someone wanting to make his way to the city can enjoy the benefits of Messalla's engineering skill as roadbuilder.

candida Alba: Vergil uses the same pun in an allusion to Alba Longa at *Aen.* 8.82. The attribute may come originally from the brightness of the native limestone.

antiquo lare: at 1.3.34 of Tibullus' own home (also 2.1.60). The age of the *lar* is complemented by its presence in a hallowed spot, traditionally founded by Ascanius, Aeneas' son.

detinet: cf. 1.3.3.

59– Two important aspects of road building: laying of a hard lower
60 bed of gravel (*glarea*) and then placing the famous pavement
stones on top. (The process is described in detail by Vitruvius,
7.1.1.ff.)

congesta: *congero* suits two aspects of the context. Messalla
had indeed heaped up wealth (as 1.1.1) but this was the source
of the (literal) pile of gravel which was strewn to make the
roadbed.

apta arte: "suitable skill," but one which also depends on
careful, tight fitting (*apo*).

61– The ordinary farmer also sings the praises of Messalla. Like
62 Osiris-Bacchus, Messalla has helped him by making his way
home easier after business in the city. We have come a long,
poetic journey from Roman triumph to Latin farmer returning
to his countryside.

agricola: the short final syllable becomes long at a moment
when the stress is strong (at the principal caesura of the line).

magna urbe: Rome (as also 2.5.56).

inoffensum: "without stumbling" because the road was
smooth. The word is a Tibullan coinage and extremely rare in
this sense. (For stumbling as a bad omen see 1.3.19–20.)

63– *Natalis*: the (birthday) Genius of Messalla (also 2.2.1, 21). We
64 return to the theme of the day which opened the poem.

per: a unique use in Tibullus in a temporal sense.

candidior: literal and figurative—literal, as the climax of a
joyous brightness which permeates the poem; figurative because
white is the color of good luck and happiness.

COMMENTARY 1. 8.

The poet knows instinctively about signs between lovers.
Marathus, stop the pretense. Your former habits are useless
now. Pholoe is lovely without any artifice. Maybe Marathus
has been bewitched. But Tibullus, to his sorrow, should know
better. Beauty needs the help of no external charms. Do not
be hard on the boy but enjoy love while you are young. He
weeps when he cannot see you: "Why does she avoid me? Venus
has taught me useless deceptions. Pholoe even fails in her promise to come which makes every approaching sound a torment."
The gods detest pride, Pholoe. Yet Marathus too once deceived unhappy lovers not realizing that the god of revenge
stood behind his head. Now he suffers from a girl's pride.

Vengeance awaits you, Pholoe. You will soon yearn to relive the present day.

We might entitle the poem "To Pholoe on Marathus" but it would be more incisive to say "To Tibullus himself on Pholoe and Marathus." The opening words project the poet's keen involvement, while the exclamation at line 23 demonstrates that he also has suffered Marathus' wiles. In fact two disparate worlds, of the *puer delicatus* and the typically elegiac *saeva puella*, both of which Tibullus knows well, clash, proving only that the trials and joys of love are universal. Artifice vies with innate beauty, vengeance stalks pride, old age dogs youth, deception is universal, superficial trappings and even *doctrina* are ultimately of little avail in any relationship. Beginning with one certainty, his ability to describe and face honestly his own emotions, Tibullus again reveals his mastery of human psychology, juggling three possible sets of relationships. Whatever the emotional fluctuations of this far from aloof *praeceptor amoris*, it is into the thoughts of Marathus and Pholoe that he enters, and his supposedly abstract notions warn them, with abundant sympathy and humor, toward, not away from each other.

1–2   Tibullus is a third party examining the signs of love between two others, with one of whom he, too, is emotionally involved.

     celari: an unusual use ("to have concealed from me") with a suppressed reflexive and followed by an indirect question (see TLL, *s.v.* 767.69–71). Since we expect some such phrase as "you cannot conceal from me . . . ," it is as much the poet's apparent weakness as the strength of his rival's wiles that is emphasized. The word order, the expressed pronoun, the initial negative, the passive-active alternation make the opening especially powerful. Compare the thought with 1.2.36: *celari vult sua furta Venus*.

     nutus verba: common signals in such a situation (see 1.2. 21–22).

     miti lenia: the words have a threefold sense. As secretive lovers' words they are soft (soothing), gentle (persuasive), even ripe (ready), and quiet. The antonyms would be such words as *acutus* and *asper*.

3–4   Tibullus, expert in amatory matters, need not resort to divination to interpret signs of love.

     sortes: see 1.3.11.

     fibra: in general, a poetic word for *exta* or *iecur*; in particular the filaments that divided the liver, watched during sacrifices (see Pease on Cicero *De Div.* 1.16).

conscia: "knowing (the thoughts of)." The only use in Tibullus with the genitive.

praecinit: apt for prophecy as well as song.

5–6 The poet himself has learned as slave and pupil of Venus (though now the pronoun is suppressed). The intensity of line 6, which *ipsa Venus* anticipates, begins with *per*, and is strengthened by litotes, while the most forceful word is held in abeyance to the end.

magico nodo: the knot that binds the hands of Venus' victims behind their backs is tied with a magic charm. (Cf. Vergil *Ecl.* 8.78, where the sorceress cries *Veneris vincula necto*.)

religatum: chosen with reference to ritual. (For the etymology of *religio* see Pease on Cicero *De Div.* 2.148.)

perdocuit: "has taught me thoroughly."

7–8 Direct address to Marathus. The subject changes slightly; pretense and unwillingness are two different things.

Amor's flame, like Venus' lash, is a commonplace, as is also the sentiment that love burns the unaccepting more deeply than others.

succubuisse: the literal meaning should not be lost sight of, given the present context.

9– The *puer delicatus*, unable to change his ways when he has
10 fallen in love with a girl.

nunc: i.e., in the new type of affair.

molles: fitting attribute for a *puer delicatus*.

disposuisse: "set in order," often after confusion.

mutatas comas: "altered," i.e., done up in a different manner or dyed.

11– *fuco*: *fucus*, in the sense of dye, was ordinarily red. Here
12 "rouge."

artificis: a barber would regularly perform this function but here the reference seems directed to Marathus.

docta manu: Marathus is learned in these superficial wiles.

subsecuisse: a rare verb ("clip," "pare"), highlighted as the last of four perfect infinitives in a row (three of which are in the same position in the pentameter), perhaps to show off Marathus' precise but precious ways, his addiction to the most minor forms of artifice.

13– Useless change is a major theme of the poem. (The verb *muto*
14 appears in lines 10, 13, and 43, and nowhere else in Tibullus).

Lines 14 and 16 are as tightly organized as the subjects they describe.

frustra frustra: the alteration of stress underscores the repetition.

ansa: ordinarily a handle, here the loop on the side of the sandal through which the lace is drawn tight. *Arta* is a transferred epithet. Tight fit was important for external show.

15– The subject, charming for beauty unadorned, is apparently
16 Marathus' girl Pholoe, who is not actually named until line 69.

inculto ore: deliberate contrast to lines 9 ff.

venerit: the erotic meaning, "come to meet," is certainly to be understood.

nitidum caput: her hair has a natural sheen without being worked over *tarda arte*, "with time-consuming artifice," the latter denoted by length and alliteration.

compserit: usually *como* would refer to hair alone; here "adorn," not simply "comb."

17– Charms and *pallentes herbae* (blanching potions) were two
18 traditional ways to induce or dispel love.

pallentibus: *palleo* here is active.

devovit: "put under a spell." Cf. also 1.5.41.

tacito tempore noctis: regular time for magic as well as illicit love-making.

anus: the *lena*, who by the nature of her trade was also a sorceress.

19– Two common uses of incantations. A prohibition against the
20 first is already in the XII Tables, *qui fruges excantassit . . . .*
(See Pliny *Hist. Nat.* 28.18; Servius on Vergil *Ecl.* 8. 99, where the same power is attributed to the magican Moeris.)

Snake-charming resulted more usually in the bursting of the victim (see F. Marx on Lucilius frag. 575 [Leipzig, 1904–1905]) while magic commonly changed the course of rivers, not serpents. Here it is apotropaic.

traducit: a boundary line or barrier is implicit.

detinet iter: prose would place *anguis* as object.

21– Another traditional accomplishment of witches (cf. Propertius
22 1.1.19). References to the chariot of the moon in Latin begin here and at Vergil *Aen.* 10.215. The wording evokes the moon's triumphal course, interrupted by magic, though the chariot apparently continues on.

On the sounding of bronze in this connection see on 1.3.23–24. (In general for the magic qualities of bronze see Pease and also R. G. Austin [Oxford, 1955] on Vergil *Aen.* 4.513).

The verbs convey the suggestion of lessening effect as the couplets progress.

faceret sonent: the tense change complements the equivalent alteration from contrary-to-fact to actuality.

23–
24   *Carmen* and *herbas* refer to line 17, but the referent of *misero* is ambiguous. Is it Marathus or, more logically, Tibullus himself who now is lovesick? Magic need not (here cannot) be advocated when *forma*, physical beauty, mesmerizes by itself.

nocuisse: cf. 1.5.47. For the "harm" of magic, cf. Propertius 2.19.32.

25–
26   The real harm comes from the physical touch of love-making, not any magic rites. The couplet is splendidly constructed with the threefold use of *sed* connecting three perfect infinitives while actually the second two prove to be examples of the first. The length of the kisses is verbalized by the separation of adjective and noun into different lines while the repetition of *femur* is the purposeful climax.

tetigisse: for *tango* in a sexual sense, see Terence *Adelph.* 686, etc.

conseruisse: cf. *conserere* (36) and Ovid *Her.* 2.58 (*lateri conseruisse latus*). The verb "links" body with body.

27–
28   Apostrophe to Pholoe, warning of Venus' enmity should she prove unyielding.

difficilis: "obstinate" (cf. 1.9.20, *difficilis Venus*).

persequitur poenis: Venus will act the role of Nemesis (for the phrase cf. Cicero *Ad Fam.* 1.9.15).

tristia: "causing grief," in this case lovesickness.

29–
30   Verbally, by means of chiastic order, she "embraces" his chill limbs in her warm bosom (hence *sinus*, originally "curve," "fold").

munera: for gifts in this connection cf. 1.4.58 ff., 1.9.11 ff., etc.

canus amator: the aging lover must more and more rely on presents.

foveat: the context suggests a double sense: literally, to warm (which anticipates *frigida*), metaphorically to bend or soften (which looks to *molli*). The erotic connotations go without saying (cf. 1.6.6).

31–
32   The initial play on the word *carior* makes the point. Gold may be expensive and the superficial attraction of riches and gifts alluring, but physical beauty is still "dearer."

carior auro: proverbial (cf. Otto, *Sprichwörter*, 49).

levia fulgent ora: the adjective and verb elaborate the more than metallic beauty of the youth. *Levia* is "smooth" but also "polished," "burnished" (as Vergil *Aen.* 5.91) while *fulgeo* is often connected with the gleam of metal (cf. the cognate *fulvo auro* at 1.1.1).

aspera barba: by contrast with *levia ora* and with the same metaphor. *Asper* is used of pieces of sculpture with raised relief on them (e.g., Vergil *Aen.* 5.267). The beard here is an unnecessary "abrasive" which would wear away rather than merely smooth out roughnesses from a surface (in this case the "rubbing" is only of bodies in an embrace).

33– To be taken closely with the preceding couplet. The gleam of
34 her arm vies with the brightness of his face, and wealth is in each case despised.

suppone: in a sexual sense (as Catullus 69.2).

despiciantur: the proverbial wealth of kings is less important than love (compare the context of 1.1.78).

35– *inveniet*: a usual change, though the manuscripts' reading,
36 *invenit*, may be defended as a type of gnomic perfect. The construction with infinitive is Greek.

concumbere: cf. 2.5.53, *concubitus furtim*.

timet: trembling of youth or maiden before a first erotic adventure is a theme used with special effectiveness by Horace (*Carm.* 1.23).

teneros sinus: cf. 1.1.46. The girl and boy are each *tener*.
conserere: see 26 above.
usque: adverbial, "continually."

37– The description is influenced by Lucretius (4.1105 ff., 1192 ff.)
38 and becomes a stock theme in elegy.

anhelanti: "panting" with eagerness (cf. Ovid *Ars Amat.* 3.803).

figere dente notas: cf. 1.6.14, Horace *Carm.* 1.13.11–12, etc.
39– The change of theme, though a reminder of 31–34, serves as
40 a warning to Pholoe: jewels and precious stones are nothing without love. (For a picture of the life of an aging courtesan, see 1.6.77 ff. and notes thereto.)

frigore sola: by a type of hypallage, "cold from being alone." *Frigus* is her only companion (*frigore* can only secondarily be ablative of time). Cf. line 30.

41– *sero*: "too late." The repetition harmonizes with the theme
42 and with the verb *revoco*.

infecit: an oxymoron: How can one stain something white?

The stain of time's passing is only the blanching of one's hair (cf. 2.2.20). This is the dye age uses.

cana: cf. line 29 and 1.1.72.

43– The repetition of *tum* parallels that of *sero* in 41–42, further
44 to dramatize the aged lover's futile attempt to restore the past and conceal the present. *Studium* has replaced *natura*. (On the bark of the nuts used to furnish dye, see Pliny *Hist. Nat.* 15.87.)

coma mutatur: cf. 10, *mutatas comas.*

dissimulet: the echo from line 7 serves to strengthen the contrast between truth and surface deception which runs through the poem.

viridi cortice: "youthful" (not literally "green," though the context might give the reader a start). Bark is an appropriate object with which to disguise the body's externals as the woman searches to renew her lost youth.

45– With the sentiment of line 45 it is instructive to compare
46 Propertius 3.25.13: "vellere tum cupias albos a stirpe capillos." In both cases there is a pun on *stirps*, "root," and the expression *a stirpe*, "utterly." *Tollere*, "remove," "make away with," "kill," enhances the double sense (cf. Livy 34.2.3: "omne genus ab stirpe sublatum esse"). Unlike *vellere* (the regular word for plucking out hair), *tollere* suggests the annihilation of a whole race or age.

The image of line 46 seems twofold. It is related to the snake who gains renewed youth after sloughing off his old skin (see 1.4.35; Ovid *Ars Amat.* 3.77). Yet it seems to have an ironic connection with proverbial phrases like *detrahere pellem* (Horace *Sat.* 2.1.64), to strip off the veneer for the truth to stand revealed (cf. Cicero *Pro Flac.* 29.70: "adfers faciem novam, nomen vetus"). *Pellis*, usually applied to animals, pointedly replaces the standard *cutis* while *dempta* further stresses the action's artificiality.

47– Characteristic Tibullan, and Horatian, motif of time's passage
48 from life's spring. (Cf., e.g., 1.1.71; 1.4.27.) By the mixture of metaphors in *labitur* and *pede*, time is personified and treated as a river (cf. ps.-Vergil *Culex* 17: *liquido pede labitur unda*). Ovid adopts the combination at *Ars Amat.* 3.65.

floret: confirms the idea of spring in the phrase *primi temporis aetas*. Greenness is now in its right place.

tardo: ironic reference to line 16.

49– The emotion of 29 ff. is restored.
50 *torque*: see 1.4.81; 1.5.5.

veteres senes: not pleonastic. *Senex* balances *puer* and echoes the mood of 29 (*canus amator*) and 42 (*cana senecta*). *Veteres* here is "experienced," "of long standing" in love's battles. It may well be meant to continue the metaphor in *gloria* and *victa*. She should challenge only love's veterans.

   dura: traditional epithet of the hardened mistress.

51–   *parce precor*: the military metaphor continues. Cf. 2.6.29 and
52   Horace *Carm.* 4.1.2.

   tenero: by contrast with *dura* and *veteres senes*.

   sontica causa: "grave reason" (for disease). The adjective appears as early as the XII Tables in the phrase *sonticus morbus*, a genuine illness which could prevent appearance in court and other things. (See Festus 290M and A. Ernout and A. Meillet, *Dictionnaire Etymologique, s.v. sons*). *Causa* has therefore both legal and medical connotations. Exaggeration adds to humor.

   luto: yellow-weed whose juice gave a yellow dye. (On yellow and the lover's pallor see Fordyce on Catullus 81.4.)

   tingit: cf. line 44.

53–   *maestas querelas*: traditional lover's complaint (cf., e.g.,
54   Catullus 64.130, Ariadne to the runaway Theseus).

   conicit: "hurls" his words like weapons against the absent beloved.

   lacrimis: Tibullus always uses the dative with *plenus*.

   omnia plena: deliberately hyperbolic in conjunction with *madent*. (Contrast the religiosity of the shepherd at Vergil *Ecl.* 3.60, *Iovis omnia plena*.)

55–   Marathus' imagined monologue to Pholoe.
56   *poterat*: imperfect indicative to express what could have happened but did not.

   custodia: same as *custodes* (as 1.2.5; 2.4.33).

   ipse deus: probably Amor (as line 7).

   dedit: construction of *dare* with an object clause more regularly finds the infinitive in the passive.

   fallere: a motif of the poem.

57–   The techniques of stealthy love are well known to the elegist
58   (and his creature). There is a near oxymoron between *nota* and *furtiva*. The delicate balance is carried over into the subsequent clauses.

   Rarely is a snatched kiss soundless. Tibullus imagines Marathus fancying himself the ideal elegiac lover.

   Venus furtiva: cf. line 35; 1.2.36 et al.

59–   He approaches the house and claims the office and power of
60   *ianitor* for himself (on the theme see 1.2.10; 1.6.12).

quamvis: "even" (with *media nocte*, when all else is still).

obrepere: "creep in," by stealth. Unique in Tibullus; elsewhere often of an enemy attacking under cover of darkness (cf. Ovid *Fast.* 3.19).

clam: he is neither seen nor heard. (Would the monosyllable, however, have suggested *clamo* to a Roman, given the present context?)

61– *artes*: in spite of his wiles her conversion is not effected.
62   *spernit*: back to the theme of line 55.

fugit puella: Pholoe, it would seem, was absent from an important rendezvous. Ferocity and flight are challenging neighbors.

ipso toro: the literal implication is that Marathus has at one time reached as far as the couch.

63– *promittit*: cf. 2.6.49: *ubi nox mihi promissa est.*
64   *subito*: the emotional action of each vignette is kept vivid.
perfida fallit: cf. Catullus 30.3: "Iam me prodere, iam non dubitas fallere, perfide?"

evigilanda: a unique use of *evigilo* in a transitive sense. Its antonym, *dormio*, is used by Catullus of death's long night (5.6). (Cf. Ovid *Ars Amat.* 1.735: "attenuant iuvenum vigilatae corpora noctes.") Marathus' only companions are evils, and those in number.

65– It furthers Marathus' fancy to imagine the sound of her coming
66   to him, in spite of boasting of his silent progress in the opposite direction (59–60).

fingo: "while I fool myself by dreaming . . ."

67– Tibullus directly addresses Marathus.
68   *desistas*: an unusual jussive subjunctive addressed to a definite person (see further Fordyce on Catullus 8.1).

frangitur: the elegiac sense of the word, "break down resistance," "soften," is illustrated in Propertius 2.18.2; 2.33.25.

lumina tument: cf. Catullus 3.17–18 (*flendo turgiduli rubent ocelli*). Alliteration makes the texture of line 68 especially tight.

69– The first mention of the name Pholoe in the poem. The crafts-
70   manship is impressive accordingly. The verb is first, the archaic, strong subject *divi* at the end, both framing apostrophe, poet's interjection, and reason. The "o" and "e" sounds are worked out so as to surround Pholoe with hatred and warning and play on her name as well.

Pholoe: the fact that the name occurs at Horace *Carm.* 1.33.7 strengthens the argument that the Albius there addressed

is Tibullus. Cf. also *Carm.* 2.5.17; 3.15.7. The name is that of
a slave (see W. Pape, *Wörterbuch der Griechischen Eigennamen, s.v.*).

fastidia: well glossed by Vergil *Ecl.* 2.14–15: "nonne fuit
satius tristis Amaryllidis iras / atque superba pati fastidia?"

nec prodest: whatever their offerings, the poet claims that
the gods do not cater to the impious and perfidious. Cf. line 9.

71– Marathus (probably his relationship to the poet is an example)
72 is guilty of the same *superbia* as Pholoe showed to him. The
sudden alteration of perspective recalls the theme and mood of
1.4.81 ff.

hic Marathus: the poet expands his scorn: "This is the very
Marathus who . . ."

quondam: once in the past, possibly with the poet though
amantes makes matters general.

ludebat: played with, only to deceive.

ultorem deum: the usual god of vengeance is Mars but Amor
(and Nemesis too) would certainly be included among *dei
ultores*. Though Cicero (In *Verr.* 2.4.87) and Caesar (*De B. G.*
1.14.5) have the phrase *deus ulciscitur*, this is the first recorded appearance of *deus ultor* in Latin (cf. Propertius
3.20.22, Ovid *Am.* 3.8.65, etc.).

post caput: the usual idiom in such expressions is *ad* or *supra
caput*. The closest parallel seems Horace *Carm.* 3.1.40 (*post
equitem sedet atra cura*).

73– *dolentis*: the grieving lover's tears form a careful juxtaposition
74 with *risisse*.

detinuisse: we would expect *detineo* to have a positive meaning, "stop the course of" (as 20), "hold back from going" (as
1.7.58). *Mora* is regularly a pretext for staying the lover's departure (as 1.3.16). Each is negated here. Marathus holds himself aloof and keeps the *cupidus* waiting with feigned delay.
Tibullus mimics the deceitfulness of Marathus; ambiguous
words expound sham reasoning.

75– *nunc*: anaphora stresses the change from *quondam* (71).
76 *odit fastus*: cf. 69, *oderunt fastidia divi*. Both will live to
regret their disdain, the poet claims.

opposita: the verb is unique in Tibullus. More than the usual
ponere seram it conveys the idea of enmity and challenge.

dura: regular designation of door and mistress (see line 50
for the latter).

77– Final address to Pholoe. *Poena* waits for her, as the *deus ultor*
78 for Marathus, unless she renounces her haughtiness.

at te: a similar phrase is used in similar fashion at 1.3.83; 1.9.65,81. Cf. also Catullus 8.14, 19.

revocare diem: Tibullus means, of course, the day in which she could have listened to Marathus' pleas and the poet's advice but did not. The thought recalls the more generalized sentiments earlier in the poem on time's passage (41).

COMMENTARY 1. 9.

"Why did you seal our relationship by oaths to the gods if you meant only harm by secret deception?" Punishment comes, though late; yet spare the boy for this first offense. Tibullus had often warned: "Do not attempt to hide your indiscretions; the truth will out." The boy swore that he would not sell faith for grand riches and Tibullus was duped. Tibullus even helped him meet his girl, thinking he was still loved. May the wife of the boy's new friend be notoriously unfaithful and his sister's house open to all! And still the boy, daring to sell the poet's affections, sleeps beside this gout-ridden old man. He will be sorry when Tibullus, released from a deceitful love, dedicates a palm to Venus.

The poem, to be read closely with its predecessor, begins with a wondering question on a lover's impulses to deceive (defying legal, religious and emotional ties at once) and ends with the fixity of a dedication for a release from this deceit. Ironically it is a golden palm Tibullus offers (but will Venus change?) and gold—the glittering attraction of concrete wealth —is a chief means of corruption and seduction, taking away beauty (17), bringing evils (18), inciting perjury, enticing infidelity (69). In this lovers' world of affections bought and sold, dissembling motivations, and petty vendettas (*poena* appears at 4, 13, and 81), noble abstractions such as faithful allegiance are of little moment in the quest for shallower goals (and the surface itself constantly deceives). The poet resorts to curse, prayer, and command: may the rival's gifts turn to ashes and water; the boy will lose his charm and beauty; may the new girl be equally flighty; may the poet's former poetic effusions be victims of fire and water. And as the catalogue draws to its conclusion, the poet claims the symbol of a triumphant victor. It is the one assertive moment (to which the bulk of the poem regularly gives the lie), and in itself ironic because, in spite of his claims of heroism, he is only a released-sufferer instead of a doer.

1–2   Direct address to Marathus. The broken statement—question at the start, object in the middle, main verb only at the end— is particularly suitable to a context illustrating hurt and violence and initiating dualities such as treachery and credulity, hidden and revealed, which run through the poem.

    laesurus amores: taken by itself the phrase would seem to parallel such expressions as *laedere fidem*. It is apparently original with Tibullus and adopted by Ovid (*Her.* 7.59; *Met.* 4.191). But *miseros* makes *amores* personal as well as abstract. *Amores* then equals the love-sick poet, injured by the callous Marathus (a common use of the word from Plautus on).

    foedera dabas: we have frequent examples of *foedus dare* and *foedus violare* (for the first, e.g., Sallust *Iug.* 104.5, Livy 9.20.8, etc.; for the second, Cicero *Pro Sest.* 15, *De Rep.* 1.31). The heightened solemnity seems to make lovers' compacts of more than ordinary moment. (For *foedus* and other political vocabulary in parallel poetic contexts, see D. O. Ross, *Style and Tradition in Catullus* [Cambridge, Mass., 1969] 80–95.)

3–4   *a miser*: Marathus, rather, will suffer for causing difficulties for the poet. The interjection *a*, rare in Tibullus, raises the tone still further. Yet the stance can be only half serious, for it is a traditional posture of the elegiac lover.

    Poena: Greek Ποινή, goddess of punishment or revenge, often associated with the Furies. Her slow arrival is traditional (see E. R. Dodds on Eur. *Bacchae* 882 [Oxford, 1960], R. M. Ogilvie on Livy 3.56.7 [Oxford, 1965]). Alliteration may illustrate her stealthy advance. (Cf. lines 13 and 81).

5–6   No sooner is the advent of Poena announced than Tibullus prays against such an event.

    aequum est: the phrase is unique in Tibullus but fits with the continuing legalistic language as does *licere*. The poet serves as advocate before the gods.

    impune: an etymological pun closely allied with the preceding line.

    numina laedere: see 1–2 above and 1.3.79–80.

    semel: the most emphatic word is reserved for last. *Formosi* should be allowed one indiscreet oath. The transition is unusually yet deliberately harsh.

7–8   Without mentioning Marathus by name until line 11, the poet embarks on the theme that all men are greedy and therefore Marathus deserves forgiveness. The farmer and the trader are common enough *exempla* for this. The anaphora (*lucra petens* anticipating *lucra petituras*, 9) insists on the idea of greed while showing how diverse are its slaves. The quest for gain is burdensome and filled with uncertainty.

habili: "manageable," though the juxtaposition with *petens* could suggest other aspects of *habeo* in the background.

durum opus: the hardship of the farmer's task is proverbial.

urget: *urgeo* is rare as a transitive verb (e.g., Horace *Sat.* 2.7.6–7). In this context we would have more easily expected *terram* to have been the object. The heaviness induced by the repeated "u" sounds is noteworthy.

9– For the theme cf. 1.3.37–40. The suspense of the adventure is
10 illustrated in the gap between *petituras* and *rates* but pervasive assonance keeps the thought moving.

The chiastic order with which line 10 ends helps the contrast between *instabiles* and *certa*. The vessels are dependent on the elements. They are unstable, while the stars are sure and the seas obedient not to the sailors but to the winds. (For the instability of ship and sea cf. Vergil *Georg.* 4.195; Caesar *De B. G.* 4.23.5).

11– The repetition *muneribus munera* within the distich helps cor-
12 relate these lines with 7–10. Again, as sound abets logic, asso-nance is remarkable, linking *muneribus* with *puer* and *meus* with *deus*.

deus vertat: in such a curse the suppliant usually prays that the object in question take the form of earth and water. For ash instead of earth see Plautus *Rud.* 1257 (with F. Marx's note [repr., Amsterdam, 1959]); Horace *Epist.* 1.15.39. For *vertat* see Servius on Vergil *Ecl.* 9.6.

liquidas aquas: probably "running" here (as line 50 below) rather than clear (as at 1.5.76). In Vergil *Ecl.* 8.101 the witch commands that ashes be hurled *rivo fluenti*.

13– There are other penalties in store for Marathus and particu-
14 larly fitting, if we may judge from the preceding poem. He will be forced to accompany his *dives amator* on a journey which will result in his loss of *decus*.

ventis coma: the phrase is a second subject of *detrahet*. To balance *pulvis* we would expect *ventis* to be in the nominative. Its place is taken by *coma* which is one aspect of *decorem*.

horrida: as often the sense is multiple ("bristling," "dis-hevelled," "rough").

15– The burning of the sun is a commonplace of erotic literature,
16 sometimes as a trial of enduring love (as Horace *Carm.* 1.22. 21–22), occasionally as a *remedium amoris*. *Sole* goes with

each verb. *Facies* and *capilli* reflect *decorem* and *coma* of the preceding distich.

invalidos: equivalent of *teneros*. Tibullus reverses the Lucretian example of a road worn away by the passage of feet (1.315–16). Only *validi pedes* could have such an effect. Note the reversal of literal and metaphorical. *Via*, which we might expect to be literal, becomes personified and metaphorical ('journey"), an active force rather than something merely worn down. *Pedes*, on the contrary, while often in synecdoche for the whole body, is here literal.

via longa: see 1.1.25–26; 1.3.35–36.

17– Tibullus remembers a warning he once gave to Marathus.
18   *pollue*: the context demands that the verb be accepted in both its literal and tropic senses. *Forma* is both Marathus' specific *decus* and beauty in general, misled by gold. (For gold as a corruptor of morals, see 1.10.7, Horace *Carm.* 3.24.48–49, and the citations in TLL, *s.v.*, 1527.50ff.)

subesse: "lurking" under the glimmering exterior.

19– *captus*: "under the spell of," tempted by. Cf. line 11.
20   *violavit amorem*: cf. line 2 above and 1.3.81. The warning is put in general terms but Marathus has already been *captus* (11) and the poet is an example of *miseros amores* (1).

aspera Venus: at 1.6.2 Amor is *tristis et asper*. For *difficilis* see 1.8.27.

21– Traditional punishments of the slave which Tibullus would
22   rather endure (or, better, have endured) than find himself in the position he has just described. Alliteration pervades the distich.

ure caput: the brand of a slave (as also 1.5.5).

intorto verbere: cf. 1.5.3–5; 1.6.46; 1.8.5–6; 2.3.84.

23– *celandi*: cf. line 3.
24   *peccare*: stumble," then, erotically, "wander astray."

deus: the god is probably Amor, though we are reminded of the role of Poena in line 4 and may well be meant to think of Bacchus in anticipation of the following distich.

25– For further details on the proverbial *in vino veritas*, see Otto
26   *Sprichwörter*, 372; Gow on Theocritus *Idyl* 29.1.

ministro: the usually silent servant, in this case the pourer of wine at a banquet who, when he himself has drunk too much, betrays what he has overheard. The slave is for a moment "freed."

lene: the corruption has yet to be satisfactorily explained.

The most common alternation is to *lingua*, though *lene* as "smoothly" is not impossible.

libera: we would adverbialize in English, "freely." Much wine frees the tongue, making the slave indiscreet.

27–
28 On sleep as a betrayer of secrets, see Lucretius 4.1018–19; 5.1158–60. The connection between wine and sleep, i.e., between the two distichs, is reinforced by the anaphora, the parallels between *permisit, ederet*, and *emittere*, etc. The idea goes back in Latin at least as far as Ennius (*Ann.* 292V³). For a full discussion see Austin on Vergil *Aen.* 2.265.

domitos: cf. *libera* (26). *Domo*, though not unusual in connection with wine, is apparently given a special Tibullan turn when used with sleep.

emittere vocem: the phrase continues the notion of freeing and releasing. Cf. Lucretius 5.1088 and TLL, *s.v. emittere* (506.47 ff.).

facta tegenda loqui: equally an accomplishment of wine (see lines 23–26).

29–
30 Tibullus now looks with shame upon his former abject attitude as suppliant lover.

nunc pudet: echoed at line 48.

teneros pedes: see line 16.

procubuisse: cf. the use of *procumbo* at 1.2.85.

31–
32 Tibullus uses two traditional illustrations of affluence, money and property, to paraphrase Marathus' former perjuries.

divitis auri: *dives*, "enriching" (as 1.10.7, etc.).

pondere: a heavy weight rather than specifically a pound.

vendere fidem: an apparently unique idiom (see TLL, *s.v. fides*, 679.71 ff.), perhaps meant to reflect the formula bona fide in matters of trade, and certainly suitable to the present context which is dealing in the economics of emotions as well as money. See lines 1–2 above.

33–
34 The idiom *pretium dare*, in the negative sense of "pay a penalty," appears as early as Livius Andronicus *trag. frag.* 1. The present meaning of *pretium*, "reward," appears first in Ennius (*Ann.* 194V³) where the context is important.

Campania terra: Campania was proverbial in antiquity for its richness (as Propertius 3.5.5).

Falernus ager: an area in northern Campania bounded by the southern slopes of Mt. Massicus, the Volturnus River and the sea. It produced one of the most prized of Roman wines (cf. 2.1.27 and the ranking in Pliny *Hist. Nat.* 14.8.62).

35– The effect of Marathus' words could have been to perform the

36   impossible. "You would snatch from me the belief that . . ."
with almost the meaning "you would snatch the stars from
heaven . . . " The drawing down of heavenly bodies from the
sky and the halting of a river's course were regular accomplish-
ments of the ancient magician (see 1.2.45–46).

puras: "clear." (Some editors read *pronas*, an alteration of
Heyne).

eriperes: a rare example of *eripere* with an object clause
(cf. Ovid *Met.* 2.483).

37– At other moments (e.g., 1.6.9) the poet would not lay claim
38   to such naïveté. For the construction *fallere doctus*, see 1.7.20.

usque: "ever" (with *credulus* but affecting the whole sen-
tence).

39– *quid faciam*: the phrase stands in place of a regular apodosis
40   (*faciam* is deliberative subjunctive). Instead of *fores* we would
ordinarily expect *esses* in the protasis of a contrary-to-fact
condition. The disjointed effect is apparently purposeful.

in amore puellae: in this case "to be in love with" seems
more logical than "to be loved by," although the Latin will
bear either interpretation. The *puella* might but need not be
Pholoe of 1.8.

sit precor: cf. 1.6.56. *Levis*, "fickle." The repetition of *sit*
helps the litany of the curse.

41– Tibullus puts himself in the servile role of *lanternarius*, ac-
42   companying Marathus with torches before (or after) his
rendezvous.

o quotiens: cf. 1.3.19; 2.3.21–23.

verbis: the exchange between Marathus and his girl.

conscius: a frequent elegiac conceit (Propertius 1.12.2).

multa nocte: "late at night," a common expression in prose
(e.g., Cicero *Ad Att.* 7.4.2; *Ad Quint. Frat.* 2.8.2).

43– *venit*: "come to a meeting," in an erotic sense (as, e.g., Catullus
44   10.5).

munere nostro: Tibullus himself served as *coniugator amoris*.
This is the right kind of *munus* (cf. lines 11–12).

post fores: proof that the house of the girl is in question,
not that of Marathus (we would then have *ante fores*).

adoperta: with head covered, apparently so as to remain
inconspicuous to those within and without. (Tibullus' only
other use of the word describes death: 1.1.70; cf. also 1.3.30).

45– *interii*: *morior* and *pereo* are more common in descriptions of
46   the elegiac love-death. The unique parallel is Propertius 2.8.18.
With the exception of Ennius *frag. sc.* 202V[3] this is the only

use of *intereo* in a hyperbolic sense outside of comedy (with *miser*, Plautus *Bac.* 836, 853).

    stulte: here, at 65, and often elsewhere of the duped lover or friend passed over for a third party.

    confisus amari: the only instance of *confido* and a single dependent infinitive (it often has an accompanying *posse*).

    poteram: as at 1.8.55, "I could have been (but was not) . . ."

    laqueos: the lover's "snares" giving concrete expression to the previous notions of restraint.

    cautior: with the exception of Livy 24.32.3, the unique use of *cautus ad* until late Latin.

47–48 *attonita*: "thunderstruck," "crazed," "maddened"—the lover and poet are one.

    laudes: more often praises of epic deeds than lovers' endearments. The tone of the whole couplet is mock-elevated.

    nostri: equivalent to *mei* but, because of the nearness to *me*, perhaps with overtones of "my relationship with you."

    Pieridum: Muses of Pieria (see 1.4.61–62).

49–50 For the curse of fire and water see lines 11–12.

    rapida: "devouring" (from *rapio*), traditional epithet of both water and fire.

    liquida aqua: see line 12. *Deleat* means "blot out" in terms of a piece of writing, "annihilate" more generally. Since *liquidus* is also an epithet of fire, Tibullus proposes a double transfer.

51–52 *tu*: Marathus. The formula of renunciation has a quasi-religious intonation. Tibullus poses as the sacred poet who avoids all taint. The ideas and their expression echo lines 31–34; the hieratic stance was initiated in 47–48.

    formam vendere: cf. the sentiments of 17 ff. as well as of 31 ff.

    pretium grande: the reward that follows on *formam vendere*.

    plena manu: see 1.5.67–68. Here, taking rather than giving is in question.

53–54 *at te qui*: we turn from the female to the male rival. This and the subsequent imprecations parallel the similar curses Tibullus hurls against his rival for Delia's affections at 1.5.69 ff.

    rideat dolis: "may your wife with impunity make you a laughingstock by her continuing deceits." No *poena* comes to her, at least here. *Rideo* with an instrumental ablative is instanced only here.

55–56 *lassaverit*: *lassus* (Ovid *Am.* 1.5.25, 3.7.80, etc.) and *languidus* (e.g., Catullus 67.21; Propertius 1.3.38) are both erotic.

usu: sc. *Veneris* (as Ovid *Am.* 3.7.3, 49).

interposita veste: cf. Horace *Epode* 3.22; Propertius 2.15.6. Word order matches cubicular arrangement.

57– "Traces (of another man) on your bed." (See further Ogilvie
58 on Livy 1.58.7; Shackleton Bailey, *Propertiana*, 81f.)

pateat domus: "may your house be always free and accessible . . . . " There is no more essential Roman symbol for personal stability and family continuity than the *domus*.

cupidis: sc. *amatoribus*.

59– The proximity of *lasciva* might suggest that *pocula amoris* are
60 meant (as Plautus *Truc.* 43; Horace *Epode* 5.38), but the next distich looks specifically to her alcoholic propensities.

soror: "her (or possibly 'his') wanton sister." We are now dealing with the sister of the wife whose husband has seduced Marathus.

emeruisse: "use up," "exhaust." (Cf. the tired gallant leaving his mistress' house *invalidum referens emeritumque latus*, Ovid *Am.* 3.11.14.) *Emeriti* were veterans who had already completed military service. The parallel with *bibisse* is intentionally humorous.

61– *convivia*: here, as often, in a negative sense (cf. Cicero *Pro*
62 *Cael.* 39, 44; *Pro Mur.* 13). Though *perducere* and *producere* are attested, the phrase *convivia ducere* is unique in classical Latin (TLL 4.883.62).

Baccho: the case is ambiguous.

rota Luciferi: Lucifer, morning star, herald of the day, riding in his chariot, a role usually given to the sun.

provocet: "summons forth." The challenge of the night's bibulous encounters continues into the day.

63– *consumere noctem*: "use up" with love, expanding upon the
64 idea of drinking in the preceding couplet (cf. Propertius 1.3.37).

operum: sc. *Veneris*. Pichon (*De sermone amatorio, s.v.*) defines *vices* here as "venereae rei genera ac figurae."

disposuisse: "arrange," often in a temporal sequence, here with variety of manner implied as well.

65– *tua*: sc. *uxor*.
66 *perdidicit*: "learn through and through." Cf. the poet at line 37.

stultissime: a similar, unobservant (old) man is the butt of Catullus' jibes at 17.20f. See line 45 above.

corpus movet: the proximity of *tibi* suggests a strictly erotic reading.

67– *disponere*: a more common use than at line 64.

68   *tenues denso*: the antonymous relationship is reinforced by
the alliteration of *denso dente* (an uncommon poetic singular)
and the chiastic order centered on *pectere*. There is a (perhaps
bitterly) humorous reverberation of "te" in line 68. In the
preceding three lines we have had *tua, tu, tibi, tu, te*. Now she
figures in the "sound" of her actions.

69–   *ista facies*: sarcastic: "that (lovely) face of yours."
70   *persuadet*: only one other example is cited of *persuadeo* and
the subjunctive without *ut* (Sallust *Iug.* 35.2).

Tyrio apta sinu: "arrayed in Tyrian drapery," i.e., with her
palla dyed in expensive purple. *Sinus* is "lap" as well as the
garments that enfold it.

prodeat: "come forth" (from your room), for obvious reasons of display.

71–   *bella*: for the more usual *pulchra* (except in Catullus who has
72   *bellus* 14 times, *pulcher* 7). There are only three other instances in elegiac poetry (ps.-Tibullus 3.4.52; 3.19 (=4.13).
5; Ovid *Am.* 1.9.6). A "popular" word may be specifically
chosen here (See B. Axelson, *Unpoetische Wörter*, 35).

devoveat: "curse," so as to ruin. The formulaic quality of
remque domumque suggests a standard imprecation (see the
examples in Macrobius *Sat.* 3.9).

73–   *vitio*: a fault of character but with elegiac overtones of in-
74   fidelity (as Propertius 1.16.47, etc.).

corpora: poetic plural for singular (as 1.8.52).

foeda podagra: gout was abhorrent as much for the remedies
used in its cure as for the disfigurement it produced. The difference between *senis* and *puella* is mirrored in *foeda* and
culta which in this instance has overtones of irony.

75–   *accubuit*: instead of the more common *concubuit* (though the
76   erotic sense of *accumbo* is attested from Plautus on).

venerem iungere: the expression seems to originate with
Tibullus and is adopted twice by Ovid. It is a grammatical
ambiguity: "I could believe that he would mate with fierce
beasts" or "I could believe that he would join Venus with wild
beasts." The latter, secondary though it is, must not be dis-
missed. It re-establishes the magic power of Marathus, announced at 35–36. He could perform the impossible. The first
meaning hyperbolically equates the old man with a *trux caper*.
At Catullus 69.6 it is rumored of a certain Rufus that *valle sub
alarum trux habitare caper*. This may be the same person who,
at 71.2ff., suffers from gout as well. Marathus either creates

or is part of an *adynaton* which may be more realistic than first appears.

77– *meas, mea*: "which belong to me" (though "given by me" in
78 the past may also be meant). The word is awarded special prominence in the arrangement of the distich. *Vendere* and *ferre* suggest humor as much as seriousness.

   vendere: see lines 32, 51.

   demens: striking epithet for one so calculating.

   ferre: a heavy verb when only *oscula* are involved.

79– *tum flebis*: conventional announcement (no doubt wishful
80 thinking on the poet's part) of the reversal of fortune.

   vinctum: for the image see 1.1.55; 2.4.3–4.

   geret regna: "hold sway," a poetic variation of such political phrases as *gerere rempublicam, magistratum*, etc. The juxtaposition *regno regna* brings out the distinction in meaning, "kingdom" and "rule," that lurks in the repetition.

81– The dedication of a palm, earned in a triumph or from a vic-
82 tory in a contest, is well attested. (On the origin of the award see Livy 10.47; Isidorus *Orig.* 18.2.4; W. H. Henzen, *Acta Fratrum Arvalium*, 36–39.)

   tua poena: cf. line 13 (and, to a degree, 4).

   Venerique merenti: the phrase parallels *bene merenti* (or *merentissimo, -ae*) on votive inscriptions.

   fixa: "attached" to the temple wall.

83– The votive inscription, like the epitaph, is a motif in elegy
84 (e.g., Propertius 2.14.27–28), rescue from the trials of love being the spiritual (elegiac) equivalent of delivery from shipwreck or other disaster. The theme is exploited by Horace in *Carm.* 1.5 and 3.26.

   tibi: assonance connects Venus and her poet.

   resolutus: the pivotal word of line 83 (as *dea* of 84), contrasting with *vinctum* (79).

   grata sis mente: "be kindly disposed." It is typical of Tibullus that the end of the Marathus affair is put in terms of future and subjunctive.

COMMENTARY 1. 10.

The inventor of the sword was himself wild and iron, bestial and with a metal heart. He fathered slaughter and war and shortened the road to death. No, we are at fault, turning against ourselves what was meant as protection against animals. Now

Tibullus is drawn to war. His humble household gods will save
him. Yet, why provoke death; the underworld is unlovely.
Better to grow old recalling the past, as country dweller with
wife and children. May Peace rule the fields. After country
festivals the farmer battles lovingly with his wife. The violent
lover deserves a military life. May nourishing Peace come and
make the country fruitful.

The many parallels in idea and expression with poem 1 bring
the book full circle. Tibullus, about to be dragged unwillingly
to war, ponders two inventors—the first swordmaker, who
unknowingly created war, and Peace, who discovered and
fosters agriculture. The litany (or rather invocation, for her
presence, though crucial, is never assumed) to Peace is only
a small part of a total prospect of ideal country living which
revolves around humble simplicity (and not ambition after
gold), continuity of tradition, religious celebrations, and
country festivals as part of a life centered on the soil. It is a
time when mild drunkenness is not a retreat from unbearable
reality. There are "battles" but these are only lovers' squabbles
and even they are of special importance, for a writer of elegies
at least, because they are concerned with the family, that touchstone against which the discontinuities, frictions, and infidel-
ities of an elegiac love are measured. Tibullus alludes not only
to the farmer-shepherd but repeatedly to the latter's son,
daughter, and wife. War brings with it untempered violence,
hardness, darkness, and death's silence, all of which man by his
greed has fostered. True there is amatory violence even in a
rustic life but, as part of his wish for an apolitical and peaceful
existence, Tibullus shows such activity as symptomatic of
fertility and not the deadly divisiveness of war against which
this poem offers a striking homily.

1–2   *quis*: "What kind of man was he who . . ."

primus: a common Augustan theme (see 1.7.20), preparing
the reader for the idea of the golden age.

protulit: the primary meaning is "invent" but in conjunction
with *enses* it reflects such military technical phrases as *proferre
signa, arma, castra*. The expression *proferre enses* is unique in
Latin (Tibullus may be remembering Lucretius 5.1293:
minutatim processit ferreus ensis).

ferus et vere ferreus: the Latin fondness for alliteration and
assonance is nowhere better illustrated than in this poem. The
punning on *ferus . . . ferreus* is as early as Ennius (*Ann.* 183–

4V³; also Cicero *Ad Quint. Frat.* 1.3.3). *Ferreus* is connected with the Homeric σιδήρεος but it is equally likely that such a savage is as "iron" as the weapon he invented.

3–4   Repetitions are again as striking as in the first couplet.

via mortis: cf. 1.3.50 (*leti mille viae*) and the contrasting *longa via* (1.1.26; 1.9.16).

dirae: originally "ill-omened," here transferred to the results of such portents, "dreadful" death.

5–6   *An* introduces a question in which an element of doubt is present. The asyndeton distinguishes between *ille* and *nos*. The original inventor of the sword might well have had a positive purpose in mind. It is we who have turned his idea to a bad purpose. The deceptive balance between *ad mala nostra* and *in saevas feras* stresses the difference.

The prominence of liquids in line 5 suggests a softening of the poet's attitude.

7–8   *divitis auri*: see 1.9.31. Note the assonance leading from *divitis* to *vitium*. That the discovery of gold corrupted man's primal innocence was held by one ancient school of thought (e.g., Lucretius 5.1423f.)

faginus scyphus. Beechwood objects are traditionally associated with the simpler life of the past or frugality in the present (Ovid *Fast.* 5.522; Pliny *Hist. Nat.* 16.185.)

9–   *dux gregis*: the shepherd or perhaps (humorously) the ram.
10   *varias oves*: sheep of different colors (as, e.g., Vergil *Georg.* 3.387 ff.). The flock is special because its master can sleep without its wandering off or any harm coming to him—a virtue of the golden age or at least of a quasi-pastoral aloofness (as 1.1.48).

securus: cf. 1.1.48.

11–   The distich is the apodosis of a contrary-to-fact condition
12   whose protasis is only implied ("if I had been alive, then . . ."). *Foret*, replacing the more usual *esset*, makes the opposition to present as well as past.

vulgi: the crux has not yet been successfully solved. *Vulgi*, with the meaning "people," goes happily with neither *vita* nor *arma*, though the latter has been cogently defended. But if *vulgus* has the meaning "herd" (as in Vergil *Georg.* 3.469), the phrase is simply a metonymy for "country living." Since one could expect an adjective to balance *tristia*, the conjecture *dulcis* has merit.

tristia arma: cf. lines 49–50.

corde micante: "with quivering heart."

13– *trahor*: the second vowel is lengthened arbitrarily before the
14   caesura. The verb suggests the poet's unwilling acquiescence
     to his ill fortune while at the same time implying Messalla's
     power. The favorite Tibullan contrast between *tunc* and *nunc*
     is nowhere more pronounced than in this poem.

     quis: unusual for *aliquis*, especially with a subsequent ap-
     positive. It results from the rare appearance of *forsitan* with
     a present indicative, adding an element of supposition to the
     sentence.

     hostis: a present-day, specific instance of the initial *primus
     ille* (1–2).

15– *patrii Lares*: see 1.1.20. The only uses of *patrius* in Tibullus
16   (1.3.33, 2.1.17, and here) are in connection with house, coun-
     tryside, and their gods.

     aluistis: nourishing by the gods is a time-hallowed religious
     notion (see commentators on Lucretius 1.2).

     cursarem: in place of *curro*, depicts the constant running of
     the child back and forth in front of the *lararium*.

     tener ante pedes: a nice variation on the usual *teneri pedes*
     (1.7.46; 1.9.30).

17– *prisco e stipite*: the earliest statues were made of wood or
18   terra cotta, another aspect of Tibullus' alleged avowal of prim-
     itive simplicity. Cf. 1.1.11. *Prisco*: best to paraphrase, "in time
     past."

     incoluistis: "give honor to" by dwelling in.

     veteris avi: "my forefather of old."

19– *tum*: in time past before luxury had taught men to break their
20   trust.

     tenuere fidem: Cicero uses the expression at *Phil.* 12.27.
     Propertius 1.18.4 is the only other instance in elegy.

     paupere cultu: cf. 1.1.19, 37. The echo of *incoluistis* (18)
     strengthens the idea that men and gods then cooperated with
     mutual benefit.

     exigua aede: the humble *lararium*.

21– *placatus*: participle: "appeased" through sacrifice.
22   *uvam*: the Ambrosianus reads *uva* (which would be instru-
     mental ablative; accusative is more direct).

     spicea serta: garlands formed from ears of grain (1.1.15–16).

23– *voti compos*: "having been granted his prayer." Horace (*Ars
24   Poet.* 76) summarizes one of the two central subjects for the
     elegiac couplet in general as *voti sententia compos*.

     liba: sacrificial cakes, as 1.7.54.

     purum favum: honey, praised in antiquity for its purity and

salubrious effects, is common in offerings. Sound carefully
links the girl and her gift.

25– A return to the present and the theme of lines 13 ff. On the
26   Lares as apotropaic divinities (the *agri custodes* of 1.1.19), see
the opening of the *Carmen Arvale*, part of a boundary ceremony.

At least one distich must be missing between lines 25 and
26 which resumes with the offerings Tibullus will make upon
safe return. On the sacrifice of a pig or sow to the Lares, cf.
Plautus *Rud.* 1208; Horace *Carm.* 3.23.4.

hara: hogsty.

27– *hanc*: the antecedent remains unclear and perhaps hidden in the
28   lacuna, though either *puella* or *hostia* is possible.

pura cum veste: an essential feature of ritual properly performed. The phrase recurs at 2.1.13. Cf. *purum* (24).

sequar: "following" and "binding" have less happy connotations in the more erotic elegies.

canistra: baskets made from reed which carried the appoint-
ments of the ceremony. Horace (*Carm.* 3.23.16) speaks of
crowning the image of the Lares specifically with myrtle,
though a myrtle wreath was festal on a variety of occasions.

29– *sic*: in the manner of one whose symbol is the myrtle of Venus,
30   offering peaceful sacrifice rather than boasting of bravery *in
armis*.

31– Unlike Ovid's more elaborate description of a similar scene
32   (*Her.* 1.31 ff.), the soldier tells his tale while the poet, by contrast, drinks and listens. Cf. 1.6.20.

dicere facta: detailing exploits of more than ordinary importance.

pingere castra: a humorous parody of *ponere castra*.

33– The silent approach of death (or its companions, old age, ven-
34   geance, sleep) was a picture of which Tibullus was especially
fond.

atram mortem: cf. 1.3.4, 5.

tacito pede: cf. 1.9.4; 2.1.90.

clam: secrecy here depends on both hearing and seeing
nothing.

35– *non seges est*: the sentiment suits the poet's present mood of
36   devotion to the quiet life on the land and complements his
description of the Elysian fields at 1.3.61.

infra: a unique usage in Latin corresponding to the Greek
κάτω.

audax Cerberus: the epithet is unique for Cerberus though regular for dogs.

navita turpis: Charon, ferryman of the Styx. Again the epithet is unique but we gain some feeling for Tibullus' choice by reading Vergil *Aen.* 6.298 ff. *Turpis* applies to character as well as looks.

37– The dead, wandering in the underworld, usually carry with
38 them marks of the way they met death and sometimes display traces of the funeral's effects.

percussis genis: cf. line 55 below and 1.1.68. For other instances of cheeks similarly marred by blows see TLL *s.v. gena*, 1764.45 ff.; 1766.34 ff.

errat: cf. Dido in Vergil's underworld (*Aen.* 6.451).

obscuros lacus: "shadowy ponds." (Cf. Vergil *Aen.* 2.135; Ovid *Ars Amat.* 3.322).

pallida turba: the epithet is traditional for the shades though used only once of death itself (Horace *Carm.* 1.4.13). Cf. 1.3.70.

39– *laudandus*: deserving the *laudes* of a hero.
40 *hic*: "this man here" who lives my sort of life. Rarely short, as here.

prole parata: "with children (already) produced" as a help for old age. (Cf. the poet's prayer for Messalla at 1.7.55–56).

pigra senecta: "old age which makes one slow" (and sluggish). Cf. 1.2.31.

41– Family affection as much as division of labor is the theme of
42 these lines (cf. 23–24 above and Horace *Epode* 2.39ff.).

comparat: the close connection with *parata* (39) stresses her foresight.

43– *candescere*: aside from a related phrase in Propertius (2.18.5),
44 this is the only use until Claudian of *candesco* in connection with old age in Latin and unique in the sense of "grow white." The regular meaning, "glisten," "glow," would suggest more strength than senility here. Line 43 is the single example in elegy of triple alliteration of two letters in one line.

temporis prisci facta: unlike the *facta* of line 31, these are the courageous deeds of those who have lived on the land in times past. *Priscus*, by contrast with *senem*, has a tone of hoary venerability.

45– A eulogy of Pax who possesses many of the qualities of Osiris
46 at 1.7.29–38 and the *ruris dei* in 2.1.37–42. Cf. H. Pillinger, "Tibullus 1.10 and Lucretius," *CJ* 66 (1971), 204–208.

arva colat: cherishes and tends.

candida: though the adjective often describes the radiance and hence goodness of the gods (see Servius on Vergil *Ecl.* 5.56), it must look as well to the goddess' white robe (68).

primum: contrast the thought and mood of line 1.

47– *aluit*: cf. lines 15 and 67, *Pax alma.*
48 *sucos uvae*: for the making of wine, no doubt.

condidit: in anticipation of the vintage later to be stored.

49– Common topics in the aretology of Peace (Horace *Sat.*
50 2.1.43 f.; Ovid *Fast.* 4.928 ff.)

tristia arma: cf. lines 11–12.

in tenebris: by contrast with *nitent. Situs* is rust from lack of use.

51– Though the change is somewhat abrupt, there need not neces-
52 sarily be anything missing between lines 50 and 51 if one men-
tally supplies *pace*, "in times of peace . . . "

luco: Servius (on Vergil *Aen.* 1.310) defines *lucus* as "arbo-rum multitudo cum religione." There are no temples in Ti-bullus' rustic world. Wagons, nothing luxurious, are the means of transportation.

male sobrius: "far from sober."

53– Unlike true *proelia* (3 ff.) or *bella* (13), these "wars" are
54 permissible, possible only in a time of peace (cf. 1.1.73 ff.)

bella calent: an unparalleled phrase, focusing several meta-phors, each applicable to the context, on a given word. *Caleo* can be used of the fury of battle but is equally at home in description of the warming effects of wine or love. These re-sults of love's battles are commonplace.

55– The conqueror in love's battles later regrets his strength (cf.
56 the sobering lover at 2.5.101–104).

subtusa: "somewhat bruised" (from *tundo*).

57– *Lascivus Amor* takes the posture of judge between two dis-
58 putants, remaining unmoved and unmoving. True to character he is *lascivus* while urging his devotees on, *lentus* once their anger is aroused (see 1.4.81). Amor is designated *lascivus* elsewhere only by Ovid (*Am.* 3.1.43) though Horace speaks of *lascivos amores* (*Carm.* 2.11.7).

59– For the proverbial connection between iron and stone in such
60 a context see 1.1.63–64. (Tibullus turns the proverb to apply to a maddened rather than an unfeeling lover.) The Titans, who sought to dethrone the Olympian gods, became proverbial for impiety. Compare the use of *ferreus* at line 2.

61– *rescindere vestem*: cf. Propertius 2.5.21 and the parallels cited
62 by P. J. Enk. (F. Solmsen, *Philologus* 105 [1961], 273–76,

proposes that the Propertius passage is a disapproving reference
to these lines of Tibullus.) *Tenuem* mitigates the violence of
rescindere.

63– *lacrimas movisse*: "cause tears to flow."

64   *quater ille beatus*: the mock solemnity of the remark may be
illustrated by comparing the serious contexts in which kindred
phrases appear (e.g., Homer *Od.* 5.306; Vergil *Aen.* 1.94).
Such a man need resort to nothing more violent than a display
of wrath to achieve his ends.

65– *manibus*: the instruments of physical violence.

66   *scutumque sudemque*: though the alliteration suggests a popular phrase, the only parallel is Juvenal *Sat.* 6.248.

    miti Venere: cf. 2.3.76.

67– The description follows closely the representations of Ceres-

68 Demeter-Terra Mater with whom Pax is regularly associated
(see 1.1.15–16, 2.1.4, and Bömer on Ovid *Fast.* 4.407 [Heidel-
berg, 1957–58]). The regular symbol of Pax was the caduceus
(see S. Weinstock, "Pax and the Ara Pacis," *JRS* 50 [1960],
44) though Tibullus' point does not depend on iconography.

COMMENTARY 2. 1.

The setting is a traditional country festival (which of several possibilities in the Roman calendar is left uncertain, but
the Ambarvalia, celebrated on May 29, is a logical candidate).
It is a ceremony of prayer and purification for crops, animals,
and farmers. Let each person attending be of good intent. Let
evil, treachery, and fear be absent. The sacrifice has proved
propitious: bring out wine and praise Messalla, the poet's inspiration as he hymns the countryside and its gods. They taught
men to build houses, to plough, graft trees, to garden, and make
wine. The ploughman invented song and dramatic play when
a goat was sacrificed to Bacchus (Dionysus). Desire, too, was
born in the country, but he should come to the festival without
his weapons. Sing the god and make private prayers. Night
comes, and after night follow sleep and dark dreams.

A superb evocation of a ceremonial day, from *lux* to *nox*,
from commanding prayer, as the rite commences, to dreams
coming after nightfall. Ordinary labor is suspended, and even
military Messalla and militant Love are drawn into an idealized
moment of hope that earth's own great cycle will renew itself.
Tibullus, in his poetry, structures ritual, and ritual gives order
to existence. The traditional stabilities of religion are comple-

mented by reference to wine, song, and dance which also permit (momentary) retreat from the cares of life and love. Religious silence leads to the noise of celebration, which in turn yields before a still more universal, unifying silence of darkness and dream. Ritual provides a fleeting escape; night suggests something more final. Cycle and stability, centered around life, love, and death and seen now as dream, now as reality, are combined.

1–2 The reader is drawn immediately into the country rite and festival, with the poet as priest. (On the re-creation of ceremony in Latin literature see Williams, *Tradition and Originality in Roman Poetry*, esp. 211–12.)

faveat: "let him be well disposed." The traditional formula is *favete linguis*, or *favete vocibus*. Cf. 2.2.2, Horace *Carm.* 3.1.2, etc.

lustramus: perform purifying, "releasing" sacrifice, which would here include walking the boundaries.

ritus . . . traditus: proper ritual adheres to inherited formulae and Tibullus was particularly conscious of tradition.

3–4 Bacchus and Ceres, divinities of wine and grain, should preside over or receive offerings at any agricultural ritual (cf., e.g., Vergil *Ecl.* 5.79, *Georg.* 1.7). The grape and grain-spike are their appropriate accoutrements while horns symbolize Bacchus' masculine strength and fertility. Their presence—the union of masculine and feminine givers of life's staples—would assure the renewal of nature which the ritual (and therefore the poem) solicits. (For the connection of Ceres with the old Italic nature-god Liber, who became identified with Dionysus-Bacchus, see A. S. Pease on Cicero *De Nat. Deor.* 2.62 [Cambridge, Mass., 1955–58]; Lucretius 4.1168).

spicis: cf. 1.1.16; 1.10.22.

5–6 All work ceases on a festal day.

luce sacra: the reason for this replacement of *festo die* will be apparent at the poem's conclusion.

requiescat . . . requiescat: the iteration stresses the difference between the (personified) *humus* and *arator*, the thing worked and the worker, created and creator, feminine and masculine. *Grave opus*, that which unites *humus* and *arator*, has two senses. The work is hard, yet heavy also because the plough presses into the earth (juxtaposition makes clear the oxymoron between *grave* and *suspenso*).

7–8 Oxen, as sacred to Ceres, would be freed from their yokes on

the Ambarvalia (Varro *De Re Rust.* 2.5.4). They are still decorated in similar manner in modern Italy on certain feast days.

praesepia: "pens" or "mangers," with implications of bounty
in either case, the one of livestock, the other of fodder.

plena: "full" (for the festival) but also with the idea of
fertility (cf. 21 and 57 below; 1.10.26).

9–   The real "work" consists in offering proper sacrifice to the
10   gods. No woman is to indulge in spinning any more than a man
in ploughing. The occupation was a symbol of chastity, but the
poet's (momentary) negativity—any such task is wrong on a
day of rest—is conveyed by *imposuisse* and *audeat*.

lanificam: "wool-working" (apparently a coinage of Tibullus).

11–   Such celibate restrictions are common (see 1.3.26). Offenders
12   against ritual are often commanded away in such fashion (as
Callimachus *Hym.* 2.2; Vergil *Aen.* 6.258). Ironically, the goddess of love (and the ordinary posture of the erotic elegist) have
no part in this re-creative ceremony.

procul: regular religious exhortation (see commentators on
Vergil *Aen.* 6.258).

13–   *pura cum veste*: see 1.10.27–28.
14   *manibus puris*: water, usually running, would cleanse the
hands of the sacrificants (see also 1.3.25).

15–   The sacrificial lamb makes its way to the gleaming altars with
16   the crowd following. The victim was usually led by a loose
rope with no knots but *eat* implies a certain spontaneity.

olea: an olive crown also adorned the priests of the Marsi
(Vergil *Aen.* 7.751) and the *ministri* of those celebrating a
triumph (cf. Festus 192M). The connection of rich oil production with a fruitful countryside is of paramount importance
here.

candida: literal, because dressed in white; metaphorical, because white is the color of purity and good fortune.

17–   The prayer of the priest-poet commences.
18   *di patrii*: the native gods, including Bacchus, Ceres, and,
especially here, the Lares as boundary gods (see 1.1.19–20 and
1.10.15–16).

purgamus . . . purgamus: repetition (and constant alliteration) as part of ritual formalism.

19–   The implicit power of crops conveyed through personification.
20   *eludat*: the metaphor comes from gaming, in particular gladi-
atorial contests (cf. also Vergil *Georg.* 1.225–26). Nature

plays a game with man (as the crop with its harvest) and could well deceive. Against the violence of the wolf the lamb in contest has no chance (a prayer that the impossible happen in this perfected landscape). Absence of fear in such a case is an *adynaton*, an "impossibility," presaging a golden age (cf. Vergil *Ecl.* 4.22–25).

21–
22 *nitidus*: "shining" with health and cleaned up, trim for the festivities.

ingeret ligna: if the festival in question is the Ambarvalia, celebrated in May, the hearth would be outdoors, if earlier, possibly indoors (certainly the words recall Horace's command to dispel the winter chill *ligna super foco / large reponens, Carm.* 1.9.5–6).

23–
24 In the amusements following the ceremony the crowd of slaves will build playhouses. Horace lists such a pastime among childhood games (*Sat.* 2.3.247). The usual meaning of *virga* militates against the interpretation that the *casae* were shelters against the sun. The slaves, like the ploughmen and animals, are also at leisure.

saturi coloni: the successful tenant-farmer.

ante: "in front of" the hearth (with *exstruet*, not *casas*).

25–
26 The *fibra*, the part of the liver under the priest's scrutiny (see 1.8.3–4), serves as "messenger" that the gods are "calm."

eventura precor: the main verb is a favorite of Tibullus, suggesting, secondarily, his insecurity about his deepest desires (especially when juxtaposed, as here, with a future participle).

27–
28 *fumosos Falernos*: sc. *cados* from 28. Wine casks and their contents, exterior and interior, were smoked in a *fumarium* (Columella *De Re Rust.* 1.6.19 f.; Horace *Carm.* 3.8.11–12, etc,). The older the better (here the consul of the vintage year is left vague). The poet is both priest and *magister bibendi*.

proferte: "bring forth" from smoking or storage room.

Chio cado: Horace (*Sat.* 1.10.24) testifies that the stronger Campanian wine was often mixed with the smoother Greek.

solvite vincla: *vincla* here are the pitch seals of the cask. (The phrase is used at line 7 of oxen released from their yokes. Wine when opened has its own power to release.)

29–
30 *vina diem celebrent*: the personification of *vina* and the unusual phraseology (we expect something like *vino diem celebrent*) may illustrate the happily disordering and commanding effect of wine already at work. (The hortatory subjunctive continues the poet's directive role.)

156 TIBULLUS: *A Commentary*

festa luce: the change from *luce sacra* (5) further suggests that the serious solemnity of ritual is giving way to less inhibiting concerns.

madere: "drip" with wine. (For the sentiment cf. 1.10.51–52).

31– Messalla is remembered even in his absence. The phrase *bene*
32 *Messallam* would be completed by *valere iubeo*. Both Horace (*Carm.* 4.5.29 ff.) and Ovid (*Fast.* 2.637–38) offer similar compliments to Augustus. Messalla's good health is crucial for the country and its inhabitants, his "divinity" more imminent than that of Ceres or Bacchus, though he is momentarily away. Hence, unlike the tone of *faveat* (1), the emphasis is on sound in the passage as Messalla's name rings out.

ad pocula: a series of toasts. The interplay of singular and plural in the couplet implies that each person honors Messalla many times over.

33– Messalla's triumph over the peoples of Aquitania is the initial
34 subject of 1.7.

celeber: this may be the first instance of *celeber* as *clarus* in Latin but the festive joy of *celebrent* (29) still rings in the reader's ears. Because of *triumphis* (generic but still conveying the continuous excitement of one moment), there are overtones of *celeber* as *frequentatus*. (See line 83 below and, e.g., Horace *Carm.* 2.12.20, in each case an attribute of divinity.)

intonsis avis: a common poetic attribute of early Romans, usually to stress primitive simplicity and a hardy courage. Messalla's prowess guarantees him a fitting place in a rite *a prisco traditus avo*.

35– Messalla is given the further compliment of serving as the poet's
36 Muse. Cf. Vergil's address to Calliope (*Aen.* 9.525) or Ovid's appeal to more general divinities (*Met.* 1.2–3). In this instance the "muse" is both alive and personally beloved. The abrupt change from *mihi* to *nostro* is perhaps a further acknowledgment of Messalla's participation. Propertius offers Maecenas a similar compliment in 3.9.

redditur gratia: the expression is rare in Latin, used before Tibullus only by Sallust (*Iug.* 110.4).

agricolis: the rare adjectival sense (see 1.1.14).

37– A new litany or, better, aretology commences as Tibullus takes
38 up one of his favorite themes, the growth of civilization. *His magistris* is tantamount to saying that the gods of the countryside were the initial educators of mankind. Early life was al-

ready a battle for survival. Its chief enemy to be routed was hunger.

vita: powerful as subject.

desuevit: "become unaccustomed to."

querna glande: since the oak requires no cultivation, the acorn was among the most primitive foods. Cf. 2.3.72–73 and, as a stage in the development of civilization, Lucretius 5.939, 1416; Vergil *Georg.* 1.147ff., etc.

39– The progress of mankind from helpless dependent on nature's
40 bounty to worker on his own behalf is epitomized in the change from cave to house (again cf. Lucretius 5.956, 1011). The narrowness of the house is conveyed by use of the diminutive of *tignum* as the matter of construction. The early use of *frons* as cover for beams in primitive society is noted by Vitruvius (2.1.3). If only for practical reasons, the leafage must be fresh.

41– Two further interconnected stages in man's development, the
42 yoking of bulls and the attachment of wheels to the wain. Neither has any connection with the golden age (see 1.3.41) which, at least to Tibullus as he writes this poem, did not any more exist in the past than it does now (cf. line 7 above). The *servitium* of the bulls is transferred to the wheel through the word *supposuisse*, one of the regular verbs in Latin for submission to a yoke or pole.

43– Wild ways give place to the development of planting and irri-
44 gation. Anaphora, perhaps to re-create the effect of ritual, is prominent in these couplets.

tum: continuing the time-scheme of lines 39–42 rather than introducing a change.

consita: sc. *est.*

45– After the uses of water, the development of wine is a logical
46 step in civilization's progress. The use of the singular (personified) *uva* and the transfer of *pressos* from *uva* to the less logical *liquores* combine the specific event with the generic idea of history. (Cf. also 1.7. 35–36).

aurea uva: the yellow grape. (Is *aurea* used because the age was "golden"?)

securo: active: "taking away care."

47– From georgic discoveries to the regular creative processes of
48 the countryside; back to the theme of 37.

calidi sideris: the Dog Star whose appearance portended the height of the summer's heat (see 1.1.27–28).

deponit comas: the shearing of earth's "hair"—the *flava*

Ceres of 1.1.15—at the summer harvest. *Depono* in this sense
is rare in Latin (the same phrase is used by Martial, 5.48.6).
Less literally it echoes the idea of birth in *ferunt* (the use is
paralleled at Catullus 34.8; Phaedrus 1.18.5, 19.4). *Coma* is
regularly used in Latin for tree leaves but the present applica-
tion to grain is apparently unique. It intensifies the personification.

49– The chronological progress of the seasons, unlike the preced-
50   ing forward march of civilization, is backward, probably to
avoid any suggestion of deterioration. Lines 45–46 depict the
autumn vintage, 47–48, midsummer harvest, and 49–50, bees
at work in the spring.

flores: apparently synonymous with *dulci melle*. Unlike the
majority of ancient writers on bees, Tibullus seems to realize
that nectar was extracted from flowers.

verno alveo: The hive expanding during the springtime.

51– Out of rustic preoccupations developed song and then drama.
52   The farmer, tired from ploughing, first sang in rhythm, though
his words were still uncouth. (Cf. Lucretius' account of the development of song at 5.1379ff.)

certo pede: "with sure foot," i.e., rhythm. Beat, a purely
physical gesture, came before exact verbalizing.

53– *satur*: after a good meal. Cf. lines 23 and 51.
54   *arenti carmen*: the phraseology is reminiscent of Vergil *Ecl.*
1.2 and 10.51 and especially of the lines alluding to the
Eclogues which Donatus claims once opened the *Aeneid*:

ille ego qui quondam gracili modulatus avena
carmen . . .

The present participle keeps vivid the moment of discovery.

diceret: "sing" (perhaps hymns to the gods whose statues he
has adorned).

55– An allusion to the primitive origins of drama.
56   *minio suffusus rubenti*: "poured over with cinnabar." This
is usually taken to mean that at the earliest stages of dramatic
performance the actors used paint for makeup instead of wearing masks. Horace (*Ars Poet.* 277) tells us that those who
acted the pieces of Thespis, "discoverer of the tragic muse,"
were *peruncti faecibus ora*. (Hence the occasional equation
of comedy and τρυγωδία, from τρύξ, wine lees. See commentators on Aristophanes *Ach.* 499–500 and, on the whole subject,
G. E. Duckworth, *The Nature of Roman Comedy*, 92–94.)

It is more likely that the farmer simply painted himself red
(hence *suffusus*, strange word for the face alone), as part of

a celebration. Pan, at Vergil *Ecl.* 10.27, is *minio rubentem* and triumphing Roman generals were painted vermilion (Pliny *Hist. Nat.* 33.111). Cf. also Priapus at 1.1.17.

duxit choros: "led the choral dances." The same phrase is used by Horace of Venus (*Carm.* 1.4.5) and of Gratia (*Carm.* 4.7.6), both spring songs. In the time of Augustus seven days preceding and including the Cerealia (April 19) were devoted to *ludi scaenici* (Duckworth, *Roman Comedy*, 77; L. R. Taylor, "The Opportunities for Dramatic Performances in the Time of Terence and Plautus," *TAPA* 68 [1937] 286–91).

57– The offering of a goat to Bacchus in connection with dramatic
58   performances complements the popular ancient etymology of tragedy from τράγος, goat (see, e.g., Horace *Ars Poet.* 220). Though the text is in question (for *curtas* the Ambrosianus reads *hyrcus*), the sacrifice is certainly part of a fertility rite.

memorabile: noteworthy in itself and because connected with an important event.

59– Tibullus proves again that he has no particular festival in mind.
60   The chief festal day for the Lares, the Compitalia for the Lares of the Crossroads, took place between December 17 and January 5. This does not harmonize, at least literally, with *verno flore*. The youth would probably have made his own prayerful offering to his *Lar familiaris*. (Cf. 1.3.34, where the poet offers monthly homage).

antiquis Laribus: Tibullus' response to the richness of many Roman traditions is readily apparent throughout the poem. Compare the contexts of 1.3.34 and 1.7.58.

imposuit: cf. line 10 and the common context of spinning.

61– From ritual to work again, this time the feminine labor of
62   spinning, to balance the farmer's ploughing. The anaphora of *rure* (cf. 47–49) and the change from *puer* to *puellis* link the two couplets. The alteration of tone may already be inherent in the verb *imposuit*. *Molle vellus* is close enough to *teneris puellis* to imply that *cura* had not yet touched the lives of the latter.

63– *femineus labor*: to remind us that women work as well as men
64   (and that their labors were also interrupted by the country festival). Cf. lines 9–10.

pensa colusque: a type of hendiadys: the "weighted" wool on the distaff.

fusus . . . opus: "the spindle that turns its work with pressure from the thumb."

65– From spinning to weaving. Minerva was the patroness of all

66   artisans and craftsmen. The weaver, like the farmer, sings as she goes about her work, in the tradition of Homer's Circe. Her own tools supply a musical accompaniment.

operata Minervae: offering service to Minerva, i.e., devoting herself to spinning.

tela: *telae* were weights which held the strings of the warp straight down.

appulso latere: both the text of *appulso* and the meaning of *latere* are in doubt. *Appulso* is regularly altered to *applauso* as if a word more specifically associated with sound were necessary in the context. But at 1.7.42 we find *crura pulsa sonent*. If *latere* is considered from *latus*, the weights strike her flank as she weaves; if from *later*, they must be considered made of baked clay. The side of the loom is another possibility.

67– The sentiment, useful as a poetic transition, is reiterated in
68   the *Pervigilium Veneris* (76ff.).

indomitas equas: mares were traditionally associated with sexual promiscuity (see on 2.4.58, and commentators on Vergil *Georg.* 3.266; Horace *Carm.* 1.25.13ff.). The hierarchy *agros, armenta, equas* is important in building up the tension from inanimate to highly emotional and *ipse Cupido* frames the whole—fields and flocks.

69– Cupido, as a fertility god of the countryside, can also be listed
70   among those who were initiators of mankind's development. *Primum* refers both to Cupid himself and to such moments as *primum* (39) and *primi* (41) describe. The word is a motif of the poem (51, 53, 56, and 59 also). The change from *indocto* to *doctas* shows him to be self-taught (cf. *docuere*, 39, and *docuisse*, 41). His virtuosity is reflected in the change from *indomitas* (68) to *perdomuisse* (72).

se exercuit: "practiced."

ei mihi: the poet's own sudden exclamation of involvement marks the transition from *illic* to *nunc*, *indocto* to *doctas* and, above all, *arcu* to *manus*. Although Desire may still use a bow, tactile impulses are of much more concern to lovers.

71– Love works like a plague, striking first the cattle and then the
72   people. *Petit*, while we expect it here to be in its literal sense, often has sexual connotations (as, e.g., Propertius 2.34.4, etc.). Ironically it is used of animals alone here whereas *fixisse* and *perdomuisse*, applied to women and men, have metaphysical overtones of "hunting" and "taming" which would ordinarily be apt literally for animals. Both are erotic commonplaces.

gestit: the verb, building on association with *petit*, suggests love's eagerness in his work.

audaces: those who might dare to oppose him (cf. the sentiments that open 1.5).

perdomuisse: cf. 68 above (*indomitas*) and, for the taming of the female, Catullus 68.118; Propertius 1.1.15.

73– Following the hints of the last two couplets we leave the coun-
74 tryside (literal and then metaphorical) and enter the world of elegy with two stock characters, the prodigal youth and ridiculous aged lover. (On the latter see 1.1.71 ff.; 1.2.89 ff.) We are no longer dealing with *rustica verba* (52).

ad: rare postpositive use.

iratae: a traditional posture for lovers of either sex, whether real or feigned. (Cf. also Propertius 1.9.22.)

75– Unlike the situation in the preceding couplet, Cupid is now
76 on the side of the young lovers, leading the girl past her sleeping guards toward the boy's house. The adventure is treated like a nocturnal sally from a beleaguered camp, with Cupid as *dux*.

custodes iacentes: either in front of her room or, more likely, the house itself.

tenebris: the first hint that evening darkness, whether elegiac (urban) or pastoral (country celebration), is descending on the poem.

77– A brilliant psychological vignette of the hesitant girl alone in
78 such darkness that the only means of feeling one's way is with feet and hand. She is standing still (*suspensa timore*) and yet moving (*pedibus praetemptat, explorat manus*) to discover the nature of her surroundings. All of this is only a moment of frozen time between *transgressa* and *venit* of the preceding couplet, as she is held off the "ground" in spiritual "suspense."

iter: for once in Tibullus, a happy journey.

79– *a miseri*: another exclamatory comment, more generic than
80 *ei mihi* (70).

graviter urget: the metaphor, which is also Catullan (73.5), would at first appear to be part of the military language which enriches the preceding couplets (cf. Cicero *Phil.* 7.14), but the contrast with *leniter* in the next line suggests that wind is also in question. (For *urgeo* in such a context see Vergil *Aen.* 1.111. The contrast between *leniter* and *graviter* appears in Cicero *Brut.* 164 to describe a speech and its delivery.)

This forms a tight transition from love as *dux* to a more generalized utterance on love's fickleness for which breezes

were a common symbol (as, e.g., Horace *Carm.* 1.5.11–12).
Propertius (2.25.27) puts the sentiment in a nutshell:
mendaces ludunt flatus in amore secundi. The sentiment helps
make a transition from elegiac stance back to rural celebration
while the repetition of *felix* and *placidus* from lines 25–26
recalls the actual rites themselves.

81– Love's arrows and torches were proverbial. Such instruments
82   of torture have no place, one would hope, at a festal board,
to which Bacchus and Ceres have already been invited in similar
terms (3–4). (For *procul* cf. the implications of line 11.)

precor: as at line 25 doubt remains concerning the efficacy
of the poet's prayer.

83– The repetition of *pecori*, the double imperatives, antithesis of
84   *palam* and *clam*, threefold use of *vocate, voce,* and *vocet* (which
in turn pick up *vos* and give an interconnecting frame to each
line) turn abruptly back to the formality of ritual prayers.
These can be uttered out loud for the flock but, lest the effect
be dissipated, individual requests—especially where Amor is
concerned—are to be made silently.

celebrem deum: deliberately vague, but Amor is probably
meant. For *celebrem* see 33.

palam clam: a favorite Tibullan duality, here in a context
not specifically erotic.

85– The open utterance of private vows is permissible after all,
86   as long as the sound is absorbed in the general din.

turba iocosa: by contrast with *candida turba* (16). Now the
noise of the ritual's aftermath is of paramount importance.

tibia curva: the instrument, though basically straight, had
a curved end of metal or horn (see further 1.7.47–48). The
"Phrygian sound" would associate the instrument with the
orgiastic rites of the Magna Mater (cf. 1.4.69–70).

87– Tibullus combines three ideas not linked before—night and
88   her chariot, the stars as her offspring, their following in her
wake. (For detailed references see Smith, *Elegies of Tibullus,
ad loc.*; R. D. Williams on Vergil *Aen.* 5.721 [Oxford, 1960].)

ludite: of "game" in every sense (see, e.g., commentators
on Catullus 61.204). In spite of latent, more negative connotations of Nox, the general picture is of sportive happiness. The
excitement of the day is transferred to a higher symbolic realm
which associates man with nature. The command, like *carpe
diem*, announces time's passage with urgency.

89– Night has less happy connotations, bringing in her train
90   *Somnus* (sleep) and then *Somnia* (dreams, but here as likely

nightmares). After playful stars we have silent sleep; *sidera fulva* yield to sleep's dark wings and black dreams. *Certo pede* (52) of the farmer's rustic song becomes something less secure, the *incerto pede* of nightmares, as life grows darker still.

Tibullus first draws a symbolic analogy between mankind and the celestial elements. But this sudden change of perspective leads only to still deeper poetic concerns. Night may bring love; it also brings sleep, dreams and, unsaid, death. Night's chariot with its followers goes its stated, mythic way, but sleep, enveloped in dark (like death, at 1.3.4–5) which in turn will surround, is the feast's last visitor. Ritual quiet in the end becomes a stillness more enduring. The poet must command the advent of Bacchus, Ceres, and Amor. Sleep comes automatically and, sometimes, with finality.

tacitus: Tibullus is fond of dark, silent, usually ominous approaches (e.g., 1.1.70; 1.9.4; 1.10.34). Hence the strangely melancholy impression here.

COMMENTARY 2. 2.

A birthday poem for Cornutus, celebrating his natal spirit, as the conclusion of 1.7 had hymned Messalla's. First we have the setting around the altar with ritual command for only proper language. The Genius himself is suitably honored with incense, garlands, perfumes, offerings of cake and wine. At the height of the ceremony the statue magically nods acceptance of Cornutus' requests. These expand on attributes of the perfect marriage, something intangible but of more value than extensive lands or abundant jewels—a love strengthened by faith, binding into old age, enhanced by children. An elegist's dream of lasting conjugal *amor* becomes momentarily possible in the midst of ritual. The next poem (among several others), where a greedy lover hunts for unbounded lands, and an ostentatious mistress shows off her Indian slaves, expounds a more realistic, or at least more elegiac, approach to Amor. We may ponder then why 2.3 is also addressed to Cornutus.

1–2   In words reminiscent of the opening of the preceding poem Tibullus announces a celebration to honor the birthday of his friend Cornutus. Structurally and emotionally the poem revolves around a prayer that the birthday spirit be present (1, 5, 21). Note the many uses of *ad* throughout the poem.

dicamus bona verba: traditional Roman formula to begin a

prayer (see Pease on Cicero *De Div.* 1.102). A contrast with
the ending of the preceding poem may well be intended.

quisquis ades: an important aspect of ritual—to embrace by
statement (here the embrace, from *lingua* to *fave*, is also verbal) everyone present at the ceremony, man or woman.

lingua fave: "speak (only) holy words." Cf. 2.1.1.

3–4 Anaphora of *urantur* (with first divergence and then conjunction between ictus and accent), assonance of *tura* (which
carries over into other sounds), alliteration of *tener* and *terra*
(where difference in length is emphasized by the short syllable
ending *divite*) give complex verbal shape to ritual progress.

pia tura: "holy" because associated with a religious ceremony linking men and gods, which will in turn become a prayer
for *fidos amores* between husband and wife, and for children.

tener Arabs: Arabians to the Romans were synonymous with
eastern luxury and hence effeminacy (cf. Catullus 11.5; Vergil
Georg. 1.57). The exotic reference seems to enhance ritual
potency.

mittit: regularly of a commercial product.

5–6 The Genius will make an epiphany, the poet prays, to see the
honors its statue has received.

visurus: future participle of purpose, rare in Latin before
the Augustan period.

mollia serta: the same offering is made (and the same words
used) to the Genius of Messalla at 1.7.52. The contexts have
much in common. At 1.3.66 the Elysian lover wears as a sign
insigni myrtea serta coma. The use of *decoro* in this connection
is as early as Plautus (*Trin.* 1.2.1). Tibullus is preoccupied
with hair, wine, binding, old age, even in religious contexts.

7–8 Compare again 1.7.50–54.

puro nardo: oil made from the root of the nard plant was
particularly attractive to the ancients and widely used on occasions such as this (e.g., Horace *Carm.* 2.11.16–17). *Puro* because undiluted and hence the more fitting for a religious occasion.

The Genius is both a statue and alive, eating the meal cakes
and growing drunk like a human participant in the ceremony.

9–
10 Tibullus pictures an interchange between Cornutus (first mentioned here) and his Genius' responsive statue. The drama of
the moment—the change from *adnuat* to *adnuit* and *rogabis* to
roga with Cornutus' hesitancy intervening—is well caught in
the brisk, conversational tone of the couplet.

cessas: "hold back."

11– Tibullus is first celebrant, now augur. The poet can put into
12   words (which a good future wife would presumably take as a
      compliment) what Cornutus would pray to—and for—him-
      self. The implication of line 12 is that Cornutus has done this
      so regularly before that more gods than his Genius have learned
      the request by heart.

13– *Fidos amores*—unusual in elegy of a wife—are preferable to
14   land or jewels, spiritual honesty to superficial wealth. The hy-
      perbole of *totum per orbem* contrasts with the one "brave"
      rustic and his "sturdy" bull.

      malueris: potential subjunctive ("would you prefer . . .").
15– Gems are singled out as a mark of riches.
16   *felicibus*: the *Indi* are lucky because they have wealth. (For
      Indi and the Eoan waters together, cf. Catullus 11.2–3. See
      also 3–4 above).

      nascitur: allusion to a theme central to the poem.

      Eoi maris unda: the sea in question is the Persian gulf, not
      the modern Red Sea and was supposedly reddened because of
      the jewels on its beaches.

17– *vota cadunt*: the metaphor comes from the fall of dice.
18   *strepitantibus alis*: "with rushing wings" (cf. the advent of
      Somnus at 2.1.89).

      flava vincula: perhaps the color of festivity, perhaps a token
      of youth, the time before hair needs to be dyed. (Tibullus'
      other four uses of *flavus* are connected with hair, 1.1.15, 5.44,
      7.12; 2.1.48).

      coniugio: "for your marriage." The bonds and yoke of wed-
      lock are proverbial. Tibullus uses them regularly of less stable
      relationships.

19– *tarda senectus*: *tarda* is both active and passive. It hobbles along
20   but it also forces others to creep at its own pace.

      inducat rugas: in connection with furrows *inducere* usually
      means to "level." Here it is simply "bring." (See TLL 1235.
      33 ff.)

21– The meaning of the couplet depends on punctuation, as well
22   as the sense of *avis*. Taking *avis* closely with *prolem* seems
      easiest: "Let the birthday spirit come and purvey offspring to
      their grandparents." The Romans were not unique in expressing
      a fear that their own children might be childless (see com-
      mentators on Catullus 64.379, et al.).

      turba novella: the adjective is more commonly used of young
      animals. We might say "youthful brood."

COMMENTARY 2. 3.

The elegist, adopting at the start an urban viewpoint, complains to his friend Cornutus that the countryside has Nemesis in its grip. He would be made of iron (would be unbending, unyielding to love and, as we learn later, driven by unreasonable ambition) who would not follow Venus into the country and play the farmer, as handsome Apollo once was forced to do. Even the gods then were open slaves to Venus. Now in this age of iron, gain, not love, is the world's chief concern—gain which leads to death in civil war, in naval battles, which battens on elaborate acquisitions, promotes noise, tames nature unnaturally. The poet espouses a simple life, but, alas, his girl craves wealth and with wealth comes the same modern world of lovers' spoils and a different, grasping Venus. Even if Nemesis is momentarily in the country only an urban setting can satisfactorily display her ostentation, with exotic fabrics (laid out like a city), foreign servants, and dyes. And in this upside-down world social categories are reversed, and slaves become kings through possession of riches—and Nemesis. A curse on crops and vines! Nemesis is seduced by them. In the good old preagricultural days of acorns and water, there was no ambition, and love was gentle, free, and open—mere dalliance in a sylvan shade—and there were no distinctions between city and country, slavery and freedom. But what use is even luxury if Tibullus still cannot see Nemesis. Lead on. He will become the rustic elegist-lover-slave after all.

By contrast with the first poem in the book we now have a negative view of the pastoral-rustic life. Instead of being healthy and harmonious, the countryside is made to seem destructive. Crops are chided, Bacchus is cursed instead of invoked, Apollo's powers are nullified by love. The whole is a splendid display of Tibullus' artistry, taking the reader full circle and running the gamut of moods from highly serious to lightly witty and ranging in theme and perspective from urban to pastoral, present to past, wide social commentary to narrow personal dilemma. The final acceptance of Nemesis' sojourn in the country, that the beginning of the poem announced, only serves to make more forceful the intervening diatribe against luxury. Yet this is accompanied by the poet's admission that wealth alone now fosters love, and, while his urban status contrasts with any urban pretension, the poet's fictitious blistered hands (a blemish on his refinement) again make light of any pastoral attitude smacking of reality.

1–2 The elegist, taking his traditional urban (and urbane) attitude, forced to look beyond this into a now bitterly real countryside where his girl has gone. There is an amused tension between the vague, generic plurals and the particular girl, "their" possession and his (*meam*). *Tenent* usually has amatory implications but, ironically, she is "held" by inanimate things. (If there is an implied glance at her new lover, it may extend to the idea of enslavement in *tenent* as well.) The same tension is implicit in line 2, treating the poet himself in general terms and yet betraying deep personal involvement by the repeated *heu*.

　　heu: a poem of exclamations (five appearances of *heu*, three of *o*).

　　ferreus: usually of someone who remains unbending toward love; here ironic because she has run off with someone else. There is no question of her begging the poet to leave. Cf. the play on words at 1.2.67 and 1.10.2.

3–4 *ipsa Venus migravit*: a compliment to (the still unnamed) Nemesis. *Migravit* implies a whole tribe. Venus has taken to the countryside with son and followers.

　　latos agros: a vague description which, however, anticipates the *multa iugera* (46) which the lover owns.

　　iam nunc: "just now," "only a moment ago."

　　verba rustica: sophisticated Amor must now also learn the language of *rura* (cf. the different approach to Cupido at 2.1. 67ff.). The paradox is engaging.

5–6 *cum* [*dum*: Heyne] *adspicerem dominam*: "when [provided] I can see my mistress, . . ." (i.e., while both she and I were in the country, I would be happy). Inspiration may come from such a vision but one wonders about the quality of the resulting agricultural adventures. A funny vignette of the elegiac plowman hopefully at work, though *illic* still keeps a Roman perspective.

　　dominam: a mere glance is sufficient for the elegiac slave.

　　quam fortitur . . . : for the wording cf. Vergil *Georg.* 1.64–65. *Valido bidente* is Lucretian (5.208). The *bidens* was a double-tined hoe or mattock. (The interlocking word order of line 6 may verbally represent the hoe coming to grips with the soil.)

7–8 *modo*: "in the manner of." Tibullus remains the elegist, no matter what.

curvum aratrum: the plough's handle was curved (Lucretius 5.933; 6.1253; Vergil *Georg.* 1.170).

subigunt arva: a Vergilian phrase (*Georg.* 1.125).

steriles boves: there is a challenge between the adjective and the masculine action in the couplet.

9–
10 The ideal (elegiac) lover possesses *graciles artus* and *teneras manus* both of which suffer from (imagined) exposure and hard work (cf. 1.9. 13ff.). These are the traditional lover's "trials" in a georgic setting. In spite of physical ineptitude complaints would be unmanly or suggest less than appropriate ardor in his love.

pussula rupta: a prosaic word to expose the vivid practicality of the poet's doubly impossible dream. The elegist's overrefinement is wittily called in question.

11–
12 Tibullus compliments himself by drawing an analogy between himself and Apollo (as he had likened Nemesis to Venus in 3). The legend of Apollo's passion for Admetus seems Alexandrian in origin (Callimachus *Hym.* 2.49). Ovid was especially fond of it (*Her.* 5. 151f., et al.). Apollo, ordinarily a patron divinity of herds, takes the menial role of herdsman. Neither his devotion nor his musical talent nor his youthful beauty served to win Admetus (for the last attribute see 1.4.38; 2.5.121). The implied comparison between Nemesis and Admetus exemplifies the ease with which ancient writers in general moved back and forth between heterosexual and homosexual themes.

13–
14 Apollo's learning in medicine is powerless to remove his own *curae*. For literal *herbae* in this connection see 1.2.62. (Propertius, 1.10.17–18, boasts of the poet's power at such a moment.)

quidquid erat: hyperbole, impersonality, and the pronounced displacement of *artis* set off by *vicerat* and *amor* poetically enhance love's victory. The abstract *ars medica* will have as much effect on the abstract *amor* as tangible *herbae* on intangible *curae*.

15
(–16) With the pentameter and probably another distich lost, any reconstruction is dubious. *Ipse* (like *ipsa*, 3) expresses further surprise at what became customary in the god's life.

17–
18 The text picks up in the middle of an *aition* on Apollo's invention of cheese. (For a more detailed look at the process see Columella *De Re Rust.* 7.8.1ff.) A verb such as *dicitur* must be supplied to complete the sense. The "process" of the discovery is paralleled in the process—and sound—of the

couplet as *miscere* becomes *mixtis* and that with which milk is mixed becomes milky.

   coagula: rennet. Tibullus is playing on assonance with *lacte* (and the subsequent *lacteus* and *liquor*) to form a sound the Romans associated with a lullaby.

19– The hardened mass is placed in a reed basket whence the whey
20   (*sero*) drips or is squeezed. (In Vergil *Ecl.* 2.71–72, Corydon reorients himself to the pastoral life by contemplating just such a task.) To focus vividly on such details in an already remote setting is a Tibullan propensity (see also 2.5.31–32).

   rara via: a transfer of epithet from *iunci* (there are few of them, i.e., they are set widely apart) or, more poetically, *nexus* (cf. *textura rara*, Lucretius 4.196), which would intensify the value of the accomplishment.

   sero: placement at the line's end looks to the process of manufacture.

21– The anaphora of *o quotiens*, especially as part of an exclama-
22   tion which seems to denote particular involvement on the poet's part, is belied by the comic tale which follows. The intensive verb and the plural *agros* supplement the meaning of *quotiens*.

   soror: Diana, who blushes for shame at her brother's doings.

23– The structure of the couplet mirrors the daring disruption of
24   of the song. *Ausae* (with the verb "to be" suppressed, un-usually) receives its noun only at the end (most emphatically). *Caneret alta* and *carmina docta* are broken up by *rumpere mugitu*, a phrase in which homophony and onomatopoeia conspire to form a direct contrast with the god's own learned songs, as bestial contrasts with divine.

   valle sub alta: the echo caused by a valley's high walls would be an especially pleasant sound (as, e.g., Horace *Carm.* 1.17. 11–12, 17).

25– The god of prophecy renders his oracular shrines useless by
26   avoiding them. The anaphora of *saepe* stresses continuous action and the plurals look to something habitual.

   trepidis oracula rebus: Tibullus varies a phrase he found in Vergil (*Georg.* 4.449) where Aristaeus seeks from Proteus *lassis oracula rebus*. *Trepidis*: "frightened," or active: "causing anxiety."

   irrita turba: the crowd is "fruitless" because the results of their search were empty. Arriving, they were leaders; departing, only a mob. There may be a pun on the first meaning of *turba*, synonymous with *confusio* (see Cicero *Ad Fam.* 6.6.13).

Turba is in any case an unusual word to apply to a group of *duces*, but Tibullus seems to associate it with ritual contexts (1.3.32; 2.1.16, 85).

27–
28 Locks, which even Juno, his stepmother (a relation proverbial for meanness), admired, his mother Latona grieves to see dishevelled. As often Tibullus puts hair in an important poetic position.

prius: emphatic from placement and uniqueness in the Tibullan corpus.

29–
30 Because he is being particularly undivine and unritualistic, Apollo lacks the fillets to adorn and tie back his hair.

aspiceret, quaereret: potential subjunctives in past time: "Whoever would look at . . . would seek (in vain for) . . ."

Phoebi comam: a play on meaning. They were seeking, and finding, the hair of Phoebus but not recognizing it as such.

31–
32 For reasons the next couplet makes clear, the situation of Apollo is seen now as present.

Delos and Delphi, both with famous oracular shrines, were Apollo's island birthplace and chief residence, respectively.

Pytho: alternate name for the town of Delphi. Apollo's priestess at Delphi was called Pythia.

parva casa: 1.10.40.

33–
34 Vision of an elegiac golden age when the immortal gods were not only epiphanic but were also slaves of Venus for all to see. Men were accordingly happy, with such a divine model to follow.

aperte: striking in view of Tibullus' constant emphasis on the furtive and hidden.

35–
36 *fabula*: a particular scandal (as 1.4.83) which in this case passed into legend as an *exemplum* of a god in love with a mortal. The generalizing (which includes the change from Admetus to *puella*) prepares for a return to Tibullus' own situation.

cura: particularized at lines 13–14, also in conjunction with *amor*.

sit: subjunctive of wish without *ut*.

37–
38 The rival, always left vague yet here very demonstrable, is as subject to Cupid as the poet. The sense of the distich is not complete. Some such sentiment as "Beware, for the same will happen to you in turn" is probably to be supplied. The lines hiss with dislike.

tristi fronte: "with severe countenance" (cf. Plautus *Asin.* 401), first against Tibullus, ultimately against his rival.

tua castra: the violent, rival lover has set up his command post, in obedience to Cupid's orders, not opposite the poet's house but in it, i.e., among other things Nemesis has now completely yielded to his rival.

39– *ferrea saecula*: chiasmus points up the present urban age of
40 iron, unlike the golden age when the gods showed public devotion to Venus. Tibullus calls himself *ferreus* (2) because he remains in the city while Venus has moved to the country. The distinction between *Venerem* and *praedam*, living divinity and inanimate object of greed, is enhanced by *ferrea* which also prolongs the military metaphor of 37–38.

est operata: "is concerned with" (with dative). Perhaps we are to think of *opus* in connection with the age of labor.

41– *praeda*: now openly personified, she goes about her evil work.
42 Cf. 2.1.47 ff.

feras acies: a coinage of Tibullus adopted by Seneca (*Ag.* 599). We would expect *ferreas*. The battle lines in this iron age are wild like beasts (cf. the pun at 1.10.2), and her "girding" with arms furthers the personification.

discordibus armis: a Vergilian phrase (*Georg.* 2.459) which may have specific reference to civil war.

cruor caedes mors: human blood, the moment of its spilling, and the final result. Verbal repetition, asyndeton and alliteration hasten the end. (On the quickening pace of death see 1.10.4 and commentators on Horace *Carm.* 1.3.32–33.)

43– A double danger confronts those who engage in naval battles
44 because of the peril inherent in seafaring.

vago ponto: "restless" but also causing others to wander (cf. 2.6.3–4 and 1.3.39–40).

bellica rostra: ships' beaks of iron to make them into warships. These give their name to the various speakers' platforms which they decorated in the Forum Romanum and elsewhere. (The initial "beaks" were taken after a battle with the people of Antium. See Livy 8.14.12; Pliny *Hist. Nat.* 34.20.)

dubiis ratibus: the ships would naturally be "hesitant" on such an occasion. They might also be unstable.

45– The devotee of *praeda* manifests his greed in a desire for un-
46 told acres, handsome homes and fishponds. The rhetoric presses the point strongly.

obsidere: the plunderer "besieges" the land he desires to possess.

pascat: the unusual transitive use of *pasco* (replacing the more regular *depascere*) gives the statement a double twist in meaning. The acreage is not being nourished but devastated.

innumera ove: though the usage is later common in Ovid, this is the first instance in Latin of *innumerus* with a singular noun which does not in itself denote number (and the only preceding example of the latter is the phrase *innumero numero* which Lucretius uses twice, 2.1054 and 3.779). The context with *immensos* and *multa* lends a touch of irony, however poetic the effect of singular for plural.

47–
48 The Roman craze for building, particularized here in the desire for exotic stone.

cui curae est: cf. line 35.

lapis externus: foreign stone, needing to be transported into the city (but also with the idea of a superficial display of wealth).

urbis tumultu: ablatives of place and manner combined.

columna: as in line 46, the poet gains his irony by using singular for plural yet juxtaposing it with the hyperbolic *validis mille iugis*. So much does the present Roman overreach, that one column might need even such forces to carry it.

49–
50 Fishponds (*piscinae* or *vivaria*), often made by cutting off a portion of ocean frontage with a breakwater, had by the time of Augustus also become a symbol of ambition and greed (cf. Horace *Carm.* 2.18.19 ff.; 3.1.33 ff.). As in the preceding distich, the hyperbole depends in part on the unnatural merging of elements ordinarily dissociable—the untamed sea is caged and made land-bound; the fish, regularly in constant motion and subject to seasonal change, is now *lentus*, careless of winter storm. The personification of sea, winter, and fish enlivens the point.

claudit: a military technical term, "invest," "blockade." But there may also be present the idea of laming (cf. Donatus on Terence *Eun.* 164 and *Adelph.* 607).

51–
52 A contrasting illustration of the simple life. Samian and Cumaean (more commonly called Campanian) ware was decorative but inexpensive.

mihi: though the manuscripts generally read *tibi* it seems more concise to bring the poet's personal interest in his musings to the surface rather than suddenly to address Nemesis or the rival lover.

trahant convivia: the expression is used for the first time in Latin. *Testae*, jugs of terra cotta, contained wine which lengthened the happy banquet (cf. 1.9.61).

ficta lubrica terra: the potter's art is nicely summarized as the earth changes from *lubrica* to *ficta* via the wheel.

53– In line 2 with the same exclamation of sorrow Tibullus gives
54 up city for country. Now he negates the thrust of the preceding couplets and accepts the idea of *praedae* and wealth, if Venus (and Nemesis) so desire. This less than serious attitude carries over into the studied ease of *iam veniant praedae* and brisk allegiance to Venus' desires.

55– *luxuria fluat*: the height of decadent living (cf. the similar word-
56 ing by Cicero at *De Off.* 1.106). Tibullus may have sensed an etymological connection between the two words (see Ernout-Meillet, *Dictionnaire Etymologique, s.v. luxus*).

per urbem: in his thinking (and with his resources) the poet has now moved Nemesis back to Rome which alone could provoke and understand such a display.

incedat: a word regularly used of a beauty's stately progress (see J. Henry, *Aeneidea* [London, 1873–89], on *Aen.* 1.405).

donis meis: the repetition of the adjective so soon after *mea Nemesis* forces the reader to relate the two nouns. The possession of one depends on the possession (and bestowal) of the other.

57– Silk stuff from the Greek island of Cos was highly prized by
58 Romans of the Augustan era and is constantly mentioned by the poets as an article of luxury and glamor.

tenues: fine in texture, light in substance, and undoubtedly erotic (see Propertius 1.2.2 also in connection with Coan silks).

vias: like *virgae*, stripes, here of gold, running in the material, imitating streets running at right angles through a city. The metaphor, begun by *texuit* and continued in *disposuit*, magnifies the humorous spectacle of Nemesis *per urbem conspicienda*, wearing material sufficiently diaphanous to prove her allegiance to a social role far different from a *matrona*.

59– Slaves, especially of foreign appearance and origin, were an-
60 other mark of luxury. Allusion to the proverbial horses of the sun adds a further exotic note.

solis: compare the posture of the rural poet-serf at line 9.

inficit ignis: a mixed metaphor. Pliny (*Hist. Nat.* 6.22.70) says of the people south of the Ganges, *"tinguntur sole . . . iam quidem infecti."*

61– Anaphora presses forward the litany of Nemesis *luxuriosa*,
62 Roman but replete with foreign trappings. It concludes in a final blaze of color. (In a list of the benefits he gives his wife,

174   TIBULLUS: *A Commentary*

Menaechmus I details *ancillas . . . aurum, vestem, purpuram*
[Plautus *Men.* 120–21], a virtual précis of lines 57–62 without
the elaborate touch.)

   puniceum: referring to a scarlet dye manufactured by the
Carthaginians (hence Punic, and from Africa).

   Tyros: Tyre, famous Phoenician commercial city and (in-
teresting for the placement) mother city of Carthage.

63– Back to (apparent) reality, *nota*.
64   *regnum tenet*: the language refers equally well to economic
or erotic achievement (for the latter sense see 1.9.80). Cf.
line 1.

   barbara catasta: a revolving platform on which slaves were
exhibited for sale. Their feet were whitened with chalk (gyp-
sum) if they were foreign (see J. Mayor [London, 1888–
89] on Juvenal 1.111). Both *barbara* and *saepe* are jibes at
Nemesis' new amour placed (ironically) next to Tibullus' own
dream of wealth dispatched from places as far away as India.

65– *at tibi*: as at 1.4.59, the beginning of a common curse. Earth's
66   crop is considered the debtor to whom seeds have been en-
trusted. Good faith is lacking in a yield only of a *dura seges*
at the end of the bargain, yet the *seges* has some power at least
to seduce Nemesis.

   dura seges: a unique phrase, perhaps with the amatory sense
of *durus* in the back of the poet's mind, as the ill-omened presence of Nemesis begins to work. *Nomen* begins to serve as
omen.

67– A curse on the lover's wine. Tibullus is careful to distinguish
68   the wine god (with pertinent adjective and notable attribute)
from his product, whose value the next couplet also calls in
question.

   consitor: a coinage of Tibullus.

   devotos lacus: the vats are cursed by Bacchus' disapproving
departure.

69– The reasoning behind the previous outburst which also down-
70   grades the vintage while honoring the god.

   tristibus agris: "accursed fields" but also with the suggestion
that such gloomy spots are not fit hiding places for *formosae*.

   tanti: genitive of value.

   musta: "vintages," perhaps with idea that some length of
time has passed.

71– The final prayer: Away with the fruits of the field, if only there
72   be no girls in the countryside! If there is no "wealth" to be
found in the country, girls will be off to the city. Back to a

more primitive (pastoral, not agricultural), noncommercial era when acorns served as food and water was drunk instead of wine. Ironically the implicit distinction between *urbs* and *rus* would then have been nonexistent.

73– What may seem primitive to some is to others a lover's golden
74 age. *Passim semper* hyperbolically suggests unending delight, topographically and chronologically.

amarunt: syncopated form of *amaverunt*.

sulcos satos: in this still happier age there is no need for the *labor* of ploughing and seeding (cf. line 8 and the intimation echoed in *nocuit*).

75– *adspirabat*: as at 2.1.35, the metaphor is that of a favoring
76 breeze but the primitive setting would also be, literally, exposed to the elements.

aperte: "openly" or "unreservedly" (cf. line 33).

mitis Venus: as 1.10.66.

in umbrosa valle: cf. Vergil *Georg.* 3.331. In spite of *aperte*, Venus, in her gentleness, provides both shade and protection. (Cf. the place of Apollo at line 23).

77– In a golden age without houses neither guardians nor doors
78 impeded a lover. Free love, even though it reinstitutes an era of water drinking, is another custom whose return would be not unpleasant.

si fas est: the prayer is apparently questionable enough to demand a regular Roman apotropaic phrase.

(79–) The missing line probably continued on the theme of happiness
80 in the past, the subject now being dress. Shaggy bodies and simple dress do not preclude love.

villosa veste: "shaggy" because made of hide. We have come a long way from our earlier luxurious Nemesis (55 ff.).

81– Back to the poet's present misery. All the luxury in the world
82 cannot bring happiness if it is impossible to see one's beloved. Because of Nemesis' imprisonment, the country takes on one of the city's worst aspects.

mea: subject while supplying an object for *videndi*.

copia: "opportunity."

laxam togam: The height of citified dandyism (see 1.6.40).

83– *ducite*: regularly a technical term for leading a slave or debtor
84 to prison. The slave-lover metaphor runs through the distich (*vincla* and *verbera* are also linked at 1.6.38). Litotes, emphatic alliteration, and chiastic order give special stress to the last line, as Cornutus (or any sympathetic third party) is drawn into the poet's final gesture of obeisance.

COMMENTARY 2. 4.

Servitude and a domineering mistress are now the lot of the unfortunate poet. Farewell to ancestral freedom. Yet better to be made of stone than suffer love's burning. Verses have no effect against greed (even though Tibullus writes personal *carmina* addressed to his mistress, not didactic or epic poetry). Tangible gifts must be procured even though sacrilege against Venus is the result. Gems, dyes, and silk are the cause of corruption, the reason for locks and guardian dogs which are opened or quieted only by suitable recompense. Beauty and greed combine good with ill, cause weeping, and give Amor an evil reputation. The curse of wind and fire (and a funeral without tears) be her lot who accepts only the moneyed lover. The unambitious mistress, though she die at a hundred years, will still have an aged lover for mourner. But true warnings fall before love's own laws. Tibullus would sell his ancestral acres and drink the deadliest of poisons, provided only Nemesis looks kindly at him.

The thought takes up briskly where the last poem left off, this time with *domina* at the beginning and *imperium* at the end. As often in Tibullus there is an ideal, rational side to the poem with kindly mistress and her aging paramour. But the poem comes full circle when the poet accepts the irrational in the form of the immediate dictatorship of Amor instead of relying on some remoter, more abstract curse. There is a slightly outlandish twist at the end. Charms instill or calm love, depending on circumstances. Tibullus neither needs the one nor wants the other. Perhaps Nemesis will in fact poison him, but if her features will at least be calm and perhaps even calming, what of his, given the situation?

1–2 *sic*: the reader is made briskly to assume past explanations for the present situation (among them the end of the previous elegy).

video: the meaning varies from "foresee" to "see" as the object changes from abstract to concrete.

dominam: context brings to the fore the elegiac double meaning.

libertas paterna: the direct address also combines abstract (*servitium*) and concrete (*dominam*) and stresses the challenge between a citizen's inherited political freedom and an elegist's amatory "slavery." *Illa* already has a distancing effect intensified by the double *mihi*. Partly because the nouns they accompany are antonymous, *paratam* and *paterna* contrast in irony.

3–4   *sed*: the position emphasizes *triste*. The chains and bonds of this "slavery" are bitter (cf., e.g., Propertius 3.15.10).

    misero: of physical and mental hurt.

    remittit: "slacken" but the idea of "release" (from slavery as well as bonds) is also present.

5–6   Towards its slave Love the torturer (and Nemesis) makes no distinction between right and wrong, a judgment the parallel clauses echo. The sudden change from singular verb to plural is as rare in Tibullus as elsewhere.

    peccavimus: originally to stumble, here to err, in an amatory sense.

    io: a pained cry for help here (though used elsewhere by Tibullus only on joyous occasions, 1.1.24; 2.5.118). But the hyperbolic playing with common elegiac vocabulary (and the implied equation of *Amor* and *puella*) suggests a less than serious tone.

    faces: on torches as a weapon of love see 2.1.82; 2.6.16. It is less often used as a metaphor for the girl herself (as Propertius 1.13.26).

7–8   The comparison to *lapis* and *cautes* (9) not only symbolizes endurance in adversity but insensitivity (in its original meaning). For *lapis* and an angry lover see 1.10.59. Chill mountains are a fit location in which to be loveless. (For *frigidus* in such a sense cf. Ovid *Rem. Am.* 492.)

    quam mallem: "how I would prefer . . . " But the choice is not the poet's.

9–   At *Aen.* 6.471, Dido, unmoved by Aeneas' prayers, is de-
10   scribed by Vergil "quam si dura silex aut stet Marpesia cautes."

    naufraga: active: "shipwrecking."

    tunderet unda: the onomatopoeia appears already in Catullus (11.4). The hyperbolic intensity bestowed on the traditionally destructive elements of wind and water puts into (humorous?) relief the poet's own private suffering. He is in reality a shipwrecked sailor, not a *cautis*.

11–   The repetitions of *nunc*, *et*, and especially *amarus* underline
12   the unceasing continuity of bitter day into still more bitter night—*omnia tempora*, in fact.

    amara: cf. Propertius 1.1.33: "in me nostra Venus noctes exercet amaras." It anticipates the taste implied in *felle*.

    tempora: appropriately ambiguous for "time" or "temples." Line 11 suggests the former translation. For the latter cf., e.g.,

Horace *Carm.* 1.7.22–23. For the usual *baccho* (1.2.3), *mero* (1.7.50), or *nardo* (2.2.7) we have only *tristi felle*, appropriate for a bitter moment unrelieved by wine (cf. 1.8.54 and 2.6.32).

13–   A succinct expression of the unfortunate difference in effec-
14   tiveness between the elegist's inspired verse and more tangible gifts in the procuring of love. See 1.4.61–62 and, more elaborate, 2.3.35–60. This is Tibullus' only mention of *elegi*.

prosunt: "help" by bringing either relief or Nemesis.

carminis auctor: the phrase is ambiguous: "discoverer, exemplar of song" or "promoter of my (i.e., Tibullus') song."

cava manu: gesture of the beggar (as Suetonius *Aug.* 91.2) or, as here, of the demanding receiver (vs. the same phrase at Propertius 1.3.24 where it must be the poet who gives).

flagitat: "duns" (for payment). See commentators on Plautus *Men.* 46; Cicero *Pro Cael.* 17; Catullus 42 *passim*.

15–   The poet needs help with love, i.e., the writing of seductive
16   elegies (which are not working), not epic.

ite procul: the matter-of-fact, intimate tone with which Tibullus dismisses his inspirers in quasi-religious language cannot be taken too seriously. (The same phrase is used of *signa tubaeque* at 1.1.76).

bella canenda: variation of a regular euphemism for epic composition (cf. Vergil *Aen.* 1.1; Lucan *Phars.* 1.1).

17–   The ways of sun and moon are two common topics of didactic
18   epic, also useless to a lover. *Errantem lunam solisque labores* are sung by the bard Iopas at Dido's banquet for Aeneas (*Aen.* 1.742; cf. *Georg.* 2.478).

The change of object after *refero* is not unusual but this is the only example in Tibullus of an indicative verb in indirect discourse.

orbem complevit: either "completed her circuit" (the image of a horse running its course is continued in *recurrit*) or "filled out her disc."

versis equis: for the horses of other astral creatures in Tibullus see 1.3.94; 2.1.87; 2.3.60; 2.5.60, 76.

19–   The elegist's real reason for writing *carmina*.
20   *aditus*: means of approach and access to.

carmina: song as magic charm.

ite procul: back to line 15, summarizing the argument.

ista: sc. *carmina*. The second person demonstrative has, as often, a sarcastic ring especially when the noun is suppressed.

21–   The poet must resort to murder or other crime in order to

22   avoid the posture of an *exclusus amator.*

      paranda: cf. line 1, linking mistress and gifts.

      flebilis: active and passive: "weeping" or "pitiable."

23– The height of sacrilege (as well as pique): to violate instead
24 of worship the shrine of the goddess of love.

      Venus violanda: her shrine is meant but there is a play on
the sexual meaning of *violare* as well. (Cf. 1.2.81 and, for
violare and the gods, Propertius 1.7.16.) The sound of line
24 is noteworthy.

25– Blame for the poet's action shifts to Venus who causes the
26 crime by giving him a greedy mistress. Hence the repetition of
facinus (21) and the reflection of *rapiam* (23, of the poet) in
rapacem, of Nemesis.

      sacrilegas manus: "hands that steal from a temple" (as Livy
29.18).

      sentiat: the personification of the goddess, hinted at in line
24, grows more vivid. Goddess and shrine are intimately associated.

27– There is a similar outburst against greed at 2.3.35 ff.
28   *legit*: there may be a punning connection with *sacrilegas* (26).

      -que: the connective is as superfluous grammatically as the
object with which it is associated is spiritually needless to the
poet.

      smaragdos: emeralds (see 1.1.51).

      Tyrio murice: for Tyrian purple see 1.7.47 and 2.3.62.

      tingit: dyeing in classical Latin poetry becomes a symbol
both of the loss of pristine purity and of luxury. The red-white
contrast is a particular Roman favorite but it is color in general that Tibullus here stresses.

      ovem: The fleece alone is meant (for a live sheep the "dip"
would be unsalubrious, not to say deadly, perhaps Tibullus'
point).

29– *Coa vestis*: the silks of Cos were a common symbol of luxury
30 (see 2.3.57–58).

      lucida concha: a shining pearl, not, of course, the oyster
itself.

      Rubro mari: Persian gulf. Contrast the reference at 2.2.
15–16.

31– Greed brought an end to the elegiac golden age of easy access.
32 The results of avarice center once more on the *exclusus amator.*
Alliteration in the distich is noteworthy.

33– But money opens all doors.

34   *pretium grande*: as 1.9.52.
       custodia: though the word echoes *custos* (32), the abstrac-
       tion now embraces *clave* and *canis*.
35–   The *sententia* is nicely worked out, as the challenge between
36   *forma* and *avara*, external beauty and spiritual blemish, ex-
       pands into the greater tension of *bonum* and *malis*.
       formam: "shape" and then, specifically, "beauty." Horace
       (*Epist.* 1.4.6–7) says, probably of Tibullus, *"di tibi formam
       . . . dederunt."*
       caelestis: this use of adjective as substantive in the nomina-
       tive is unique in classical Latin. Its position emphasizes the adja-
       cent nouns.
       malis: sex is unspecified but feminine plural is most likely.
       Abstractions follow in the next couplet.
37–   The noises that Amor arouses reflect either sadness or wrath,
38   not joy.
       denique: summarizes the reasoning in the last two couplets
       why a god, especially a god of love, should be characterized
       as *infamis*, disreputable.
39–   *pretio victos*: "overcome by the price," i.e., unable to pay the
40   price she demands. The thought returns to line 33.
       eripiant: cf. 23 and 25.
       ventus et ignis: fire and water are the more usual combina-
       tion in such curses (as 1.9.12, 49–50). Here wind fans the
       flames and, as we learn from the next couplet, water could,
       but in this case will not, put them out. Personification enhances
       efficacy.
41–   Youths who might ordinarily be her lovers will rejoice as the
42   flames destroy.
       tua incendia: the adjective is ironic (especially by contrast
       with lines 5–6). This is all she will have left.
       spectent: i.e., they merely look on.
       lenti: both sound and placement stress their sluggishness.
       addat aquam: "pour water (on)."
43–   Nor will anyone mourn her death.
44   *seu*: equivalent of *vel si*, "or if."
       munus: either intangible or tangible, the most usual form of
       the latter being perfumes and flowers, not to speak of tears (see
       Daremberg and Saglio, *Dictionnaire des Antiquités, s.v. funus*,
       p. 1395, esp. n. 11.)
       exequias: here the funeral rites themselves.
45–   The subject changes from curse to positive statement, from

46 the greedy mistress—the topic begun at line 29—to the good
one. The implication of the concessive clause, however, reminds us that for most people who have reached a hundred
years few mourners will be around, especially for one whose
profession depended on remaining youthful.

> *flebitur*: balances *nec ullus* (43): everyone will mourn.

47– From funeral to tomb. In the case of the *bona* the lover him-
48 self grown old will remember old love. The alliteration and
syllabic interconnection from *senior* to *amores* is remarkable
and perhaps meant to reflect the intimacy of the love itself.

> *veteres*: not so much "of long ago" as "of long standing,"
as old as the *senior* himself.

> *veneratus*: the possible pun here, on the etymological con-
nection of *veneror* with Venus, appears as early as Plautus *Rud.*
1349.

> *annua serta*: there would be several yearly opportunities for
such display but the anniversary of death is probably meant.

49– A poetic variation of the prayer *sit terra tibi levis*, so often
50 found on Roman sepulchral monuments.

> *placide quiescas*: Vergil (*Aen.* 1.249) tells how Antenor, in
old age or death, *placida compostus pace quiescit*.

51– After curse on the greedy and praise of the good mistress we
52 return to Amor himself and the poet's perplexed admission
that a moral code of apparent value in the long run has little
effect on momentary greed.

> *prosunt*: cf. 13 and 15.

> *illius*: either Amor or his legislating disciple Nemesis.

53– *sedes avitas*: ancestral "seat." The reference need not but
54 could be taken autobiographically. (Cf. line 2 and Tibullus'
other allusions to inherited wealth, e.g., at 1.1.42; 1.10.18;
possibly 2.1.2). The subject of *iubeat* is still in doubt.

> *imperium*: i.e., under someone else's control, possibly the
auctioneer's.

> *titulum*: notice of sale.

> *Lares*: there is no more essential symbol of the Roman house.

55– Tibullus claims he will drink any conceivable poison (in this
56 case a love charm) if only Nemesis prove kindly. In the Latin
authors, Circe and Medea are more notorious for their prowess
in witchcraft. (For Medea in a similar context see 1.2.53.)

> *Thessala terra*: the land of magic *par excellence*. (For further
references see commentators on Propertius 1.1.24, 1.5.6, etc.)

57– For a more detailed explanation of *hippomanes* see Vergil

58   *Georg.* 3.280–83.

   indomitis gregibus: see 2.1.68. The mares had still not experienced sex when the phenomenon in question occurs.

   Venus adflat: "when Venus breathes loves on . . . " See
2.1.80. In Vergil's account (*Georg.* 3.270–79) mares become
pregnant by wind alone.

59–   The only direct mention of Nemesis in the poem which makes
60   the couplet all the more emphatic, especially with the striking
final *bibam*. We are left with the paradox of the calm (and
calming) features of Nemesis the sorceress, luring the bewitched poet to drink poison (perhaps to arouse love or cause
death). The subject of *iubeat* (53) is now clear.

   placido vultu: cf. line 49 and *placidus Amor* (2.1.80) who
breathes lightly on the happy lover and the *blandos vultus*, the
seductive but misleading looks which Amor bestows on the
poet (1.6.1.). Is he willing to settle here for Nemesis only
looking at him?

   herbas: as at 56, 1.2.53, etc., the plants from which potions
are made.

COMMENTARY 2. 5.

   A hymn to Apollo in honor of the induction of M. Valerius
Messalla Messallinus, Messalla's eldest son, as one of the
quindecimviri sacris faciundis (see introduction pages 4–5).
"Phoebus, look with favor on your new priest and come in
triumph with cithara and songs to your rites. As god of prophecy you allow Messallinus to touch the pronouncements of the
Sibyls." One Sibyl foretold to Aeneas a future Rome when
Romulus and Remus had not yet lived and cattle grazed the
Palatine: "Aeneas, brother of Love, the Laurentine fields await
you. Victory flies over your ship, and death is readied for barbaric Turnus. Soon this Palatine pasture land will rule the
world." So the Sibyls prophesied and foretold as well the signs
of a violent war in the distant future. This too is now past and
Apollo, mild again, sends now good omens for a prosperous
agricultural year. The farmer will drunkenly celebrate the
Palilia on Rome's birthday. Apollo should now be without his
arrows and Desire—who has wounded the poet for a full year
—weaponless as well. Nemesis, spare your sacred bard so he
can sometime sing Messallinus' triumph as his father looks on.
Apollo and Diana are to make this a reality.

   This is Tibullus' most "Roman" poem, moving with subtlety

between past and present, city and country, war and peace, history as passing event and landscape-ritual as an aspect of nature's continuity. The whole is presided over by Apollo as war-god become god of poetry and prophecy. The immediate setting is the temple of Apollo on the Palatine, vowed by Octavian for his victory over Sextus Pompeius and dedicated in October, 28 B.C. Apollo was said to have overseen the battle of Actium and a Roman would have felt an explicit analogy between king Saturn, exiled by Jupiter, and Antony defeated by Octavian. He would have also recognized (perhaps with Vergil's help) the portents which foretold the murder of Julius Caesar, the event which precipitated the final years of civil strife. In between, Tibullus has us watch Aeneas reach Latin lands assigned by Jupiter, with Victory accompanying his ships and Turnus slain. But to balance this Jupiter-Aeneas-Augustus analogy we have a different, pastoral Rome where Pan could appear and love-making was common on the spot where now stands the city's commercial center.

Moreover by putting Messallinus at the beginning and adding his father to the composition at the end of the poem Tibullus effectively balances them with Augustus, reflecting the semi-detached view of both poet and patron. Another point of interest: Tibullus seems to use the same vocabulary in both a dignified and a less lofty manner, as if to warn the reader that such subjects have both a serious and a lighter side (or, with some irony, that such high themes deserve a certain under-cutting). The two sides of Apollo, as god of war and poetry, are paralleled in an archetypal Roman myth of Mars without his weapons seducing Ilia. Perhaps in Tibullus' own Sibylline hopes past Rome can be restored by fertility rite and he himself make happy love the way the young do, once the ritual is over. Perhaps Apollo and Diana, who together usher in the new golden age in Horace's *Carmen Saeculare*, will nod approvingly on the poet's idealistic designs.

1–2   A prayer to the god, in whose temple on the Palatine the installation is taking place, to bless the ceremony with his presence. There are as many dactyls as possible in the distich, reflecting the briskness of a ritual entrance.

fave: of a religious rite (see 2.1.1; 2.2.2).

novus sacerdos: Messallinus himself, newly appointed *quindecimvir*.

cithara carminibusque: Apollo as god of music and proph-

ecy, possibly a reference to the famous statue of Apollo Citha-
roedus of Skopas which Augustus had installed in the temple.
(See Pliny *Hist. Nat.* 36.25 and the description in Ovid *Met.*
11.165–71.)

3–4   *vocales chordas*: strings which sing.

impellere: ordinarily a verb of violent action (a passing look
at the martial side of Apollo?), this is its first use in Latin in
connection with a musical instrument. It is imitated by Ovid
(*Met.* 10.145). See 1.1.3–4 and 1.3.23–24.

flectere verba: the idiom, which originates in Latin with
Tibullus (see TLL, *s.v. flecto*, 895.80f.), appears in Greek as
"trope," in English as "turn." Again a regular military image
is directed toward a more spiritual pursuit.

ad laudes meas: "to the praises which I am to deliver."

5–6   *triumphali lauro*: referring, in the past, to the victory of the
Olympians over the Titans and, more recently, to Augustus'
triumph at the battle of Actium. It was in honor of this victory
(over which Apollo was thought to have presided) that the
temple was dedicated on October 9, 28 B.C.

tempora: accusative of respect.

cumulant: the indefinite subject ("they") is unusual in classical Latin. Cf. also 1.3.35.

7–8   The implication of the couplet is that there were other occasions in which Apollo could appear dishevelled, i.e., when
playing the warrior (or wooing Admetus, as 2.3.26–30). Present circumstances require the handsome god of music.

sed: "yes, and . . . "—a colloquial use which lightens the
tone and makes humorous the string of commands, growing
in intimacy, which mortal has just given divine, especially a
poet to the patron god of music.

sepositam: "laid aside," because either reserved for special
occasions or not used for a long time.

longas comas: standard attribute of Apollo.

9–   Though no parallel is quoted for Apollo's song to Jupiter after
10   his victory, the situation can easily be imagined along with its
modern parallel. Song and celebration follow battle.

concinuisse: the verb conveys the notion of group participation as well as of the god's own accompaniment.

11–   We turn from Apollo as god of song to god of prophecy with
12   brief mention of the four chief ways of divination open to a
Roman—augury, *sortes*, *haruspicina*, and Sibylline books.

augur: the etymology of the word is in doubt but, like the
clearer *auspex*, the original connection with *avis* is patent.

provida: there is a play on the original meaning of the word: "foreseeing" (linked with *procul* and *vides*) as well as "cautious" (in the face of challenge).

13– *sortes*: for divination by lot see 1.3.11–12.
14 *haruspex*: a diviner from signs on entrails. The etymology of the word is still debated.

lubrica: the literal slipperiness of the entrails is a figure for their uncertainty which the diviner interprets.

deus: Apollo, momentarily at a distance, working through his priest.

notis: "signs," to be deciphered, known only to Apollo.

15– Though there were numerous Sibyls scattered throughout the
16 ancient world, the reference here is probably to the Sibyl at Cumae who appears in the sixth book of the *Aeneid* (which, though not yet published, Tibullus would probably have known). She was said by tradition to have sold the original *Libri Sibyllini* to Tarquin. (For further details see Pease on Cicero *De Div.* 1.4; 2.110–11; R. Merkelbach, "Aeneas in Cumae," *MH* 18 [1961], 83–99; B. Cardauns, "Zu den Sibyllen der Tibull 2.5," *Hermes* 89 [1961], 357–66.)

frustrata: sc. *est.*

senis pedibus: the Sibylline oracles were all in Greek hexameters.

17– There is a tradition (noted by Vopiscus in his life of Aurelian,
18 chapter 19) that the priests touched the books *velatis manibus.* Nothing further is known about the procedure of selection. The first direct mention of Messallinus is coupled with a final prayer linking the god and his priest.

canat: both literal and figurative ("foretell"). Cf. Vergil *Aen.* 3.444 of the Cumaean Sibyl.

19– The chronology of the Sibyl's revelation to Aeneas is appar-
20 ently different from Vergil's not yet canonical version. The Sybil spoke immediately upon his withdrawal from Troy, not after his arrival at Cumae. Tibullus follows a tradition that the Sibyl came from an Erythrae located originally not in Euboea but under Trojan Mt. Ida (see Dionysius of Halicarnassus 1.55). There is literary evidence for Aeneas carrying his father and the *sacra* from Troy as early as Stesichorus (c. 600 B.C.).

Lares: here probably standing for the *sacra* as a whole, including the Penates.

21– The immediate spectacle of Troy in flames belies the Sibyl's
22 assurance of a Rome in the distant future. The circumstantial

cum, implying continued action, underlines grammatically the hero's *maestitia*.

ab alto: "from the deep."

ardentes deos: the statues of the gods and hence their burning shrines.

respiceret: often used of looking back in longing (cf. 1.3.14 and Vergil *Georg.* 4.491 or *Aen.* 5.3 as Aeneas looks back at Dido's flaming pyre).

23–   Romulus, descendant of Aeneas and child of Ilia and Mars,
24   founded Rome traditionally in 753 B.C. Mention of *moenia* elicits the subsequent phrase, recalling that Romulus killed his twin brother Remus for leaping over the wall.

aeternae urbis: the first mention in Latin letters of a phrase which was to become standard under the Empire. See K. J. Pratt, "Rome as Eternal," *JHI* 26 (1965), 25–44.

formaverat: "gave (appropriate) shape to." We would expect the word to go with some form of *urbs* but instead Tibullus gives it to *moenia* which in fact did outline the city.

consorti: brother and coheir but, ironically, not a sharer in Romulus' lot.

habitanda: an enlivening transfer of epithet, which we would expect to go with *urbs*.

25–   A favorite Augustan contrast of Rome then and now. There
26   was a time when the Palatine was a pasture and the Capitoline, which held among others the splendid temple of Jupiter Optimus Maximus, was covered with lowly huts. We are not meant to forget that the initial setting for the poem is the new temple of Apollo on the Palatine, one of Augustus' exceptional buildings (Suetonius *Aug.* 29.1–3).

Palatia: Tibullus is punning on two ancient (but probably false) etymologies, from *pasco* (see Festus 245.3M; hence the proximity of *pascebant*) and Pales (as Solinus 1.45 and probably Velleius 1.8.4; this anticipates her mention in line 28). He is also reminding us that Augustus' mansion was on the Palatine (and we are therefore to think of the origin of the generic *palatium*, "palace.") There is a connection with the preceding couplet because the traditional foundation date for Rome was April 21, the feast of the Parilia, honoring Pales.

27–   The features of special antiquity here are the offering of milk
28   (to Pan) and the making of a statue from wood. For the libation of milk to Pan see Gow on Theocritus *Idyl* 5.53.

madens: a word more usually associated with wine (as at

2.1.29; 2.2.8), the regular poured offering. The participle personifies the statue.

ilicis: ilex and especially pine were sacred to Pan. The resonance with *illic* is on purpose (as is that between *facta* and *falce*).

falce: a wooden statue carved with a pruning hook would be particularly roughhewn.

Pales: ancient Italic goddess of shepherds and shepherding (see 1.1.35–36).

29– The god in question is perhaps Silvanus (hence *silvestri*) but
30 more likely Pan to whom the offering of a shepherd's pipe would be particularly appropriate.

vagi: a shepherd is continually on the move, each day and each season, a characteristic he shares with Pan and Silvanus, both extra-boundary deities.

fistula: the so-called Panpipe, consisting of a series of reeds decreasing in length (as described in the next distich). In line 30 alliteration supplements meaning.

31– The detailed description of the pipe, with its lessening order
32 described in two ways, has the effect of focusing directly on this simple shepherds' world devoted to religion and music. (Line 32 is reminiscent of Vergil *Ecl.* 2.32–33: "Pan primum calamos cera coniungere pluris / instituit . . . ")

cera: the stalks were held together by wax.

33– The Velabrum was the area between the northwest corner of
34 the Forum Romanum and the Forum Boarium through which ran the *vicus Tuscus* and the *vicus Iugarius*, main arteries from the river into the Forum Romanum. The Palatine and Capitoline loom on either side but the Velabrum itself is low ground, sloping toward the river and constantly menaced by its overflow.

regio: simply "area," without the technical sense of the Republican four *regiones* of the city (or the fourteen Augustus was to designate in 7 B.C.).

pulsa aqua: probably by oars (as by the body of the swimmer at 1.4.12) or by the boat itself (cf. 1.4.46).

linter: a skiff formed by hollowing out a log.

35– The girl came on a feast day from the city to the country where
36 her shepherd-lover lived. The *gregis magister* and *iuvenem* are probably one and the same. The rival rich lover, constant elegiac figure, enters even this primitive scene.

est vecta: "sailed."

37– Such glowing *munera* of an agricultural civilization are dif-
38 ferent from those Tibullus often bemoans in his more sophisticated society, but the expected effect was undoubtedly the same.
Cheese and lambs are common in such catalogues.

39– Back to Troy and the Sibyl's words (line 19).
40   *impiger Aenea*: the epithet is unique for Aeneas but it is
liberally applied to other heroes in Latin letters (as Achilles,
Hector, Hercules).

    volitantis: love also travels.

    frater Amoris: an elegiac, perhaps slightly ironic touch re-
minding us that the subsequent prophecy cannot be taken
completely in the high tone, say, of Jupiter's words at *Aen.*
1.257–96. Aeneas (we think of Dido or Troy in flames) and
his brother both have in common a certain agility. (There is
an echo from line 36 in line 40 which may not be wholly
accidental.)

    Troica sacra: the Lares and Penates (see line 20 above).

    profugis ratibus: cf. the description of Aeneas at *Aen.* 1.2,
fato profugus.

41– We move from Troy to what in Tibullus' time was regarded as
42 Aeneas' traditional landing place on the south shore at the
mouth of the Tiber.

    Laurentes agros: the land on which Aeneas established the
Laurens castrum (49). Contemporaneously Livy uses the same
phrase telling how "Aeneam ... ab Sicilia classe ad Laurentem
agrum tenuisse" (1.1.4). (On the relationship between *ager
Laurens* and Lavinium see Ogilvie on Livy 1.1.10.)

    adsignat: technical term for the designation of land to
colonists.

    hospita terra: only after the treaty with Latinus (as Livy
1.1.6).

43– The deification of Aeneas at the waters of the Numicus, mod-
44 ern Rio Torto, was traditional by Tibullus' time. (The best
introductions to the area and its many topographical problems
are B. Tilley, *Vergil's Latium* [Oxford, 1947] and A. McKay,
Vergil's Italy [Greenwich, Connecticut, 1970].)

    deum indigetem: the meaning of *indiges* is still debated but it
probably conveys the sense of "native-born divinity." (For
detailed information see G. K. Galinsky, *Aeneas, Sicily and
Rome* [Princeton, 1969], 149 f.) Aeneas is so described at
Aen. 12.794.

45– Traditionally Victory flew between opposing forces until choos-
46 ing the winner. Since the Trojans are not associated explicitly

with any sea battle we are undoubtedly meant to think of Aeneas' years of wandering, but the reader's attention should probably also be directed again vicariously to Actium.

ecce: the anaphora (like the repeated *iam* at 41–42) keeps the future scenario vivid.

fessas puppes: Vergil twice uses the phrase *fessas navis* of Aeneas' ships (*Aen.* 1.168, 5.29).

superba: "haughty." There is perhaps a punning association with *super* in the preceding line.

47– No burning of the camp of the Rutuli exists in the Aeneas
48   legend as we have it, but the killing of Turnus is the subject of the final book of the *Aeneid*. (The Ambrosianus reads *rutilis*. The text is not beyond debate.)

mihi: "before my eyes."

barbare Turne: the address has its ironies not least being that both the Sibyl and the Trojans were foreigners. Turnus is thus subtly placed in the tradition of the Titans (and Antony).

49– A précis of the initial foundations made by Troy in Latium,
50   *Laurens castrum* and Lavinium by Aeneas (see 41–42), Alba Longa by his son Ascanius. (Line 50 is paralleled, verbally and thematically, at *Aen.* 5.597 and 8.48.) The situation of Alba Longa is still in question but the candidate most often suggested is Castel Gandolfo on the western shore of present-day Lago di Albano.

Alba Longa: note the deliberately lengthy separation between the two words.

51– The Vestal virgin Ilia and Mars were the parents of Romulus
52   and Remus. The allusion reverts chronologically to lines 23–24 and is as far ahead in history as the Sibyl goes. Reference to a *sacerdos* who forgets her vows, however momentous the results, comes amusingly in a poem devoted to the initiation of another *sacerdos*.

placitura: an elegiac touch not without irony (cf. line 35).

focos: There is a punning connection with Vesta (Greek Ἑστία), goddess of the hearth.

53– Given the context, the detail furthers the humor.
54   *furtim*: a very elegiac situation, unlike the episode at 35 ff.

vittas: symbols of her priestly office, thrown off instead of worn.

ripas: traditional spot for the tryst (see the beautiful fragment from Ennius' *Annales* quoted by Cicero at *De Div.* 1.40).

55– Back first to the thought of lines 25–26, then into a broad
56   prophecy of the future.

septem montibus: the first literary reference to the famous seven hills of Rome is in Varro *De Ling. Lat.* (5.41), a work written some twenty years before this poem.

dum licet: cf. such diverse contexts as 1.2.75; 1.5.76.

57– In her grand vision the Sibyl addresses the city of Rome di-
58   rectly. Her words have much in common with the vista of the breadth of Roman dominion that Anchises opens up before his son at *Aen.* 6.781 ff.

nomen: a rich word meaning both reputation and the power on which it is based, the *nomen Romanum*.

fatale: "destined" (with gerundive of purpose in the dative).

sua arva: i.e., the whole world.

59– Rome is destined to rule east as well as west, the extent of the
60   sun's course.

patent ortus: two ideas are uniquely combined, the "open-ing" of the gates of dawn and the "rising" of the sun. For the first see Ovid *Met.* 2.112.

abluit amnis: the ascent of the sun's chariot from the ocean's waters at dawn and descent to them at dusk form a common ancient poetic notion.

61– Reborn Troy will be amazed at its new image.
62   *vos*: Aeneas and his companions.

bene consuluisse: "to take good care of," i.e., to have her best interests at heart (the idiom derives at least from Plautus *Trin.* 635).

longa via: "by so long a voyage." Rare instance in Tibullus of a positive journey.

63– The final pronouncement of the truth of her prophecy in the
64   form of a reverse curse, introduced by *sic* and outlining qual-ities she expects to retain, since she is telling the truth, but which would otherwise be lost. If she were lying, the inspiring laurel would do her harm and she would lose her virginity, an essential of ancient prophetesses, parallel in longevity to the age of the city (23).

innoxia: the implication being that it could hurt others.

vescar: a rare example of *vescor* with the accusative, un-paralleled in classical Latin poetry.

65– The violent physical effects of inspiration on the seer. This and
66   the impressive catalogue of Sibyls lend more general validity and power to the brief but vivid prophecy of lines 71–78.

Phoebe: the vocative recalls the poem's initial setting.

fusas comas: cf. 1.3.8.

caput ante: the only example of the postposition of *ante* in Tibullus.

67–
68 According to Servius (on *Aen.* 6.72), Amalthea was the Sybil who originally sold the books to Tarquin. Herophile, supposedly the name of the Erythraean Sibyl, came from Marpessus under Trojan Mt. Ida. Phoeto was the Sibyl of the island of Samos. (For further details on a rather confusing picture see Cardauns on 15–16 above).

69–
70 Tiburs, the Sibyl from Tibur (modern Tivoli), has usually been identified with Albunea, following the authority of Servius (on Vergil *Aen.* 7.83). (For strong arguments in favor of a different location for Albunea near ancient Lavinium see B. Tilley, *Vergil's Latium*, 103–11.) Tiburs, in any case, was probably to be found somewhere near (Tibullus almost wants us to say in) the famous falls of the Anio above which is located the small round "Temple of the Sibyl" of Sullan date.

portarit pertuleritque: "carried and brought through." The situation is mysterious but may well be connected with the waterfalls. (*Portarit*, syncopated from *portaverit*.)

71–
72 Suddenly we are in the year 44 witnessing the portents that followed upon the death of Julius Caesar (described at greater length by Vergil at *Georg.* 1.464–88).

cometen: a universal sign of violent change, for good or ill. The comet in question, which Vergil (*Ecl.* 9.47) calls *Caesaris astrum*, appeared while Octavian was performing games in honor of his adoptive father in July of that year.

multus lapis: a rain of stones is mentioned among these signs by Appian (*Bell. Civ.* 4.4.14).

deplueret: (sc. *fore* with *ut.*) Apparently a coinage of Tibullus (and rare later) to emphasize the heavy fall of the stones.

73–
74 Tibullus switches to a more general "they" in reporting the remaining portents.

arma strepitantia: the rare use of the frequentative of *strepo* suggests the volume and continuity of the sound.

lucos praecinuisse: the phrase evokes the mystery of both portents, that things are heard but not seen (in this case disembodied voices issuing from groves, always an object of awe to the ancients).

fugam: "rout," applicable to either side at moments in the civil struggles to come but perhaps in particular to Antony at Actium.

75– The change from *ferunt* to *vidit* with the year itself as subject

76   adds further directness to the description (and a certain irony
      because what the year saw was dark).

      pallentes equos: the ordinarily blazing horses of the sun
      grew pale, reinforcing the description of line 75.

      nubilus annus: the adjective in this context can be both literal
      ("cloudy") and figurative ("gloomy").

77–   Apparently the first mention in Latin of a crying statue. They
78   usually sweat (see Pease on Cicero *De Div*. 1.98).

      tepentes: inanimate statues of metal or stone shed warm
      tears as if corporeal.

      vocales boves: cattle with (human) voices. Cf. line 3.

      praemonuisse: like *praecinuisse* (74) the prefix sets the time.
      Cf. line 114.

79–   The implication is that Apollo, once less gentle, will look
80   kindly on the present era and blot out ill-omened occurrences.
      The same effect is achieved here by *iam* as by the double *nunc*
      at 7–8.

      indomitis aequoribus: the cleansing as well as obliterating
      power of water is a universal concept.

81–   A new happier era will dawn, predicted by the happy crack-
82   ling of laurel during the ceremony. (For the omen see com-
      mentators on Propertius 2.28.36 and Livy 40.37.3). The allit-
      eration in line 81 is remarkable and can be compared with
      similar descriptions at Lucretius 6.154–55 and Ovid *Fast*.
      4.742.

      laurea: sc. *arbor* or the equivalent.

      sacris . . . sacer: the flames reflect the year (ten out of the
      twenty-one occurrences of the word in Tibullus are in this
      poem, not unexpectedly).

83–   *Bona signa* instead of *mala signa* (71) for this new epoch.
84   *coloni*: here all dwellers on the land (more technically,
      tenant farmers).

      Ceres: see 58 above, 1.1.15 and 2.1.4.

85–   First grain and now wine, two staples of existence, are cele-
86   brated.

      oblitus musto: "smeared with (the) juice."

      dolia: storage jars where the juice fermented. The *lacus* was
      a vat near the press which caught the juice (as 1.1.10).

      dum: "until." (Note the alliteration which caught Tibullus'
      fancy in all his descriptions of the wine-making process, 1.1.10;
      1.5.23–24; 1.7.35–36; 2.1.45–46.)

87–   The Parilia (or Palilia), feast of Pales on April 21, saw the

88   purification of flocks and shepherds alike (see lines 25–26).
      a stabulis . . . lupi: except for *tunc*, this could be the shepherd's ritual cry. (With *procul este* cf. 2.1.11, etc.)

89– The most specific moment of the rite as the shepherd, now
90   appropriately (and perhaps necessarily) *potus*, leaps through the sacred flames. For further details see Smith, *Elegies of Tibullus, ad loc.*
      stipulae: straw.

91– Human productivity is last and most important.
92   *fetus*: apparently the first instance in Latin of *fetus* applied to human beings. The usage may have deliberately rustic associations or be merely another Tibullan way of linguistically taking the reader from one sphere to another.
      comprensis auribus: a universal gesture of affection.

93– A charming vignette, unique in ancient literature. In the pre-
94   ceding distich the focal figures had been parents and young child. Now we see the discrepancy in age between the child and his aged grandfather (*senem*, which indirectly implies long life and continuity, is given particular emphasis).
      advigilare: "keep watch over." The verb is rare and used here for the first time in Latin with the dative.
      balba verba: "baby talk," and yet the kind of chatter that comes naturally to age as well (for the adjective in this connection see, e.g., Horace *Sat.* 2.3.274, *Epist.* 1.20.18).

95– Youthful merrymaking after the ceremony.
96   *operata deo*: "honoring the god" (cf. 2.1.9).
      levis umbra: we might say "darting shadows" (there is a punning connection with *cadit*).

97– If they lack trees they make canopies from their own garments
98   and tie them together with garlands.
      coronatus calix: crowned (with garlands), though the Homeric sense ("filled to the brim") is not out of the question (see Williams on Vergil *Aen.* 3.525–26).

99– The tables and couches are made of turf, as befits a country
100 celebration.

101– *ingeret*: "pour out upon" or "throw at."
102   *potus*: cf. line 89.
      maledicta: a universal effect of alcoholic overindulgence. Disharmony here is minor.
      votis: to his girl at a later time (*postmodo*).
      irrita: "invalid," cancelled.

103– *ferus*: to be taken in conjunction with *suae*.

104   *mente mala*: we might say "of unsound mind," but "in-
        fatuated" is what is meant (cf. Catullus 15.14 and 40.1; Prop-
        ertius 3.24.19 for *mens bona*). Cf. 1.10.55 ff.

105–   Comparison with the other appearances of Apollo's name will
106   show how carefully the poet has changed themes throughout
        the poem (1, 17, 65, 79, 121).

        pace tua: ablative of attendant circumstance ("in a peace
        of your making").

        inermis: if the arms of war are put aside, love too must be
        weaponless. Love may have no power but he still wanders
        ubiquitously. (The alliteration in line 106 is noteworthy.)

107–   *ars bona*: hunting or making love in an era before Cupid dis-
108   covered arrows?

        sibi: emphatic. He had never had them before.

        heu heu: the iteration usually occurs where Tibullus is com-
        plaining of love's trials (e.g., 1.4.81; 1.6.10).

        dedit malum: a traditional phrase going back in literary
        remains at least to the famous riposte of the Metelli to Naevius
        (*dabunt malum Metelli Naevio poetae*), if this is genuine.

        ars ista: *bona* now is perverted into "of yours," with a sting.

109–   *iaceo saucius*: a regular posture of the "wounded" lover,
10   elegiac or otherwise (cf. Catullus 64.250; Vergil *Aen.* 4.1;
        Ovid *Her.* 12.57).

        annum: probably merely a long period of time, as Propertius
        1.1.7; 3.16.9.

        faveo: "take pleasure in."

        cum iuvat: a rare use of *cum* causal with the indicative.

111–   Nemesis is the inspiration for his verse (a common elegiac
12   stance, as Propertius 2.1.4; Ovid *Am.* 3.12.16). The unusual
        cadence of line 111, three bisyllables at the end of the hexa-
        meter, is carefully chosen to sketch the poet's search for *iustos
        pedes*, an "appropriate" rhythm.

        usque: "continually."

113–   A prayer to Nemesis to spare her inspired poet, which cannot
14   be taken completely seriously in a context where the Sibyl has
        twice been styled *vates* (18, 65).

        divum tutela: the protection of poets by the gods, a common-
        place notion (as, e.g., Horace *Carm.* 4.6.33).

        praemoneo: the repetition from line 78 amusingly links
        Tibullus, elegiac lover-poet, with the grand portents accom-
        panying Caesar's demise. The same may be said more gen-
        erally of the word *sacro* (see 81–82 above).

115–   Anticipation of an event which actually did occur in 11 A.D.

16 (see Ovid *Ex Pont.* 2.2.75ff.)

oppida victa: in apposition to *praemia*: the floats represent-
ing the conquered towns which were borne along in the triumphal procession.

117– The soldier, crowned with laurel like his master, will sing the
18 hymn of triumph.

io: a shout of joy (1.1.24) or sorrow (2.4.6).

lauro devinctus: the repetition from line 5 brings the poem
full circle and links Messallinus with his present patron,
Apollo.

119– Messalla dies in 8 A.D., three years before his son's triumph.
20 *meus*: it was the poet's affection for the father, not the son,
which probably caused the present poem to be written.

pia: because of the father's devotion to his son.

pater: alliteration, chiastic order, and placement give the
word special pre-eminence.

121– And in conclusion back to Apollo, this time addressed, as often,
22 with his sister Diana. The phraseology is similar to the Sibyl's
prayer at 63–64. Cf. the use of *sic* at line 63. The implication
here is that the devotees hope the gods will retain their attributes, if the prayers are fulfilled.

intonsi capilli: one of Apollo's chief attributes (cf. line 8).
casta: Diana's virginity was celebrated.

COMMENTARY 2. 6.

Macer is about to become a soldier. Will love go with him
and not call back his errant slave? Tibullus too will give up
love for war—as if such a boast were possible when he cannot
even tear himself from his unresponsive mistress' door. Hope
alone, which makes even the slave's lot bearable, keeps the
poet from suicide with the (futile) promise that hard Nemesis
will be easy. From curse to prayer: "Spare me because of
your dead sister." She died young, was dear to Tibullus, and
might well send nightmares or appear as she herself looked
in death. But such a spectacle would hurt Nemesis. Rather a
curse on the *lena* who makes false excuses for Nemesis before
the poet and sharpens his sorrow.

A desperate vision with few relieving moments. Present
reality seems more unfulfilled and unfulfilling than usual, and
the bridge to perfection shakier than ever. War is no escape
and suicide impossible. Even the prayer to Nemesis involves
untimely death. In between imprecations upon Amor and

Nemesis' procuress is a hymn to Hope, but even this, while it begins on a positive note, proceeds to offer the goddess praise primarily because she deceives unsuspecting creatures and lightens a slave's tortures—small consolation. It is fitting that the last poem of Tibullus' two books (noteworthy stylistically for constant ordering through repetition and anaphora, as if control over the irrational were of special importance here) should end in a curse.

1–2 The meaning is that Macer either is about to pursue the career of soldier, or that, as poet, he intends to turn from elegiac to epic themes. The conflict between elegiac love and military life is a favorite theme of Tibullus and already present in the life of Cornelius Gallus, as portrayed by Vergil in *Ecl.* 10. (For a discussion of which Macer is in question, see E. N. O'Neil, "Tibullus 2.6: A New Interpretation." *CP* 62 [1967], 163–68.)

3–4 The adjectives *longa* and *vaga* tender the poet's feelings on such journeys, usually negative (as 1.1.26 and 1.3.39–40).

    telis: ambiguous: love's "weapons" become a soldier's arms.

    ad latus ire: a military phrase but with sexual implications (see 1.5.61–62).

5–6 *ure*: the implication is double: brand as a slave and burn with love. Sc. *eum* or the equivalent.

    quaeso: the poet reveals his own involvement.

    tua otia: plural for singular: "your life of leisure" (vs. the *negotium* and ferocity of the real soldier). Tibullus' only use of the word.

    erronem: a vagabond soldier or slave. Amor is the real commanding general (the possessor of elegiac *signa*) and master.

7–8 As the poet shifts dramatically to himself, the two realms of reality and metaphor clash wittily in the repetition *militibus . . . miles.*

    levem aquam: "shifting water." The epithet is often applied to the fickle lover (Catullus 72.6), but the water should be "light" also because the lover turned soldier has little strength. (He is, after all, *macer* like any elegiac lover and *tener*).

    galea: the helmet doubles as container for water (as Propertius 3.12.8).

9– Wishful thinking, and an amusing touch, on the part of this
10 most unwarlike of poets. Incidentally this is the only appearance of *vis* in Tibullus, as if sudden appeal were necessary to an ordinarily absent attribute.

    mihi facta tuba est: the phrase is bothersome and often obelized. If read literally, it must be taken as a call to war with which Tibullus often associates the tuba (1.1.75; 1.10.12; 2.5.73).

11– The alliterative repetitions pinpoint *mihi* (and thereby give
12   the lie to the boast of 10). The lover's bravery consists only of words which have little power against the hard facts of *clausae fores*.

   excutiunt: the personification of *fores* is effectively bold. They "shake out" the poet's brave words. The metaphor may be from shaking clothes but military overtones, possibly of a siege, are more likely. Doors are stronger than words. They more easily repel or dispel the enemy.

13– Another contrast between saying and doing, words and deeds,
14   which the repetitions from hexameter to pentameter bring into relief.

   rediturum: sc. *me*.

   ipse: "of its own accord." The poet shifts the blame for his emotion to his foot. Body is uncontrolled by mind.

15– After provoking love with the epithet *acer*, the poet mitigates
16   his prayer with the disarming *si licet*. Love's weapons, inflicting "wounds" and "burning" desire, are truisms (on the latter see 2.4.6, and for the combination, 2.1.81–82).

   acer: an unusual designation for Amor, in strong contrast with *tener* (1).

17– On love, or the lover, as torturer, see 1.4.81, 1.5.5, etc.
18   *dira precari*: "call down curses upon"—a desperate vision though only words.

   nefanda: things that have no right to be uttered. The juxtaposition with *loqui* is almost an example of litotes.

19– Suicide would have ended suffering had not hope lent strength.
20   With the aretology of Spes we may compare the praises of Pax at 1.10.45 ff.

   credula: "inspiring belief" (with a hint to be taken from the preceding lines that perhaps the poet is a bit credulous).

   fovet: in elegy often with a sexual sense.

   cras semper: the juxtaposition is ironic because today never is good (at least in terms of the present elegy).

21– On the connection of Spes with farming see 1.1.9. The image
22   is drawn from banking.

23– There is a decrease in optimism as well as a lessening of trust
24   in the efficacy and quality of Hope's methods. The verbal progression from *alit* (21) to *negat* (27) illustrates the point.

   captat: "seek to catch" rather than actually seize.

   ante: "in front."

25– Still gloomier. Hope brings comfort to the afflicted bondsman
26 (as does Bacchus in 1.7.41–42). There are two competing
sounds: the clanging of chains and the singing of the slave(s).
27– Worst of all: Hope promised that Nemesis would be *facilis*,
28 i.e., willing, easily won (as 1.3.57; 2.4.19). But the couplet
is built on antitheses. Hope promises, Nemesis denies; instead
of being malleable Nemesis is really *dura*. Hence there may
be a direct play on the meaning of her name. By leaving the
poet hopeless she gets her "revenge." The lines are a warning,
however, that by challenging Spes Nemesis might have drawn
down the goddess' own form of revenge. Hence the poet's
exclamation of sorrow.

spondet: with implications.

ne vincas: second person optative subjunctive used in a
(negative) command.

29– *parce precor*: cf. 1.8.51 and Horace's plea at *Carm.* 4.1.2.
30 *immatura*: the transfer of epithet from *soror* stresses the
untimely aspect of the sister's death which came when she was
not yet fully grown (*parva*). For the prayer and its variations,
see 2.4.49–50.

tenera humo: since *levis* is the usual word in such phrases
(regularly *sit terra tibi levis*), *tenera* may be said to reflect the
tender quality of the girl herself. (The same words are used
of the inexperienced earth at 1.7.30.)

31– The anaphora of *illa* recalls the repetition of Spes at 20, 21,
32 25, and 27 as if to note structurally the difference between
Spes, her creature Nemesis, and the latter's dead sister. See
also 2.4.48 for the placing of garlands on a tomb. *Dona*, *serta*
and *supplex* (33) may be meant to recall happier moments of
the elegiac lover and therefore stress the sadness here.

33– *sedebo*: regular posture of the suppliant.
34 *muto cinere*: the phraseology and tone may be borrowed
from Catullus (101.4) where he addresses the ashes of his dead
brother in words which can receive no response (or, as here,
give no comfort in return).

35– The poet assumes the role of *cliens* to the dead girl (as *patrona*)
36 and takes upon himself to give to her sister commands which
he claims to have heard.

illius verbis: "according to her words."

lenta: "slow" to yield or make love (cf. 1.4.81 and 1.10.58).

veto: the poet now emphatically claims the position of power.

37– A favorite way for the dead to display emotion was by send-
38 ing dreams. For the dead sister herself to appear would be the

most impressive of all. (The most famous dream sequence in elegy, perhaps even in Latin literature, is elegy 4.7 of Propertius where Cynthia comes to him in his sleep. It begins *Sunt aliquid Manes . . .*)

mala somnia: we may compare the *saeva somnia* that delirium brings on (1.5.14) and night's ordinary *somnia nigra* (2.1.90).

ante: "in front of," i.e., at the head of.

39– A macabre picture (perhaps meant to be amusing, at the least
40 startling) with the suggestion that her fall from a window ended only in the lakes of the underworld. The change from the top (*excelsa*) to the bottom (*infernos*) is expanded by the plethora of prepositions, alone and as prefixes. Assonance is also prominent.

If we may judge from Hector's appearance to Aeneas (*Aen.* 2.270ff.), the spirit often returns looking exactly as did the body at the moment of death.

41– Tibullus now commands himself to stop the description lest
42 it only sadden Nemesis again.

tanti: genitive of value.

43– The contrast between *puella* and *lena* (the girl is good after
44 all; it is the procuress who does the harm) leads to a curse upon the latter with which the poem concludes.

oculos loquaces: a delightful expression which finds a partial parallel in Delia's *nutus loquaces* (1.2.21). A rare reference in Tibullus to his mistress' face.

45– Compare 1.5.47–56 for a similar denunciation. The name
46 Phryne was used by both Greek (Propertius 2.6.6; Quintilian 2.15.9) and Roman (Horace *Epode* 14.16) courtesans. It may be to Tibullus' point that the Greek word means "toad," a hint at both the texture and color of her complexion. The elegiac *lena* frequently serves as letter-carrier.

tabellas: wooden tablets covered with wax on which a message was written. The edges were raised so that when the tablets were folded and tied the words would not rub off.

occulto sinu: The fold is "concealed" because this is the hiding place of the tablets.

itque reditque: her busyness, portrayed verbally (cf. Catullus 3.11).

47– A vocalic and linguistic connection between *dominae* and
48 *domi* unifies the distich. The procuress' patent falsehood is verbalized in the alliteration of (and partial antinomy between) *dulces* and *duro*. Hearing is different from seeing. The

door (hard like Phryne and perhaps Nemesis herself) is more real than voices to the lovesick poet. He spares his mistress by transferring her qualities to the door and the *lena*.

49– The promising of nights is a natural elegiac platitude.

50   *languere*: ambiguous: to lie faint or already to be satiated with love.

    aliquas minas: probably as vague as Nemesis meant it to be.

51– The harping on death in this poem is out of the ordinary, even
52   for elegy, and the abruptness of the ending cannot be denied. He repeats the pattern of 29–44: death, dream, *lena*.

    perdita: the poet claims the double loss of rationality and mistress, yet the distich is one of his most artful.

    quot modis: the meaning is of course sexual (cf. Ovid *Am.* 2.8.28).

53– He gives the final curse to the *lena* and not Nemesis. For
54   the phrase *precor diras* cf. line 17. Amor had forced Tibullus to curse himself before. He now uses the same words against the *lena*, perhaps as surrogate for the god whom he cannot curse.

    anxia: seemingly mild but sometimes the anticipation (and imagining) of disaster is worse than the event itself (cf. 1.2.25). Such worry is a characteristic of Tibullus.

    e votis: a rare construction with *pars* instead of the genitive.

    pars quotacumque: the rare pronoun focuses attention on the phrase. Even if only a small part of the curse works she should have trouble enough.

SELECTED BIBLIOGRAPHY

Commentaries

André, J. *Tibulle: Elegies, Livre Premier*. Paris, 1965.

Postgate, J. P. *Selections from Tibullus*. 2d ed. London, 1922.

Smith, K. F. *The Elegies of Albius Tibullus*. New York, 1913; reprint, Darmstadt, 1964.

Concordances

Della Casa, A. *Le Concordanze del Corpus Tibullianum*. Genoa, 1964.

O'Neil, E. N. *A Critical Concordance of the Tibullan Corpus*. Am. Phil. Assoc. Monograph # 21. 1963.

Books and Articles

Alfonsi, L. *Albio Tibullo*. Milan, 1946.

Axelson, B. *Unpoetische Wörter*. Lund, 1945.

Buchheit, V. *Studien zum Corpus Priapeorum*. Munich, 1962.

Carter, J. *Epitheta Deorum*. Leipzig, 1902.

Cartault, A. *Le distique élégiaque chez Tibullus, Sulpicia, Lygdamus*. Paris, 1911.

———. "Horace et Tibulle," *RP* 30 (1906), 210–17.

Copley, F. O. *Exclusus Amator: A Study in Latin Love Poetry*. Am. Phil. Assoc. Monograph # 17. 1956.

———. "*Servitium Amoris* in the Roman Elegists," *TAPA* 78 (1947), 285–300.

Daremberg, C., and E. Saglio. *Dictionnaire des Antiquités*. Paris, 1877–1919.

Dawson, C. M. "An Alexandrian Prototype of Marathus," *AJP* 65 (1946), 1–15.

———. "The Iambi of Callimachus," *YCS* 11 (1951), 1–168, esp. 32–39.

Day, A. A. *The Origins of Latin Love-Elegy*. Oxford, 1938.

Delatte, L. "Key-words and poetic themes in Propertius and Tibullus," *RELO* 1967, issue 3, pp. 31–80.

Duckworth, G. *The Nature of Roman Comedy*. Princeton, 1952.

201

Eisenberger, H. "Der innere Zusammenhang der Motive in Tibulls Gedicht I.3," *Hermes* 88 (1960), 188–97.

Elder, J. P. "Tibullus: Tersus atque Elegans," in *Critical Essays on Roman Literature*, ed. by J. P. Sullivan. Cambridge, Mass., 1962. Pp. 65–105.

––––––. "Tibullus, Ennius, and the Blue Loire," *TAPA* 96 (1965), 97–105.

Enk, P. J., ed. *Propertius. Book 1*. Leiden, 1946.

Ernout, A., and A. Meillet. *Dictionnaire Étymologique de la langue Latine*. Paris, 1959.

Gaisser, J. H. "Structure and Tone in Tibullus 1.6," *AJP* 92 (1971), 202–16.

––––––. "Tibullus 1.7: A Tribute to Messalla," *CP* 66 (1971), 221–29.

Galinsky, G. K. "The Triumph Theme in the Augustan Elegy," *WS* 82 (1969), 75–107, esp. 77–80.

Grimal, P. "Hésiode et Tibulle," in Fondation Hardt, *Entretiens sur l'antiquité classique*. Vandoeuvres-Geneva, 1962. Pp. 271–87.

––––––. "Le roman de Délie et le premier livre des Élégies de Tibulle," *REA* 60 (1958), 131–41.

Hanslik, R. "Tibull I,1," *WS* 69 (1956), 297–303.

Hart, C. R. "Tibullus, Lover of Nature," *CB* 28 (1952), 67–68; 29 (1953), 68.

Henzen, W., ed. *Acta Fratrum Arvalium*. Berlin, 1874.

Herter, H. *De Priapo*. Giessen, 1932.

Heyne, C. G., ed. *Tibullus*. Leipzig, 1817.

Highet, G. *Poets in a Landscape*. New York, 1957. Ch. 5.

Klingner, F. "Tibulls Geburtstagsgedicht an Messalla (I 7)," *Eranos* 49 (1951), 117–36.

Leumann, M., J. Hofmann, and A. Szantyr. *Lateinische Grammatik*. Munich, 1963–65.

Levy, F. "Der Geburtstag des Freundes," *SIFC* 7 (1929), 101–11.

Littlewood, R. "The Symbolic Structure of Tibullus 1," *Latomus* 29 (1970), 661–69.

Luck, G. *The Latin Love Elegy*. 2d ed. London, 1969. Esp. chs. 4 and 5.

Musurillo, H. "The Theme of Time as a Poetic Device in the Elegies of Tibullus," *TAPA* 98 (1967), 253–68.

Nash, E. *Pictorial Dictionary of Ancient Rome*. London, 1961.

Nisbet, R. G. M., ed. *Cicero in Pisonem*. Oxford, 1961.

Norden, E. *Agnostos Theos*. Leipzig, 1923.

O'Neil, E. N. "Tibullus 2.6: A New Interpretation," *CP* 62 (1967), 163–68.

Otto, A. *Die Sprichwörter der Römer*. Leipzig, 1890.

Pape, W. *Wörterbuch der Griechischen Eigennamen*. Braunschweig, 1875.

Pichon, R. *De sermone amatorio apud Latinos elegiarum scriptores*. Paris, 1902.

Platner, S., and T. Ashby. *A Topographical Dictionary of Ancient Rome*. London, 1929.

Pöstgens, P. *Tibulls Ambarvalgedicht*. Dissertation, Kiel. Wurzburg, 1940.

Putnam, M. "Horace and Tibullus," *CP* 67 (1972), 81–88.

———. "Simple Tibullus and the Ruse of Style," *Yale French Studies* 45 (1970), 21–32.

Quinn, K. *Latin Explorations*. London, 1963. Esp. pp. 136 ff.

Schuster, M. *Tibull-Studien*. Vienna, 1930; reprint, Hildesheim, 1968.

Sellar, W. Y. *Horace and the Elegiac Poets*, 2d ed. Oxford, 1899. Ch. 2.

Shackleton Bailey, D. R. *Propertiana*. Cambridge, 1968.

Solmsen, F. "Propertius in his Literary Relations with Tibullus and Vergil," *Phil.* 105 (1961), 273–89.

———. "Tibullus as an Augustan Poet," *Hermes* 90 (1962), 295–325.

Steidle, W. "Das Motiv der Lebenswahl bei Tibull und Properz," *WS* 75 (1962), 100–40.

Ullman, B. L. "Horace and Tibullus," *AJP* 33 (1912), 149–67.

Vretska, K. "Tibulls Paraklausithyron," *WS* 68 (1955), 20–46.

Williams, G. *Tradition and Originality in Roman Poetry*. Oxford, 1968. Esp. pp. 495–505, 535–38.

Wimmel, W. *Der frühe Tibull*. Munich, 1968.

———. *Kallimachos in Rom. Hermes* Einzelschrift 16. Wiesbaden, 1960.

INDEX